Introducing Translation

Connecting theory, practice and industry, this innovative introduction to the complex field of translation takes a can-do approach. It explores the latest advances in both research and technology, considers the importance of different genres and contexts, and takes account of developments in our understanding of the mental and physical processes involved. Chapters cover four main areas: what we know and how we acquire knowledge about translation, what translation is for, where and how translation happens, and how to do it. There are forty illustrative exercises throughout, designed to cement understanding and encourage critical engagement, and recommendations for further reading are provided to allow more in-depth exploration of specific topics. *Introducing Translation* is a cutting-edge resource for advanced undergraduate and graduate students in languages, linguistics and literatures.

Kirsten Malmkjær is Emeritus Professor of Translation Studies at the University of Leicester. She has pursued her interest in translation throughout her academic career, developing the approach known as Translational Stylistics and designing translation programmes at several UK universities. She has published widely in the field, including *Translation and Creativity* (2020) and *The Cambridge Handbook of Translation* (2022). She edits the Cambridge short works series, Elements in Translation and Interpreting.

Introducing Translation

KIRSTEN MALMKJÆR
University of Leicester

Shaftesbury Road, Cambridge CB2 8EA, United Kingdom

One Liberty Plaza, 20th Floor, New York, NY 10006, USA

477 Williamstown Road, Port Melbourne, VIC 3207, Australia

314–321, 3rd Floor, Plot 3, Splendor Forum, Jasola District Centre, New Delhi – 110025, India

103 Penang Road, #05-06/07, Visioncrest Commercial, Singapore 238467

Cambridge University Press is part of Cambridge University Press & Assessment, a department of the University of Cambridge.

We share the University's mission to contribute to society through the pursuit of education, learning and research at the highest international levels of excellence.

www.cambridge.org
Information on this title: www.cambridge.org/highereducation/isbn/9781108494151

DOI: 10.1017/9781108657167

When citing this work, please include a reference to the DOI 10.1017/9781108657167

First published 2025

Printed in the United Kingdom by CPI Group Ltd, Croydon CR0 4YY

A catalogue record for this publication is available from the British Library

A Cataloging-in-Publication data record for this book is available from the Library of Congress

ISBN 978-1-108-49415-1 Hardback
ISBN 978-1-108-71398-6 Paperback

Contents

Preface

Introducing Translation is a coursebook for use in translation and translation studies classes, those which form part of undergraduate and postgraduate taught programmes in translation (studies), as well as translation classes and exercises that form part of programmes in linguistics and in language(s). The book will also be of interest to many students and teachers involved in taught programmes in literature(s) and comparative literature, because these often include components on translation and translation studies or explore translated literature. The book can also be used for independent study by aspiring or practising translators.

Introducing Translation is inspired by my experience within three different types of British university (redbrick, Oxbridge and 'new') where I have designed, led and taught courses and modules on translation and translation studies. My students have included undergraduates and postgraduates on a variety of study paths: undergraduate Modern Languages and Literature programmes, postgraduate programmes on Translation and Translation Studies or Applied Linguistics and Literature. I have guided numerous PhD students and visiting scholars. For some, translation was a familiar activity; for others, it was totally new. Many were surprised that a theory of translation existed and that it could inform practice, and that their practical experience turned out to be directly relevant to the formation of a theory. Many were delighted to see that a synergy exists between this most ancient and essential of human endeavours and other core areas of our humanities and science.

While *Introducing Translation* assumes no prior experience or knowledge of translating or translation studies, it does assume advanced skills in more than one language. The exercises, which are integrated in the chapter text, are designed to be used in groups, but individual use is also possible. The exercises enable readers to put into practice the knowledge and skills that the relevant chapter section presents, and they will also enhance understanding of issues in research, in ethics and in theory. Users will be able to use whichever languages they have advanced skills in, and many exercises encourage discussion and comparison of translations between different language pairs.

Unlike some coursebooks on translation, *Introducing Translation* is not structured in terms of the components of language, or in terms of the levels of language, or in terms of the history of translation and translation studies, or in terms of different approaches to translation. Rather, the structure of *Introducing Translation* reflects five central aspects of the translation phenomenon: First, what we know about translation and how that knowledge can be derived; secondly, the purposes translations may be made to fulfil; thirdly, the social, linguistic and human contexts that surround translation acts; fourthly, the practicalities and tools of translating; and fifthly, the processes of working with individual texts in different media. Throughout, translating is treated as a professional practice which demands both considerable skill and immense cognitive engagement, and which is therefore of interest both within academia and well beyond it, in the spheres of commerce and enterprise. The final chapter sums up, considers the status quo, and suggests what may lie ahead for translating and translators. The focus is not on solving translation problems but on the total translation process, including the physical, behavioural and cognitive aspects of making translations, the use of translation technology, and the practical aspects of translation management whether within translation agencies or by individual translators working on a freelance basis.

Each chapter begins with a preview and closes with a summary. Chapters also include suggestions for further reading and there is a full list of references at the end of the book.

Acknowledgements

I would like to thank Rebecca Taylor of Cambridge University Press for inviting me to write this textbook and for her constant encouragement and support.

I also very much appreciate the help and encouragement provided in so many ways by Isabel Collins, Jacqueline Grant and Melissa Shivers.

The book has been long in the making, and, as always, my children and grandchildren have brought me immense joy throughout the process: indeed, Storm and Inigo have joined the family along the way.

So this book is dedicated to Inigo, Storm, Sol, Viggo, Magnus, Max and Elliot, their lovely parents, and their aunt Krista and uncle Nils.

Finally, and most of all, I thank my husband, David, for simply everything.

Introduction: On Translation

The term 'translation' has many uses. For example, in geometry, a translation is a transformation that moves every point in a figure the same distance in the same direction so that the shape and size of the figure is not altered. In biology, the term refers to a process that takes place in living cells. In the social sciences, the term 'translation' has been used to refer to the movements of people and peoples, with their identities, to new sociocultural settings, and to the adjustments that this demands. In the philosophy of language, the term has been used to cover all interpretation of the speech of another; and in the performing arts, it may be used to refer to the representation in one medium of a work originally produced in another.

In this book, we are concerned with translation between texts in different languages. This seems to be the most commonly employed usage of the term: among 100 tokens randomly produced by a search of the British National Corpus, only twenty-one terms referred to other senses of translation: six to matters of finance, four to computing, three to the work of lawyers, two each to medical matters, scientific activities and number, and one each to data and technology. But it is difficult to define translation between languages precisely, because definitions so easily run into other terms that are themselves difficult to define precisely

Exercise I.i

A. Write down a definition of translation as you understand it.

B. If you are working in groups, compare your definitions and discuss the differences between them.

The understanding of translation employed in this book is the following:

Translators use a text in one language, following its own rules and spoken and used for writing in certain sociocultural and temporal settings, as the basis for

> making a text that can function in the same or a very similar way to the first text in another language with another rule system, usually in another location and often at a different time.

This understanding of translation reflects or even conceals a dilemma that translators are regularly faced with, which arises from the circumstance that a translation almost always needs to satisfy two common expectations that consumers of translations generally have. These are (1) that there will be strong semantic similarity between a text and its translation (they will mean the same), and (2) that there will be weak physical similarity between a text and its translation (the translation will not look or sound like the text it is a translation of). If we come across a translation that does look or sound like the text it is a translation of, we often accuse the text of displaying 'translationese', that is language use that does not sound quite natural and which may betray the text as a translation.

Exercise I.ii

Consider the following text, which is taken from a tourist brochure:

> [Place Name] offers fantastic nature experiences, where you will get real close. This gives feelings for nature. The feelings should preferably be reflected in our actions in the everyday, so that we will make progress in taking care of the nature. Thus the main efforts of [Place Name] point to the future in order to make everybody take better care of nature.

A. Can you identify instances of translationese in the text above?
B. Suggest how the text might be improved.

Together, expectations (1) and (2) can be challenging for a translator because physical, linguistic details almost always contribute significantly to meaning; therefore, it can be difficult to keep meaning stable when linguistic detail varies, as the two expectations demand. After all, languages differ. No wonder, therefore, that books on translation commonly dwell on the problems translators face and, of course, on providing solutions to these problems. This book takes a more optimistic approach, choosing to see translating as a fascinating task that offers multiple opportunities for creativity on the translator's part, and to encourage translators to adopt an attitude to the texts they are dealing with which is closely related to the attitude to art that Scruton (1974/1988) calls 'aesthetic'. The aesthetic attitude to an object *X* is interest in the object for its own sake, and this amounts to

> a desire to go on hearing, looking at, or in some other way having experience of *X*, where there is no reason for this desire in terms of any other desire or appetite that the experience of *X* may fulfil, and where the desire arises out of, and is accompanied by, the thought of *X*. . . . If I am interested in *X* for its own sake, then I shall respond to the question 'Why are you interested in *X*?' with the expression of the thought that provides the reason for my continued interest – in other words, I shall respond with a description of *X*. (Scruton 1974/1988: 148)

I have argued (Malmkjær 2020) that translation may be considered the kind of description that Scruton proposes – but of course a description of a text. Some such descriptions are very accurate, other descriptions less so. The comparison between the object of Scruton's aesthetic attitude and a text to be translated also suggests that a translator would do well to adopt the aesthetic attitude to that text, that is, to afford it considerable attention. However, the moment the decision is taken to translate, or the thought is even entertained of translating the source text, the aesthetic attitude, which is supposed to be disinterested except in the object of the attitude, is, if not forgone, then at least imbued with functionality, and therefore it is not completely identical to Scruton's disinterested concentration on the object. Nevertheless, I think it is not too far-fetched to suggest that translating requires the translator to attend aesthetically to the source text, as well as to the translation being created; and this translation is, in a certain sense, a description of the source text.

A second effect of a decision to translate a text is that the translator's process of reading the text (even a first read-through) differs from the process of reading for information or for pleasure (Jakobsen and Jensen 2008). This is likely to be at least partly because the translator, who knows they are going to be translating the text, bears in mind both languages involved, that of the source text and that of the translation-to-be, and is already beginning to make reasoned choices from that second language in view of what they are reading. So translating makes considerable cognitive demands on the translator beyond reading and writing, and some of the research that we will consider in Section 1.3 has attempted to investigate and chart these demands. This book, in contrast, is intended to help you respond to them. To this end, the book offers you a number of exercises throughout its chapters.

CHAPTER 1

What We Can Know about Translation and How We Can Come to Know It

Preview

In this chapter, I describe some traditional ways of thinking about translation, before testing them against evidence about how translators translate; this evidence is provided by empirical investigations of the translation process. Questions about the translation process have attracted increasing attention from both scholars and practitioners, because they realize that if translator training and translating automation are to move ahead, it is crucial to understand how translation happens. Martin Kay, a prominent member of the International Committee of Computational Linguistics and a pioneer of machine translation and of systems providing machine-assisted translation, put it like this: 'The trouble with research on machine translation is that we don't know enough about translation' (quoted in Harris 2011: 11). Indeed, it is no longer true that '*how* translation happens is still a somewhat peripheral question', as O'Brien (2011: 1) put it, nor that 'What the translator actually does is an under-analysed concept' (Jones 1989: 184). Rather, the questions of how translation happens and what translators actually do have taken centre stage in research in translation studies since the second decade of the twenty-first century, although it has shared that position with a number of other, related, issues. In fact, as we come to understand more and more aspects of our discipline better and better, talk of centres and peripheries turns out to make less and less sense. In the past, when translation studies was a young subject and a little insecure, there may have appeared to be safety in asserting its independence and ability to compete with other academic subjects. Now that we can feel more secure, cooperation, knowledge sharing and recognition of mutual interests are the order of the day.

1.1 Translation: Beliefs and Attitudes

The term 'translation' is sometimes used about both written and spoken text. In this book, however, 'translation' is only used of written text, whereas spoken translation is referred to as interpreting. This is in line with the practice of many large organizations' translation departments. For example, the European Commission explains on its Translation web page that it 'deals exclusively with written texts' (European Commission's Directorate-General nd); and the United Nations translation website clearly indicates the same, adding that 'The translation of the spoken word, whether simultaneously or consecutively, is referred to as "interpretation"' (United Nations DGACM nd). Similarly, the Institute of Translation and Interpreting (ITI) in the United Kingdom says on its website that 'Translation can be defined as the process of converting written text or words from one language to another, whereas interpreting is the process of orally converting spoken words from one language to another, or between one language and another' (ITI nd). I will not discuss interpreting in any detail in this book, but see Setton and Dawrant (2016) for a course in conference interpreting and Cirillo and Niemants (2017) for information on the teaching of dialogue interpreting.

Steiner (1975/1992: 248–249) divides 'the theory, practice and history of translation' into four periods. The first begins with Cicero (46 BCE) and Horace (c. 19 BCE) and ends with Hölderlin (1804). Robinson (1997) does not mention Hölderlin, perhaps because, as Constantine (2011: 81) has it, 'Hölderlin propounded no theory of translation and had no fixed way of translating either'. According to Constantine, Hölderlin merely produced a 'few explicit remarks', expressing what he refers to as 'the writerly attitude toward translation, which boils down to "What's in it for me?"'. In fact, as Steiner points out (1992: 248–249), in this initial period in his historical divisions, writings on translation theory grew directly out of translators' own experience of translating. These writings include famous examples such as Martin Luther's *Sendbrief vom Dolmetschen* (Open letter on translating) (1530) which concerns Luther's translation of the Bible (and biblical translation in general). Clearly, reading records of translators' experiences of translating is one way of coming to know something about translating, and biblical translation continues to provide much food for translation-theoretical thought, as expressed prominently by scholars affiliated with the Summer Institute of Linguistics (now SIL International) and the American Bible Society; scholars affiliated with SIL International include, for example, the late Eugene A. Nida (1914–2011) and Ernst-August Gutt (see e.g. Nida 1964; Gutt 1991).

Many consumers and commissioners of translations tend to assume that the main purpose of a translation is to represent all aspects of the source text as closely as possible; that is, they expect a text that is equivalent to the source text. However, translators of texts which are designed to have a global reach may need to adjust the wording to ensure that the text will have appeal and relevance to the various reader groups. This concern is at the basis of one of three prominent understandings of what is commonly termed 'equivalence' in translation studies, namely the conception of equivalence developed by Nida (1964). Nida's distinction between formal and dynamic equivalence will be discussed below, along with the understandings of the equivalence concept developed by John Cunnison Catford (1965), and by Gideon Toury (1978/1980). An alternative approach to engaging the audience for one's translation, not based on equivalence but on the notion of purpose, was developed by Hans Vermeer (1978), who refers to it using the Greek term, *skopos*. This alternative approach nevertheless shares something with Nida's in its focus on adjusting the text to ensure its appeal to its audience; as Vermeer (1989/2000: 226) points out, in an advertisement, for example, audience appeal and persuasion are more important than close linguistic equivalence between the original text and the translation, which 'may diverge from each other quite considerably, not only in the formulation and distribution of the content but also as regards the goals which are set for each' (1989/2000: 223).

Writings on translation that focus on equivalence between two texts often refer to these as the source text (the original) and the target text (the translation). These terms are used to avoid any suggestion that the pair of terms 'original' and 'translation' might encourage, that one text (the original) is somehow superior to the other (the translation). This view has prevailed from time to time in the not-so-distant past. For example, Richards (1979: 4–6) explains that when the eighteenth-century German author and statesman Johann Wolfgang von Goethe suffered writer's block, he engaged in literary translation because this was after all literary work 'even though of a subordinate kind'. Similarly, jingles like the Italian 'traduttore, traditore' ('translator, traitor'), recorded by Giusti (1873), imply that a translator must inevitably betray the original. Furthermore, if a translation is beautiful, it has been suggested, then it must be unfaithful to its original. This sentiment is encapsulated in the term 'Les Belles Infidèles' which the seventeenth-century French scholar Gilles Ménage applied to the very free translations made of the classics by his near contemporary, the French translator Nicolas Perrot d'Ablancourt (Giroud 2010: 1216; see Brodie 2022 and Merkle 2022), and which the French linguist, translator and semiotician Georges Mounin uses as the title of his book on translation theory (1955). The expression of course assumes that translations resemble women in being incapable of being both beautiful and faithful, and is therefore at least as insulting to women as it is to translators and translations. For further discussion of equivalence, see Section 5.3.

The terms 'source text' and 'target text' carry their own difficulties with them, though. It has been pointed out that the term 'target' may easily connote the hoped-for destination of a bullet or an arrow and is therefore an unfortunate, bellicose term to use for an item such as a translation, which is most often intended to promote and enhance interpersonal understanding. To avoid this unpleasant connotation, this book will use the pair of terms 'first-written text' and 'translation'. Another reason for selecting these terms is that they reflect the view we adopt here that nothing distinguishes the two texts *qua* texts other than the simple fact that one was typically written before the other – although there are cases of translation, notably in the European Union, for example, where no text involved in a translation situation is officially designated or acknowledged as written before the other and where text drafts flit back and forth between language sections so that it is difficult to distinguish any full text as the 'first' with respect to its associates, and where the term 'language version' is preferred to the term 'translation' (see Koskinen 2008; Wagner, Bech and Martínez 2002: 7–9).

Steiner's second period of translation theory, practice and history begins with the publication of two essays around twenty years apart. The first of these was written by the Scottish advocate and Edinburgh University Professor of History, and of Greek and Roman antiquity, Alexander Fraser Tytler. It was published in 1792 under the title *Essay on the Principles of Translation*. The second essay was written by the German theologian, philosopher and biblical scholar Friedrich Schleiermacher. It was published in 1813 under the title *Ueber die verschiedenen Methoden des Uebersetzens* (On the various methods of translating). This is the period during which theorizing about translation began in earnest, in the sense that the theoretical writings published then were no longer tied to the writers' own experiences of translating particular texts. Instead, writers began to probe the phenomenon of translating in general and also its relationship to other disciplines that focus on language and the human mind. The pursuit of this relationship, or these relationships, has by no means ended, as we shall see in Section 1.3, but it began to develop a more scientific edge when the first attempts at machine translation were made at the end of the 1940s, and scholars began to understand the complexity of the translating endeavour. After that, says Steiner (1975/1992: 249), 'we are fully in the modern current', which is the period that this book focuses on. In this modern period, translation studies was named (Holmes 1972/1988) and achieved recognition as a discipline, so that it became possible to specialize in translation in its own right, rather than as an extra asset, relevant or related to certain aspects of a scholar's other, main, pursuit, as the quotation above from Richards (1979) clearly implies that it is.

In the early part of this modern period, it is possible to identify at least two major topics of discussion concerning translation studies. One centred on the place of translation studies within what we might loosely call the academy: was it an art or a science? The second, not wholly separate from the first, concerned the relationship between translation studies and other disciplines; for example, should translation studies consider itself a branch of comparative literature (and thus, arguably, be classed as an 'art') or should it align itself with linguistics (and thus, arguably, be considered a science)? Nida (1964) famously presents the case for the second position. It is his intention to provide 'an essentially descriptive approach to the translation process', and this approach, he believes, commits him to grounding his study in linguistics: 'The fundamental thrust', he writes, 'is, of course, linguistic, as it must be in any descriptive analysis of the relationship between corresponding messages in different languages'. Nevertheless, he adds, the focus 'is by no means narrowly linguistic, for language is here viewed as but one part of total human behavior, which in turn is the object of study of a number of related disciplines' (1964: 8).

The view of translating as an art is encapsulated in the title of Selver's book, *The Art of Translating Poetry* (1966), and eloquently made by Jones (1989), according to whom translating, especially translating poetry, 'could be called the art of compromise' (197). Jones discusses the translation of poetry with particular reference to his own experience as a translator of poetry, but points out that 'discussions with other translators and participation in translation workshops have shown [his experience] to be fairly typical' (1989: 185). Jones refers to translating as 'recreativity', a process of 'creating a new text along the model of an existing one' conceding, nevertheless, that 'all translation is a form of creation' (1989: 184). On the basis of his personal experience, Jones develops a model of poetic translation, which, in common with many models of translation, has three main phases, which Jones refers to as (i) understanding of the source text, (ii) interpretation, which is 'the search for cross-text equivalences' and (iii) creation, 'the construction of a target text' which comes to stand 'in a relationship of greater or lesser equivalence to the source text' (1989: 187). Bell (1991: 62–75), similarly, suggests three parts to the translation process, basing his model on the translation of a poem. His first phase is Analysis (reading the source-language text), which is followed by a phase called Preparing to Translate, and the final phase is called Synthesis, during which the target text is written. Bell's model depends 'on insights from linguistics and cognitive science', and he comes down on the science side of the debate about where translation belongs, apparently because the vast majority of translating is made of 'technical, medical, legal administrative' texts and 'the vast majority of translators are professionals engaged in making a living rather than whiling away the time in an agreeable manner by translating the odd ode or two on winter evenings' (1991: 5). Amusing though Bell's defence of translating as a scientific endeavour may be, it seems odd to imply that the translation of an ode cannot be approached scientifically, and that the type of the text that is undergoing translation should determine the translator's approach to its treatment; and Bell himself in fact presents his scientific account of the translation process on the basis of the translation of a poem. Be that as it may, accounts of translation as a tripartite process are very common indeed; for example, Nida (1964: 241) proposes that 'Technical [translation] procedures consist essentially of three phases: (1) analysis of the respective languages, source and receptor; (2) careful study of the source-language text; and (3) determination of the appropriate equivalents.'

A so-called integrated approach to translation studies was proposed by Mary Snell-Hornby (1988/1995), whose view is that text type does not determine the severity of what she refers to as 'any translator's dilemma', namely the tension between reproduction and recreation (Snell-Hornby 1988/1995: 1). It is Snell-Hornby's hope that by replacing the traditional dichotomies in translation theory between, for example, word-based and sense-based translation units, proposed by Cicero, and between different types of equivalence, for example dynamic versus formal equivalence, proposed by Nida (1964; see below), with 'a holistic, gestalt-like principle based on prototypes dynamically focused at points on a cline' (Snell-Hornby 1988/1995: 2), 'the multi-dimensional character of language with its dynamic tension of paradoxes and seemingly conflicting forces becomes the basis for translation' (1995: 2). This is a good place to begin to examine this and other theories of translation that have been based, more or less firmly, on a particular linguistic theory. In Catford's case, that of Halliday (1961) and in Nida's case that of Chomsky (1957). Snell-Hornby herself is especially enchanted by Charles Fillmore's scenes-and-frames semantics (1977).

The title and subtitle of Catford's book, *A Linguistic Theory of Translation: An Essay in Applied Linguistics* (1965) is about as specific as it is possible to be about the nature and purpose of a piece of work. Catford wants to provide 'an account of what translation *is*', as he puts it in his preface (1965: vii), and because he sees translation as 'an operation performed on languages', he believes that the translation theory he has set out to develop 'must draw upon a theory of language' (1965: 1). This is perhaps slightly odd, given that the object to be investigated is translation, not language; and is translation not rather a process performed *with* language? Arguably, a formulation like Catford's runs the risk of obscuring the nature of the item being investigated (the 'operation') by prioritizing a description of the object that the so-called operation is said to be 'performed' on. Indeed, Catford's first chapter is an account of the general linguistic theory he has chosen to work with, as presented by Halliday (1961) and by Halliday, McIntosh and Strevens (1964). This theory is social in its conception, insofar as it considers language to be 'a type of patterned human behaviour . . . perhaps the most important way in which humans interact in social situations' (Catford 1965: 1). Therefore, the starting point for the Hallidayan grammar that Catford builds his translation theory on is social: 'Our starting point', he begins 'is a consideration of how language is related to the human social situations in which it operates' (1965: 1). Such a situation will include a speaker/writer, whom Catford refers to as a *performer*, as well as at least one other participant, an *addressee* (1965: 1; italics in the original). The medium of communication may be spoken or written and may therefore be realized phonologically or graphologically, and its abstract levels of theorizing are grammar and lexis (vocabulary). The relationship between grammar and lexis on the one hand and the situation on the other is context (Catford 1965: 3). Context is a concept that has occupied the minds of most, possibly all, linguists concerned with language as a social phenomenon, and which in the later decades of the twentieth century also made its way into cognitively oriented theories of language like that of Dan Sperber and Deirdre Wilson (1986) and the account of translation derived from it by Ernst-August Gutt (1991).

Catford (1965: 20; italics in the original) defines translation as '*the replacement of textual material in one language (SL) by equivalent textual material in another language (TL)*', where 'SL' stands for source language and 'TL' for target language. Translation equivalence obtains between linguistic items (of various lengths and ranks) for situational rather than formal reasons, namely when they are '*interchangeable in a given situation*' (Catford 1965: 49; italics in the original). Therefore, the aim in translation is mostly 'to select TL equivalents . . . with the greatest possible overlap of situational range' with the source-language items (49). It happens, of course, that aspects of the situation where the ST operates cannot be matched very closely, or at all, with the situation where the translation is to operate, in which case translators may take various measures like annotation, explanation or simply borrowing; borrowing occurs in situations where the term is not translated at all, as in the case of *pizza*, for example, which has been borrowed from Italian for use in English and numerous other languages.

The units of Hallidayan grammar are (from smallest to largest; smaller units make up units at the level immediately above) morpheme, word, group, clause and sentence. So morphemes make up words, words form groups, groups form clauses, and clauses form sentences. Such a grammar is 'rank based' and its organizing principle is a 'rank scale'. The Hallidayan group corresponds to what most other grammars refer to as a 'phrase'. 'Below' the grammar is phonology and 'above' grammar is text. 'Below' and 'above' here are obviously place indicators metaphorically only; they are used to highlight the borders or limits of grammar. It is true that sounds (phonemes) make up words, but the ways in which they do so are studied within phonology, not within grammar; similarly, the ways in which sentences compose texts is studied as text analysis, not as grammar (text grammars have been proposed, but will not detain us here; see Van Dijk 1972). The main drawback of a theory of translation that is based on a theory of grammar might be expected to be that the upper limit of grammatical description is the sentence, whereas translation decisions very regularly need to be made on the basis of phenomena that span across sentences in a text. However, the theory that Catford draws on also takes lexical relations seriously, including those generally known as collocation and lexical sets: 'A collocation is the "lexical company" that a particular lexical item keeps' Catford 1965: 10) and 'a *lexical set* is a group of lexical items which have similar collocational ranges' (1965: 11). For example, he points out, 'sheep' collocates frequently with 'field', whereas 'mutton' collocates frequently with terms like 'roast'; so the two terms belong to different lexical sets. In contrast, 'chicken' belongs to the same lexical set as 'mutton' insofar as both collocate strongly with 'roast'. These concepts have proven immensely helpful in translation theory because, among other facets, they pinpoint both that and why it is that several terms with similar senses (e.g. high, tall) are often not interchangeable either within or across languages. For example, a building can be both high and tall in English, but a person can only be tall (if a person is high, they are intoxicated in some way, but may be either tall or short). In Danish, in contrast, 'høj' does duty for tall versions of either phenomenon, buildings and persons (as well as for intoxicated people, although these can also be described using the adjective 'skæv'). 'High' and 'tall' have different collocational ranges in English, and a translator needs to know what these are when translating the Danish term 'høj' into English. In order to come to know this, a translator can explore a corpus of English texts. A corpus, in the relevant sense, is a collection of texts, usually stored and searchable electronically. A search of such a corpus for the terms 'high' and 'tall' will illustrate their most frequent collocates, and it is likely that the collocates for 'tall' will include many more references to human beings than the collocates for 'high' will.

Exercise 1.1 Corpus exploration

In this exercise, you will practise using a corpus of English. You can use the British National Corpus (BNC, www.english-corpora.org/bnc/), or any other corpus of English.

A. Look up the terms 'tall' and 'high' in the corpus to test out the assertion made just above that the collocates for 'tall' include many more references to human beings than the collocates for 'high' do.
B. Think of a term in a language other than English which presents the same need for an informed choice in translation into English as the Danish term 'høj' does. Use a corpus to test your sense of what would be the most appropriate translation into English of the term you have identified. What is it that determines which term is the appropriate translation?

Comment

You can repeat this exercise with as many terms and languages as you like. This will make you adept at exploring a corpus, and it will remind you that the lexicons (vocabularies) of languages do not correspond one-to-one, and that some language 'rules' are 'just there' – like the 'rule' that people can be blonde, but cars cannot. If you type 'blonde car' into your search engine, it may give you a set of pictures of a blonde woman in or with a car.

The rank scale arrangement of the grammar (the principle of smaller units making up units at the rank next above) has given rise in translation theory to the notion of translation shifts (Catford 1965: 73–82). Translation shifts may take place when, for example, grammatical marking of tense by bound morphemes, as in English generally, is translated into time adverbs – words – in Mandarin Chinese, which has no bound morphemic markers of tense (Li and Thompson 1981: 184, 320); or when the word 'fortnight' is translated into the nominal group (noun phrase) 'to uger' (two weeks) in Danish; or when the Danish word 'døgn' (a day and a night) is translated into the nominal group (noun phrase) 'twenty-four hours' in English. The notion of the translation shift, and Catford's emphasis on the contextual influences on translation decisions remain relevant in translation studies, and Catford's definition of translation equivalence forms the starting point for the definition adopted by Gideon Toury (1978, 1995; see below).

The linguistic theory that inspires Nida (1964) is that of Noam Chomsky (1957), but it is important to note that despite the fundamental linguistic 'thrust' of his inspiration (Nida 1964: 8), mentioned in his introduction, Nida lists a number of disciplines that are 'related directly and indirectly to problems of semantic and linguistic correspondence' (1964: 8). These include anthropology, philosophy, psychology, psychiatry and philology as well as biblical interpretation, the latter being relevant because Nida's book is concerned especially with Bible translating. The attraction for Nida of Chomsky's theory is that Chomsky views language not 'as some fixed corpus of sentences, but as a dynamic mechanism capable of generating an infinite series of different utterances' which every normal adult speaker of the language will be able to understand, even though they have never heard them before (1964: 9). Catford and Nida thus complement one another in a similar manner to the way Halliday and Chomsky do: Halliday and Catford are primarily focused on language as a social phenomenon that can be interpreted in light of its relationship to the environment, the 'situation' of utterance; Chomsky and Nida consider language primarily as a psychological phenomenon that can be interpreted in light of speakers' shared humanity. These two foci are of course not in opposition to one another; they are merely different approaches to a phenomenon, language, which can surely be approached from both a social and a psychological vantage point.

Nida posits two types of translation equivalence, formal and dynamic. Formal equivalence obtains when items in the translation match source text items as closely as possible from a formal point of view, that is, when genre matches genre, sentence matches sentence, and concept matches concept. Nida gives as an example the phrase from Romans 16:16 which means 'holy kiss'. In a formal equivalence translation, this expression would be rendered using whatever terms in the language being translated into that would mean the same, that is, that would denote a kiss and ascribe to it the property of being holy. This phrase might then be annotated to explain 'that this was a customary method of greeting in New Testament times' (Nida 1964: 159). Dynamic equivalence, in contrast, would provide 'complete naturalness of expression' and refer to customs and behaviour that a translation receptor is familiar with from their own culture. Nida (1964: 160) refers to J. B. Phillips' translation of Romans 16:16. Here, the Greek expression that means 'greet one another with a holy kiss' is translated into 'give one another a hearty handshake all around' (Phillips 1953). When it is considered necessary to adjust a translation in this way (relative to the first-written text) for it to be suitable for a given audience, a translator may either alter, as in the case of Phillips, or subtract, or add. Each of these processes is 'designed to produce correct equivalents' (Nida 1964: 226). Equivalence, then, is a relative concept – relative to the occasion and to the user of the translation – in Nida's generally source text [first-written text] oriented theory of translation.

Clearly, early-twentieth-century translation theorists realized the contentious nature of the notion of equivalence, which was so difficult to define, and to which we shall return in Section 5.3. There was general agreement about how translation ought to be undertaken, namely by proceeding from an analysis of the first-written text to the production of the translation, and about what the goal of translation was, namely to produce a text that was in some way equivalent to the pre-existing first-written text; and Nida's flexibility notwithstanding, the concept was left relatively undisturbed until the late 1970s and early 1980s, when it was assaulted from two directions: through the work of Gideon Toury in Israel and through the work of the so-called Skopos theorists in Germany, including, prominently, Hans Josef Vermeer (1978) and Katarina Reiss (1971/2000). One of the meanings of *skopos* (Greek *σκοπός*) in its original Greek language-home is 'goal' or 'purpose', and Skopos theorists were at pains to point out that a translation, be it ever so accurate, is useless for a client who has commissioned it if it is incapable of encouraging the behaviours in its readers that it was meant to encourage. For example, advertisements are normally meant to encourage a person to buy a certain product or to engage in a certain action (e.g. visiting a museum or donating to a charity), so it is important to present the product or experience in such a way that people are attracted to it or that it seems useful to them. Therefore, advertisements often vary between different locales in ways that reach beyond language variations; fitting an advertisement to a new locale often requires more significant adjustment to content than would be demanded by the different modes of expression that languages embody and by pragmatic considerations, for example of politeness and generally good linguistic manners, alone. This is also evident in the case of products that have more than one function. For example, on the Vetsend.co.uk website, which is aimed at owners of animals, the antiseptic cream Helosan is advertised as seen in the box.

Helosan

Helosan is an antiseptic skin cream with a hydrating and moisturising effect suitable for horses, dogs and cats.

Helosan makes the skin soft, supple and resilient. Helosan can be used as an intensive restorative for dry and damaged skin.

Use

- Clean the skin well with cold or warm water.
- Apply Helosan where needed.
- Helosan may be applied several times a day.

Composition

Aqua (fats), Liquid Paraffin, Glycerin, Cetearyl Alcohol, Glyceryl Stearate, PEG-100 Stearate, Polyaminopropyl Biguanide, Eucalyptus globulus, Propylparaben.

On Amazon.co.uk, in contrast, the product is not aimed at animals only (both accessed 7 June 2024).

Exercise 1.2 Advertisement analysis

This exercise will enhance your awareness of how the cultural characteristics of the locale in which an advertisement is to function may influence its content and form.

A. Identify a pair or set of language versions of an advertisement for the same product, and see whether the versions reflect cultural stereotypes and/or different cultural realities.
B. If you are working with others who have different language pairs or sets, compare your findings. Is there a pattern in the degree of differences you see between language pairs or sets?

Comment

This exercise illustrates that translations often differ more from their sources than you might expect, for good reasons. Unless translation is being used as a test of a person's language skills, it involves a great deal more than matching term for term and sentence for sentence. It requires understanding of cultures and their behavioural and other norms. If you are working with others, you may find that the variations between the translations and the source may be greater, the greater the differences and distances are between the language cultures involved.

As Nord (1988/2005: 9–10) points out, the importance of ensuring that a translation is fit for purpose in the sense of appealing to its projected readership in turn highlights the need for the commissioner of a translation (that is, the person who needs the translation or who asks for it on behalf of the end user) to provide the translator with a detailed translation brief, that is, a clear outline of the target situation, including, prominently, information about the end user, the purpose the translation is to serve, and the medium in which it is to appear. Vienne (1994: 55) provides a detailed account of what he terms an 'analysis of the translational situation', including a set of questions for the requester (the person who has asked for or requires the translation) and a set of consequent actions to be taken and strategies to be adopted by the translator. Such requirements remain as crucial for the success of a translation effort as they were when the works by Nord and Vienne were published.

A potential difficulty that commissioners of translations may encounter in this respect is that they do not necessarily know what the needs of the prospective user of the translation are, because they do not know how a certain purpose is achieved, textually, in the culture where the translation is to be used. Therefore, it is important for a translator to be thoroughly familiar with the culture that the translation is to function in – with its textual conventions, including genre conventions, politeness strategies, and linguistic and cultural taboos; and because these may change over time, it is important for a translator to keep in close touch with the cultures of each of their languages. The translator must also be prepared to argue for their translation choices in case these are questioned by a requester or commissioner. The translator needs to act appropriately and convincingly as an expert in the shaping and wording of a text that will be appropriate to the purpose it is meant to fulfil.

Many translators often face time restrictions, and these can be challenging to deal with. Because of strict deadlines, it can be difficult for translators to carry out the types of preparatory work that theorists recommend. This does not mean that there should not be a focus on such work during the education and training of translators, however, because trainee translators and those newly qualified will learn from such a focus much that can be transferred to future situations in which it may not be possible to undertake detailed text and situation analysis. Such analyses, however, can be significantly aided and enhanced by the availability of the internet, which is a gigantic textual resource, as well as by the availability of large, machine-stored and machine-readable corpora, some of which consist of specialized texts, and others of more general written language. Corpora of spoken language also exist. In Chapter 4, we will explore corpus use for translational purposes.

As discussed above, publications like those by Vermeer, Nord and Vienne relinquished a focus on equivalence in favour of a focus on text purpose and situatedness, concepts that remain central in translation studies and translation practice (see Suojanen, Koskinen and Tuominen 2015). Nevertheless, it has to be possible to name the relationship between two texts which stand to one another in the relationship of text T and translation of text T by way of a briefer term than the lengthy description I have just provided; and the term 'equivalence' has occupied that position for a long time. Perhaps, then, it may be possible to reconceptualize the notion of equivalence in a way that does not prioritize linguistic relationships over textual and contextual relationships, and which can accommodate the important concepts of function and text receiver or text user too. One such approach to the notion of equivalence was developed by Gideon Toury in the late 1970s.

Toury points out that most translation theories before the time when he was writing were oriented towards the source text (ST) and the source language (SL). They consider translation to be a reconstruction of the source text in the target language (TL)

> in such a way and to such an extent that TT [target text] and ST are interchangeable according to some preconceived definition of this interchangeability. In other words, they concern themselves mainly with *potential* translation ... rather than with *actual* translation, hence with the *act of translating*, which actually proceeds from ST, rather than with *translations* as actual textual-linguistic products ... which belong first and foremost to the system of texts written in TL. (Toury 1978/1980: 35)

This, he continues, makes such theories 'totally unable to supply a sound starting point and framework for a descriptive study of actual translations'. What we need is a TT-oriented approach to the study of translations as empirical phenomena. As mentioned above, the *sine qua non* of translation is the relationship between the texts involved, which we shall call equivalence. In his discussion of this notion, Toury turns to Catford's general definition (1965: 50, italics in the original) '*translation equivalence occurs when a SL and a TL text or item are relatable to (at least some of) the same features of substance*'. To this definition, Toury (1978/1980: 37) adds the important notion of relevance: 'Translation equivalence occurs when a SL and a TL text (or item) are relatable to (at least some of) the same relevant features.' The notion of relevance, he points out, is relative in two ways: first, relevance is always relevance for something or from a certain point of view; and secondly not all features are of equal relevance from every point of view and for every purpose. We should therefore 'speak in terms of *hierarchies of relevance*, rather than of absolute relevance' (Toury 1978/1980: 38, italics in the original). Features that are relevant from the point of view of the target culture may not be those that are relevant for the source culture. In addition, from the point of view of the target text, equivalence is 'not a postulated requirement, but an empirical fact, like TT itself: the *actual* relationships obtaining between TT and ST' (Toury 1978/1980: 39, italics in the original). This conception, then, allows for the use of 'translation equivalence' as a descriptive term to denote an empirical phenomenon: the relationship that actually obtains between the texts; that relationship can then be examined, as can, indeed, the target texts themselves, which function as translations. The questions to be asked in translation studies then focus on the type and degree of translation equivalence that obtains between the texts (Toury 1978/1980: 47). Here, Toury employs the notions of acceptability and adequacy, and the position of a translation, or a corpus of translations, relative to these concepts depends on the norms that govern translation in a given culture. It is the study of norms, therefore, that should 'be the focal concept in any study of literary translation' (Toury 1978/1980: 50). It is important to note that Toury (1980: 7) explains that he 'regards most of the mechanisms dealt with [in his 1980 collection of articles] as pertaining not to [literary] ... translation alone, but to translation in general, as a type of *semiotic* activity and product' (italics in the original).

With the work of Gideon Toury, the notion of equivalence is laid open to examination in a manner that was not enabled by previous, source text-oriented theories of translation. Equivalence *is* the relationship between texts that stand to each other in the relationship of first-written text and translation, and there are degrees and types of equivalence. Equally, translations are those texts which societies accept as translation, and these, too, are available for examination in ways that we will explore in the following section.

1.2 Empirical Investigation of Translation Products

In Section 1.1, we looked at what translators and theorists say about translating as an important way to get to know something about the translation phenomenon. A second important way in which we can come to know something about translation is to examine the tangible product of the process of translating, namely translations, perhaps in the contexts of the first-written texts that the translations represent in different languages. I understand a text to be a stretch of language, of any length, composed to tell, ask, request, or carry out any other act and, often, many such acts, by way of language. Acts carried out by way of language were named 'speech acts' by John Langshaw Austin (1911–1960) (see Austin 1962 and see Chapter 2 Section 2.1), but I use the term in this book to include acts carried out through written texts. A text may be, and often is, illustrated and accompanied by other outcomes of acts of meaning-making (music, film, photographs, paintings and so on). In such cases, the text will interact with these other acts of meaning-making to contribute to the unique meaning generated momentarily when a person engages with the translation in its situation; but it is helpful to be able to isolate for discussion the textual contribution to this situation. For this reason, I do not adopt here Adami and Ramos Pinto's broader definition of text as 'any multimodally composed meaningful whole' (2020: 73).

Translated texts can be investigated in isolation from the first-written texts they represent, or they can be investigated in the contexts of these first-written texts. Both methods have been used to describe translations and to make claims about the nature of translation. The main methods for investigating translations are traditional close reading by humans, and machine searches through electronically stored and electronically readable corpora of texts. Human close reading is limited in its scope by time and human endurance; machine storage, searching and analysis are in principle unlimited. However, they require considerable human effort to determine what to search for, to design the corpus, and to interpret the findings, and are therefore no less reliant on human endurance and ingenuity than investigations unaided by machines. Machine-aided investigation is likely to be more accurate in the search phase, but its susceptibility to human frailty in the phase of interpreting the findings of the search is as great as that of human close reading. Nevertheless, machine-aided searches and the results derived from them may be more safely explored for the drawing of generalizations than more limited, human-only searches, because machines do not fail (given reliable programming and definition of search terms) during phases of identifying items of the type that is of interest

Human searches can focus on any feature of text, whereas there are restrictions on the foci of machine-aided searches. A computer cannot, for example, be asked to search for metaphors, metonymies, jokes or sarcasm; only clearly identifiable, graphic forms and combinations of such forms can be searched for by an a-cognizant mechanism. Of course, graphic forms such as '... like ...', 'What do you call ...', and 'Oh, that's very ...' may signal the presence of the kinds of phenomenon just mentioned, but the phenomena are not limited to taking these forms. Nord (1988/2005) presents a detailed model for undertaking translation-oriented text analysis which does not necessitate the use of electronic devices; the model draws on Skopos theory and on text-linguistics. Boase-Beier (2006, 2020) presents a number of stylistic approaches to translation analysis and practice, and I (Malmkjær 2004, 2011) present a method called Translational Stylistics (which will be further examined in Section 5.4). Each of these methods is devised to be used for detailed analysis and interpretation of individual texts or a set of texts in preparation for translation, or when comparing texts – whether a first-written text and one or more translations of it, or only the translations. Some or all of these texts may of course exist in machine-readable form and be searched in that form; but for translational stylistic purposes, the extent of texts needs to be limited to a size that is manageable by a human reader and interpreter.

Large machine-readable and machine-analysable corpora have been designed for numerous languages and language pairs or sets (see for example McEnery and Wilson 1996 and McEnery, Xiao and Tono 2006). These are all useful for translation and translation-related purposes. Monolingual corpora (corpora of one language) can provide information about the use of a specific term in a specific language, so that if a translator is wondering which of several candidate terms to use on a specific occasion, they can search for these terms in a corpus to see a selection of the contexts in which the terms have occurred in the relevant languages. Aligned parallel corpora (corpora of first-written texts and their translations into one or more languages) can provide evidence of past translation candidates for terms. Five hundred ready-to-use corpora in more than ninety languages, each of up to 30 billion words, can be explored through the Sketch Engine website, which also contains information on how to design and use such corpora for translation purposes. Examples can also be found in Anderman and Rogers (2008), Bernardini (2000, §3), Grainger, Lerot and Petch-Tyson (2003), Hasselgård and Oksefjell (1999, section III), Kenny (2001: Ch. 5) and Laviosa (2002). Search tools include Antconc, freely available at the time of writing, paraconc, and WordSmith Tools. See also the Concordancers website, which gives information about a number of concordance programmes, and go to WebCorp in order to access the web as a corpus (see Further Reading at the end of this chapter for addresses). For translation-related research methods in general, see Mellinger and Hanson (2017), Saldanha and O'Brien (2013), and Williams and Chesterman (2002).

There are several possible goals of text investigation for translation and translation-related purposes. One is very practical and has already been mentioned: looking at how translators have translated in the past can help translators of the present to select their own equivalents, although it is important to remember that the past does not necessarily resemble the present closely, nor does the past limit what may happen in the present and the future. Furthermore, the translation of a term may vary with text type and text purpose. Close source text analysis can also be used by a translator, as Nord (1988/2005: 1) points out, to ensure that a text that is to be translated has been 'wholly and correctly understood', though it is clear from more recent empirical studies that not all translators follow the practice of ensuring that they have wholly and correctly understood the text that they are to translate. For example, the preferred reading strategy exhibited by a translator whose gaze behaviour was observed by Jakobsen (2019b) was 'as little [reading] as possible' or 'only as much [reading] as necessary' (105).

Another purpose of text analysis in translation studies is to identify features characteristic of translated text, such as explicitation (Toury 1976/1980; Blum-Kulka 1986; Øverås 1996, 1998), simplification, normalization, interference, and avoidance of repetition (even when repetition is a feature of the text being translated) (Toury 1991). Avoidance of repetition was identified by Toury (1977: 113–236) in a corpus of literary translations into Hebrew, but is familiar to many readers of translations and their first-written texts, since it is 'one of the most persistent, unbending norms in translation ... irrespective of the many functions repetition may have in particular source texts' (Toury 1991: 188). It is important to keep in mind that repetition may have such functions, and that carrying these functions over into the translation might result in a more appropriate translation than avoiding repetition might.

Explicitation is the 'almost general tendency – irrespective of the translator's identity, language, genre, period, and the like – to explicate in the translation information that is only implicit in the original text' (Toury 1976/1980: 60). This tendency often leads to a translation that is longer than its source. Mona Baker (1993: 243–244) provides an excellent example of this phenomenon: a single, simple sentence of ten words in English is rendered into a paragraph in Arabic, consisting of four sentences of varying complexity in which it is explained that Truman, briefly mentioned in the original sentence, was the American president who succeeded Roosevelt and that he had appeared to be unsuitable as a leader, but proved to be immensely effective, something that the translator suggests might also happen to the one-time third president of Egypt, Muhammad Anwar Sadat (1918–1981).

Simplification in translation was identified by Dagut (1971) and defined by Blum-Kulka and Levenston (1978/1983: 119) as 'the process and/or result of making do with *less* words' in contexts where there are no precise equivalents in the target language for a source text item. This can reduce the lexical variety and density of the translation compared with the first-written text. That is, the vocabulary of the first-written text may be more varied than the vocabulary of the translation, and the information load may be less in the translation than in the first-written text because there are fewer lexical words (words that carry 'concrete' meanings) than grammatical words (function words, which serve to hold the text together but which do not 'add' meaning) in the translation than in the first-written text (Zanettin 2013: 22).

Normalization is defined by M. Baker (1997: 183) as a tendency 'to exaggerate features of the target language and to conform to its typical patterns'. In other words, translators tend to make choices which are 'more conventional from the target language point of view, than are those made by original writers from the source language point of view' (Kenny 2001: 55). Malmkjær (1998) identifies normalization in a set of translations into English of Hans Christian Andersen's story usually titled *The Steadfast Tin Soldier* in English. The Danish term for 'born', 'født', which is used in the Danish first-written text about the tin soldiers the story centres on, is translated into 'born' in only one of a set of ten translations she examines (other terms used are 'made', 'come', and 'sprung').

Interference from the first-written text in the writing of a translation is unavoidable in the sense that the translation is based, at least to some extent – usually to a large extent – on the first-written text; if it were not, it would not be a translation. However, the term 'interference' is normally only used in situations where features of the first-written text and of the source language are obviously mirrored in the translation and where this causes the translation to sound unnatural or odd in the language being translated into, and/or in the text type in question in the culture where the translation is to function. For example, a leaflet that provides information about Gaudi's Expiatory Temple of the Sagrada Familia in Barcelona, Catalonia, explains that eight bell towers 'of more than 100 m high' have already been built. The quoted stretch is clearly a direct translation of the Catalan 'de més de 100 m', albeit with the addition of 'high', whereas the natural expression in English would have been either 'more than 100 metres high' or 'more than 100 metres tall' or 'of more than 100 metres in height'.

Exercise 1.3 Interference

This exercise is intended to enhance your awareness of interference in translation.

A. Examine a set of texts and translations for signs of interference. What aspects of the translations are affected by the interference (e.g. lexis, grammar, cultural conventions)?
B. Retranslate the texts or parts of them so that they display no signs of interference.
C. What action did you take?
D. If you have access to the first-written texts for any of the translations, double-check to see whether the phenomena that you have noticed are in fact interference or simply the reflection of a poorly written first-written text.
E. Not all poor translation leads to poor translations. Or does it? Should a translator produce a well-written text even if the first-written text is badly made? Never? Always? Sometimes? Argue for your opinion.

Comment

Try to look out for signs of interference in the translated texts you come across in your everyday life, and think about how you might produce interference-free versions of these.

A further possible outcome of the analysis of translated texts is the identification of terms and expressions specific to particular text types and particular topics. This process is known as term extraction, and Sketch Engine, mentioned above, offers an automated method for translators to extract terms from their own text corpora. Sketch Engine will also help translators build a corpus if they do not already have one. Of course, it is also possible for a translator to compile term banks themselves on the basis of their growing experience with different text types and, importantly, different clients, who often have their own personal or company style, which includes sets of specialized terms. The academic field concerned with terms is called 'terminology', and Sager (1990: 2) defines this as 'the study and field of activity concerned with the collection, description, processing and presentation of terms, i.e. lexical items belonging to specialized areas of usage of one or more languages'. He points out that terminology data banks have existed in many organizations since the early 1970s, and insists 'that the only practical means of processing lexical data is by computer' (1990: 129). As mentioned above, Sketch Engine offers an automated method of term extraction, but as Sager (1990: 131) reminds us, 'terminology compilation is an ongoing and repeated activity', because language and its specialized sub-languages change over time.

Having considered research directed at translation products, we will now consider how the mental acts that translators perform to create these products have been investigated.

1.3 Empirical Investigation of Translation Processes

A number of methods are used to identify the cognitive processes and efforts that are involved in making translations. The most prominent and earliest of these methods is the think-aloud protocol (TAP), which involves recording translators' verbalizations of their thoughts and considerations during or after translating. Early examples of such investigations tended to focus on instances in the translation process when translators encountered problems and on identifying the strategies translators have used to deal with these problems. For example, Lörscher (1986: 279–282) identified fourteen strategies employed by German university language students of English in fifteen oral translations. These ranged from 'RP': realizing a translation problem, through the formation of 'PSH': problem-solving hypothesis, to 'VKT': verbalizing translational knowledge. There were also sub-strategies of many of the main strategies together with a bewildering array of patterns of combinations of these. Krings (2001) and Shih (2006, 2015, 2023) have used the introspective method to investigate translators' revision and editing strategies, and Krings (1986) and others have built models of the translation process on the basis of TAPs. These show that the translation process is not straightforwardly linear: many translators look back and forth in both texts, the first-written text and the translation. This finding has stood the test of time. As Jakobsen (2019b: 71) puts it:

> if we are looking over the shoulder of the translator, we can see that production is jerky. Sudden bursts of production are followed by shorter or longer intervals with no typing activity while the source text (ST) is scrutinized.

Exercise 1.4 Investigating the translation process using TAP

This exercise enables two people to work together. It is intended to familiarize you with a popular method of investigating the translation process and to raise your awareness of decisions taking during translating.

If you are working through this book alone, you can record yourself speaking out your thoughts during translating, and think about your TAP afterwards.

A. If possible, pair up with a colleague. Take turns to be researcher and translator. The translator translates a text of around 200 words, speaking out their thoughts and considerations as they go along. The researcher can decide whether to allow the translator to use reference materials (internet, electronic dictionaries . . .). The researcher records (you can use a mobile phone or any other recording equipment) what the translator says, making a TAP. The researcher develops a set of questions to ask the translator about their TAP. The researcher can refer to the translation that has been made when asking questions.
B. Do you see any patterns in the TAP, or TAPs if you are a pair? Can you identify mention of any obvious strategies that the translator has employed?

There are certain disadvantages associated with the introspective method. Requiring translators to speak their thoughts aloud while translating is asking them to work in an unfamiliar way, since translators do not habitually speak their thoughts aloud while translating. Engaging in this unusual behaviour might distort the process that is being reported on; for example, the flow (Csikszentmihalyi 1990) of a translation experience will clearly be interrupted so that the translator may work with shorter segments of texts than they normally would and experience less enjoyment from both the text and from translating it. The request to speak aloud may be experienced as a pressure, either because of anxiety to 'get it right' or because the translator wants to please the researcher. For either reason, the translator may be an unreliable witness when reporting on their own thinking.

Arguably, the main disadvantage of the TAP method is that it cannot cast light on passages during which a translator experiences no problems and therefore says little or nothing; but such passages are perhaps the most interesting when we are trying to discover the nature of the translation process, because, we might assume, they occur when translating proceeds in a natural, untroubled fashion. Bernardini (2001) provides a thorough survey and critique of TAP studies undertaken until around 2000, and Jääskeläinen (2002) provides an annotated bibliography.

An alternative method of investigation which does not depend on translators' own impressions of the translation process relies instead on logging translating translators' behaviour – their typing behaviour and their eye and gaze movements. Typing behaviour can be recorded using a computer program developed by Arnt Lykke Jakobsen and the then fifteen-year-old Lasse Schou (see Jakobsen 2016, 1998, 1999; Jakobsen and Schou 1999). The program is called Translog, and it operates as follows (Jakobsen 1999: 11):

> When a subject translates in *Translog*, the source text appears in the top half of the screen ... The translator's target text is written in the bottom half of the screen ... Whenever a key has been touched, *Translog* records the time of day and stores the information. In sum, *Translog* creates a log of every key that was pressed during the composition of the target text, of all revisions made, all (electronic) dictionary lookups, all typos and errors – and when it all happened.

In a footnote, Jakobsen (2017: 29) tracks the development of Translog as follows:

> The first *Translog* version was developed in 1995 (in DOS). The first word-based version appeared in 1999. The 2006 'Academic' version was developed in the context of the EU Eye-to-IT project (2006–2009) and has been widely distributed. In 2011, it was superseded by M. Carl's development of a Translog II version. [Carl 2012]

A database of projects undertaken using Translog, known as the 'CRITT Translation Process Research Database (TPR-DB)' is publicly available (see Carl, Schaeffer and Bangalore 2016).

Of course, the data obtained by means of Translog is external behaviour, which is interpreted as evidence of internal processing; but Translogging does away with the need for translators to self-report. Some studies have used both methods (e.g. Hansen 1999), and others have used a combination of retrospective protocols (translators are asked *after* the event about their thoughts while they translated), keylogging and tracking translating translators' eye movements (see e.g. Alves, Pagano and da Silva 2010).

Eye movements have been used in reading research since the 1800s. According to Wikipedia,

> In 1879, the French ophthalmologist Louis Émile Javal used a mirror on one side of a page to observe eye movement in silent reading, and found that it involves a succession of discontinuous individual movements for which he coined the term saccades [Javal 1878]. In 1898, Erdmann & Dodge used a hand-mirror to estimate average fixation duration and saccade length with surprising accuracy [Erdmann and Dodge 1898]. (https://en.wikipedia.org/wiki/Eye_movement_in_reading; accessed 7 June 2024)

Technology has advanced since these pioneering studies. By 2020, the preferred method of recording eye movements in translation research was to employ sensor technology that enables a computer to track where someone is looking on a computer screen; and the preferred machine for enabling this was the TOBII eye-tracker (see www.tobii.com/; accessed 23 January 2024).

Eye tracking provides information about the typical duration of eye movements and fixations and about factors of text that influence them, such as word familiarity, word predictability, length, complexity and ambiguity. Such data, of course, is still external evidence in the form of physical behaviour; researchers interpret the data as evidence of internal cognitive processing. It suggests that translators make use of the fact that the source text remains available for them to consult throughout the translating process. The permanence allows the translators to concentrate all their efforts on individual translation decisions without having to rely on their short-term memory since they can look at the text items again whenever necessary (Jakobsen 2019b: 107).

The method assumes that the translator is busy processing what they are gazing at, and not, for example, staring at a stretch of text while thinking hard about a previous stretch or about where they spent the previous weekend. The method has inherited this so-called eye–mind assumption from reading theory (Just and Carpenter 1980: 331), namely that what is being looked at is what is being processed. This assumption may be reliable in experimental situations, where the subjects who take part are likely to do their best to concentrate on the task at hand. Further, it can be difficult to look at text without reading it. Jakobsen (2019b: 73) adds that 'it is fair to assume that pausing as part of the typing process is a … meaningful indicator of cognitive processing' and that (2019b: 74) 'longer pauses indicate greater mental effort'.

A number of studies using eye tracking have suggested that the reason why someone reads affects the way in which they read, including how fast they read (Schaeffer et al. 2017: 38); in particular, it can take a reader twice as long to read a text that they have been told they will be asked to translate later than it takes them to read a text that they have been told they will have to answer comprehension questions about later. The number of eye fixations and regressions (re-readings of passages) is also greater if a person thinks they are reading for translation (Schaeffer et al. 2017: 39). According to Schaeffer et al. (2017) this is partly because two language systems are activated from the beginning of the reading when a reader knows that they will be translating the text, an assumption that supports and is supported by Jakobsen and Jensen's suggestion (2008: 116) that 'a fair amount of pre-translation probably enters into the reading of a text as soon as it is taken to be a source text for translation'.

There have also been studies on 'translation in the brain', as Alves, Szpak and Buchweitz (2019) put it. These studies focus on identifying the areas of the brain that are involved in translating, using positron emission tomography (PET), functional magnetic resonance imaging (fMRI), or functional near-infrared spectroscopy (fNIRS), for example. Arguably, the brain is rather closer to whatever we mean by 'mind' than the gazing eyes and the typing fingers are, so the evidence obtained by this method can be interpreted as more closely related to the cognitive processing that the translators who are the experimental subjects engage in than both eye tracking and keyboard logging are.

PET imaging works by scanning the blood flow in a person's brain. The subject has a dye with radioactive tracers injected into the bloodstream and is placed in a body scanner. In contrast, fMRI uses a magnetic field and radio waves to take a large number of images of the brain, milliseconds apart, and can show how the brain responds to different stimuli; the scanner is effectively a large magnet. Unlike these scanners, fNIRS technology can be worn on a person's body, and this means that changes in blood oxygenation and blood volume can be monitored over extended periods without interfering with the person's behaviour and environment (Lu and Yuan 2019: 109). According to Lu and Yuan (2019: 110), research using these methods suggests that there is a hemispheric lateralization process involved in translation. This is hardly surprising, since the different roles played in language use by the two hemispheres of the brain have long been recognized, and translation is, as García (2019: 76) puts it, 'necessarily rooted in linguistic mechanisms'.

García (2019) provides a detailed account of the brain and its functions in connection with what he terms 'interlingual reformulation' (IR), including translating and interpreting. As he points out, 'much of our current knowledge about neurocognition comes from the investigation of dysfunctional systems – in particular, lesion models' (2019: 99). Studies of brain-damaged bilinguals have shown four types of translation-related potential effects of injury: (i) compulsive translation (immediate, involuntary translation of one's own utterances or the utterances of others), (ii) inability to translate, (iii) paradoxical translation behaviour (for example ability to translate into a language that one cannot produce spontaneously but inability to translate into a language that one can produce spontaneously) and (iv) translation without comprehension, that is, the ability to translate an utterance that one does not understand (García 2019: 100–114). These studies show very clearly that translating is dependent not only on what we think of as the mind but, like all language use (and indeed this 'mind'), also on its main physical manifestation, the brain. Importantly, they also indicate that 'translation subsystems are neurofunctionally independent from those engaged during L1 and L2 tasks' (García 2019: 118), In other words, being bilingual is not tantamount to being a translator, something quite a few bilinguals agree with, in my experience, and a good reason for considering translation as a skill that has to be learnt and practised for expertise to be achieved.

Finally, there is growing evidence that emotion is centrally involved in the translation phenomenon (see Jakobsen 2017: 39; Hubscher-Davidson 2018) and that emotion combines with cognition in ways that may differ between individuals. Hubscher-Davidson (2018: 2) identifies 'three distinctive areas where emotions influence translators: emotional material contained in source texts, their own emotions, and the emotions of source and target readers'. Translators themselves testify to the role of emotion in translating. As Boase-Beier and de Vooght (2019: 17) put it,

> Translation ... is never about getting it right, about approximating the form or content of the original, about making a copy for those who do not speak Yiddish, or Latvian or French. It is about recognising someone else's story, understanding the way the teller has chosen to tell it, and passing it on to others.

Studies like those reported here provide impressions of the complexity of the enterprise of translation. It is important for translation practitioners, students and researchers alike to build awareness of their métier and interest as a complex topic of interest to the language sciences and to other human sciences too. This should endow translators with a keen sense of self-worth and enhance their sense of themselves as professionals engaged in an activity that is of great scientific interest as well as of considerable practical and commercial value.

Summary

The focus of this chapter has been on how scholars have tried to come to understand what translation involves, both in terms of textuality (translations as products) and in terms of the cognitive processing involved. We have explored the place of translation in academia, and identified important concepts in translation theory, including equivalence, shifts, collocation, skopos; and features that are frequently identified in translated texts, such as explicitation, simplification, normalization, interference and specialized terminology. We have noted that translations as products may be investigated with or without the aid of computation, and discussed the relative merits of each choice: machine investigation enables searches of vast quantities of data, whereas human investigators are limited in their processing powers. The interrelation between the two has been stressed: a mass of data is only as useful as its human interpreters' ability to manage it.

Influential figures in the establishment of translation studies as an independent discipline have been introduced (Catford, Nida, Toury, Reiss and Vermeer, Snell-Hornby). Ways of exploring the cognitive processes involved in translating have been described (TAPS, keylogging, eye tracking, PET, fMRI and fNIRS), and we have touched on the role emotion can play in the translation process. Chapter 2 will focus on the genres of translation and on commissioners and consumers of translations.

Further Reading

Hinchliffe, I., Oliver, T. and Schwartz, R. (eds. and compilers). (2014). *101 Things a Translator Needs to Know*. WLF Think Tank. United Kingdom: WFL 101 Publishing.

This small book contains a selection of practical tips compiled by three successful practising professional translators, and advertised as for beginners as well as seasoned professional freelance and staff translators – relevant to any translator at any stage of their career.

Li, D., Lei, V. L. C. and He, Y. (eds.) (2019). *Researching Cognitive Processes of Translation*. Singapore: Springer.

This book contains eight chapters in two parts. The three chapters in the first part focus on theory (of translation studies, of bilingual language processing, and of machine translation post-editing) and the five chapters in the second part focus on expert translators' segmentation behaviour, ways of investigating brain activity during translation (two chapters), how to measure translation difficulty, and the relationship between teaching translation competence and teaching L2 writing.

Meylaerts, R. and Marais, K. (eds.) (2023). *The Routledge Handbook of Translation Theory and Concepts.* Oxford: Routledge.

This handbook contains a collection of twenty-three chapters covering the foundations of the translation studies discipline and approaches to it.

At the time of writing, search tools mentioned in this chapter are available at the following addresses, all accessed 5 June 2024:

Antconc www.laurenceanthony.net/software/antconc/
Paraconc https://paraconc.com/
Sketch Engine https://sketchengine.eu
WordSmith Tools https://lexically.net/wordsmith/
Concordancers http://martinweisser.org/corpora_site/concordancers.html gives information about a number of concordancing programs.
WebCorp www.webcorp.org.uk provides access to the web as a corpus.

CHAPTER 2

What Translation Is For

Preview

In this chapter, we examine the notion of genre in order to distinguish different kinds of translation made for different purposes (Section 2.1). Genres that are examined in some detail include brochures, tourism texts, community information materials, instructions for use, legal texts, medical texts, official documents, scientific writing, news texts and subtitles. Localization, which is the adaptation of texts to their environment, is also introduced. Secondly, the chapter discusses the relationships between translators and those who pay translators for their services (Section 2.2), and finally it examines the relationships between translators and the people who are the projected and actual readers of the translations (Section 2.3).

2.1 Translations and Their Genres

According to Swales (1981: 10, 2011: 4), a genre is 'a more or less standardized communicative event with a goal or set of goals mutually understood by the participants in that event and occurring within a functional rather than a social or personal setting'. The analysis of genres, known as genre analysis, is, in turn, defined as 'a system of analysis that is able to reveal something of the patterns of organization of a "genre" and the language used to express those patterns' (Dudley-Evans 1987: 1). Bringing these insights together, we may define a genre, broadly, as a text or discourse type which is recognized by its users as being of that type, by way of certain features of its structure and language use, and which has certain recognized uses, users and settings within a community. For example, a sermon is typically used in the setting of a place of worship, by a person in a pastoral role, to address a congregation, typically composed of believers, on various matters, secular and/or religious, from a religious point of view. It differs from an academic lecture, for example, in that the academic lecture is usually delivered in a university setting, by an academic, to an audience of students and/or colleagues, on a specialized topic relevant to the audience's subject of study or specialism, with the intention, usually, of informing the audience and encouraging them to undertake their own reading and research on that topic. The reason that discussions of genres tend to focus on aspects of structure and setting rather than lexis is that lexis is easily shared across genres; for example, if the topic of a lecture is religion, the lecture can be expected to include an amount of terminology typical of sermons. There will always be this possibility of lexical overlap between genres, given that lexis is closely related to topic, and topics float freely between genres; a newspaper leader, like a sermon, can in principle be on any topic, whereas a topic is closely tied to its lexis – you cannot easily discuss gardening, for example, without mentioning soil, positioning and names of plants, digging, beds, seeds and sowing. Of course, a few particular genres are closely tied to only one particular topic; for example, weather forecasts cannot be weather forecasts without focusing on the weather.

The analysis of genres is useful for translators because, as Miller (1984: 151) puts it, 'an understanding of genre can help account for the way we encounter, interpret, react to and create particular texts'. Translators often want to ensure that the readers of a translation can share the experience of encountering, interpreting and reacting that the first-written text provides for its readers; so being able to recognize and write according to the conventions of genres in each of their languages and cultures is important for translators. However, the forms and conventions of genres differ both within and across cultures and languages. For example, British recipes tend to employ the imperative mood (e.g. 'whisk to a smooth batter', from the BBC Good Food recipe for pancakes) whereas Danish recipes tend to employ passive voice (e.g. 'Æg og mel piskes sammen' (Eggs and flour are whisked together), from a pancake recipe from the website of DK-Kogebogen).

Exercise 2.1 Recipe analysis (emphasis on structural text conventions)

This exercise is intended to enhance your awareness of the different norms governing one text type, the recipe, in different languages. Many text types take different forms in different languages, but recipes tend to be especially clear examples of this phenomenon.

A. Select a recipe (you can either use a cookbook or look for a recipe on the internet). Identify its different parts, such as title, brief paragraph of information about the dish, the number of people it will serve, the list of ingredients (which may be divided into different parts), and the procedure, which tells you what to do (e.g. whisk) and how to do it (e.g. vigorously). Not all of these sections may be present in all recipes, and some recipes will have more and/or different parts.
B. Do the same for a recipe in a different language, for a dish as similar as possible in kind to the first.
C. Compare the structure, grammar and vocabulary of the two. How do they differ?

Among the most studied genres in both the Translation Studies community and the Language for Specific Purposes community are scientific texts, legal texts, instructions for use, manuals, brochures, tourism texts, recipes, official documents and texts of various literary genres. Literary texts probably account for fewer than 10 per cent of translations across the world (Kingscott 2002: 247; Byrne 2010: 2) but are nevertheless among the most visible and the most closely scrutinized and criticized kinds of translated texts. However, it is difficult to generalize across literary text genres, and I will not discuss their translation here. Excellent works on literary translation include Balmer (2013), Boase-Beier (2006, 2020), Boase-Beier and de Vooght (2019), and Maher (2011). Malmkjær (2022) includes chapters on the translation of a number of literary genres. Translated texts of other genres are rather less visible as translations, except when something is wrong with them and they end up, for example, on internet sites to be laughed at (try Googling 'funny translations' or similar). However, non-literary translations are ubiquitous. Many products and services are marketed and sold internationally, and international standards require that information about them and their uses be available in the languages of their destinations (Byrne 2010: 2). Furthermore, the significant migrations of peoples that have taken place in the twenty-first century (and before) mean that the population internal to a country may not all speak the country's national language(s), so that translation of messages meant for use within a country's borders is often necessary to ensure that the whole population can participate in the life of a nation.

It is generally agreed among theorists and teachers, and also generally among translators, that translators of specialist texts benefit from an understanding of the topics of such texts. Topic-specific information can be offered in programmes of study and/or be honed through professional practice. However, given that no programme of study (or textbook) can provide an understanding of every potential specialist subject, it is important for translators to develop a capacity to transfer skills used in the translation of specialist topics between such topics. Among transferable skills, text analysis and genre analysis are especially helpful for translators. Section 5.4 in Chapter 5 will introduce a method of text analysis, Translational Stylistics, developed especially with the analysis of translations and of texts for translation in mind.

A second feature of specialist texts that needs careful consideration before translation of them is offered and/or undertaken is that some texts have the potential to cause harm to their users if they contain errors; in this respect, legal documents, medical texts, and instructions for use of machinery and electrical goods stand out especially.

In the sections that follow, we will examine a selection of text types that are regularly translated, including brochures, tourism texts, community information materials, instructions for use, legal texts, medical texts, official documents, scientific writing and news texts. There is some overlap between these types of text, and one document may contain a selection of text types. For example, some tourism texts are brochures, and some brochures that advertise or accompany various types of items may contain instructions for use.

2.1.1 Brochures

A brochure may be produced to give information or to promote and advertise an object, place or event, and brochures vary greatly depending on what it is that they promote or inform about. Technical brochures, for example, tend to include technical data sheets (see Olohan 2016: 93), whereas tourist brochures tend to include descriptions and pictures of places. The amount of text in proportion to illustrations or other visual features varies between brochures, but whatever the proportion, it is crucial that the right piece of text is placed with the appropriate visual. For example, if the text refers to 'the illustration on the page opposite', then it is important to have the illustration positioned on the page opposite to the page with the text on it. Obvious though this may seem, it does not always happen, especially if the translator does not have the opportunity to check the brochure before it goes to print, and if the designer does not understand the language of the brochure.

Exercise 2.2 Brochure analysis (emphasis on specialist terminology and illustration)

This exercise is intended to enhance your awareness of the different norms governing the text type brochure. Brochures often employ specialist terms; like recipes, they may be illustrated, and the illustrations may be especially important in conveying place, time and usage information.

A. Select a brochure (you can obtain a brochure from a place of local interest or from your local library, or you can use a brochure or guide to the use of an object, or you can visit your local doctor's surgery to find an information text; other options are available too, including on the internet). How is the brochure structured? Does it use specialized terminology? Is it illustrated? Is it available in different language versions? How do the illustrations (if any) relate to the text? Are the illustrations suitably positioned relative to the text?
B. If the brochure you have chosen is multilingual, how are the illustrations (if any) related to the different language versions? Are the different language versions of roughly similar length? Are they equally prominent in the brochure?
C. If the brochure you have chosen is monolingual, translate it. Did you encounter any difficulties?
D. If the brochure you have chosen is multilingual, compare the versions and discuss the relationships you identify between them.

2.1.2 Tourism Texts

There are many sub-genres of tourism texts or texts that tourists might use, ranging from full-length books purchased in book shops, through still fairly substantial publications available, sometimes gratis, in tourist information offices and many other places like motorway services and cafés, to much smaller brochures. In mainland Europe, these almost always include translations into English; in

Britain, translations are often confined to non-European languages, on a par with the community advice website we shall examine in Section 2.1.3. Tourism destinations are of course also advertised on the internet or in other electronic forms, and portable devices make the use of these convenient, so long as there is regular access during one's travels to opportunities to charge the devices.

Tourism texts share a predilection for adjectives and adverbs, because it is their purpose to attract people to places and activities, and these are therefore portrayed as desirable; major players in this portrayal, along with attractive photographs, are positively loaded adjectives and adverbs. Other adjectives and adverbs refer to characteristic features of hotels and other types of accommodation (e.g. cruise ships and holiday cottages), for example, 'en-suite', 'single', 'double', 'twin' (see Pierini 2009); terms related to special offers (e.g. 'special', 'free', 'complimentary', 'unlimited') are also prolific across the sector. Tourism texts are of considerable economic importance because they can entice tourists to visit historically and culturally significant places, thus bringing valuable income to a country or location. Nevertheless, they are often rather poorly translated, a characteristic that they share with restaurant and café menus. For example, *Get Around Town* of June 2018, an otherwise exceptionally high-quality publication printed on very substantial paper (almost card-like), advertising the attractions of the town of Aarhus in Denmark, allows itself numerous mistranslations, like the following, from a feature focusing on an ice cream shop:

Danish first-written text:
Fordi gelato laves af mælk og de bedste råvarer, får du den fulde smag og kun halvt så mange kalorier som i klassisk is.

(Because gelato is made of milk and the best raw materials, you get the full taste and only half as many calories as in classic ice cream).

English translation:
Because gelato is made of milk and the best commodities, you get the full taste and only half the calories, as in a classic ice cream.

The selection of the term 'commodities' where raw materials is meant is odd; but worse than that, the Danish text explains that gelato contains only half as many calories as normal ice cream, whereas in the translation into English we are told that like classic ice cream, gelato contains only half the calories, which (a) does not make sense and (b) may be understood to claim that gelato and classic ice cream contain the same number of calories, namely half [of what?], which is the opposite of the message the Danish first-written text conveys. The same feature translates 'kugler' (scoops, in the context of ice cream) as 'bowls', which is perhaps a misspelling of 'balls'; but 'balls' would be the wrong word to choose as a translation of 'kugler' in this context anyway, since, in English, ice cream comes in scoops and not, as in Danish, in 'kugler' (a 'kugle' can be a bullet, a cannon ball, a child's marble or similar spherical objects, but not a ball to play ball games with, which is called 'bold' in Danish).

Of course, some tourism texts are exemplary. For example, the Greek holiday accommodation provider Kedros Villas on the Greek island of Naxos provides information in flawless English via a Tripadvisor webpage:

> Kedros Villas is situated on a gently sloping hill in the Stelida area, providing easy access to Laguna Beach (550 m.) – ideal for windsurfing – and Agios Procopios Beach (1.2 km.), famed for its white sand and crystal clear waters. In its amphitheatrical, leafy location, Kedros Villas – comprising twelve holiday homes with fully equipped kitchens and four suites with outdoor hot tub or private pool – boasts a panoramic view of the seascape. Set in the shade of elegant cedars, our villas enjoy excellent temperatures during the summer months. Wherever possible, natural materials have been used both for their construction and décor … white marble flooring strikes a cool contrast with rich oak fittings … wooden furnishings … elegance, simplicity, comfort. Kedros Villas embraces all three. The wild, natural beauty of the landscape, unspoilt by the passage of time, undulating sand banks, the restless and glimmering sea. All these combine to inspire us. www.tripadvisor.co.uk/Hotel_Review-g805487-d1109410-Reviews-Kedros_Villas-Agios_Prokopios_Naxos_Cyclades_South_Aegean.html (accessed 24 January 2024)

Note the number and nature of the adjectives and adverbs in this text:

> Gently sloping; easy (access); ideal; famed; white (sand/marble); crystal clear; amphitheatrical; leafy; fully equipped; outdoor hot (tub); private (pool); panoramic (view); elegant; excellent; natural; cool; rich oak; wooden; wild; unspoilt; undulating; restless (sea); glimmering.

Only 'restless' has negative connotations, but since it modifies 'sea', all the romantic notions of outward yearning and adventure that the sea can evoke are transferred to 'restless' and transform its potentially negative connotations to positive ones that harmonize well with the notion of a holiday on one of Greece's approximately 3,000 islands.

Exercise 2.3 Tourist information text analysis (emphasis on adjectives and adverbs)

This exercise is intended to enhance your familiarity with a much-translated genre, the tourist information text. Such texts make liberal use of adjectives and adverbs, word classes that can pose particular challenges for translators. The exercise will allow you to practise translating these word classes in a context in which they are especially highlighted and in which they are especially important to the goal of the text.

A. Select a tourist information text. Write a list of the adjectives and adverbs in it. Are they positive or negative in meaning?
B. Adjectives and adverbs can be challenging to translate because close equivalents between languages can be difficult to identify. If the tourist information text you have chosen is multilingual, consider and comment on the adjectives and adverbs it contains.

2.1.3 Community Advice Materials

Community advice is very varied. Much community advice is freely available on the internet and in hard copy in libraries, community centres and some doctors' surgeries. When it is translated, the translation is usually intended for use 'by, and for, institutions, organizations and people who share the same nation, territory, public space and attendant services' (Taibi and Ozolins 2016: 39). Therefore, it may be counterproductive to translate the names of local institutions and phenomena except as a matter of glossing, because the users of the translation will encounter and need to be able to recognize these institutions through the language of the community in which they live. It is important to add, however, that certain temporary communities, which may be extremely diverse internally, both linguistically and culturally, may form in special locations at certain times, for example during major sporting or religious events; for such communities, translation of references to local phenomena may be important. As Taibi and Ozolins (2016: 97–99) point out, temporary communities can present particular challenges for translators in situations where the members of such communities are unfamiliar with their surroundings and living conditions, and because translators may have had little time to anticipate and prepare to meet their needs.

Here, we will look at the 'Find Answers' page which forms part of the city of Liverpool's internet-based Community Advice on Immigration (https://ellis.custhelp.com/app/answers/list/c/645; accessed 5 June 2024). The page is headed by what looks like a family photograph, and there is a navigation bar on the left. The page itself has headings, in purple, with information below the heading in smaller but easily readable grey font. Clicking one of the purple headings takes you to a page with more detailed information. Downloadable forms are available in ten non-European languages in addition to English, the assumption being, presumably, that any speaker of a European language seeking advice will be able to understand English well enough to be able to complete the forms in that language.

Exercise 2.4 Community advice materials (emphasis on translation for co-located people)

This exercise is intended to heighten your awareness of the specific features of translation for co-located people, particularly the names of offices and institutions.

A. Go to Liverpool's Community Advice page or select the Advice page of a different local authority of your choice. If the page is not available in one of the languages that you know, translate it into that language.
   i. What issues does the making of your translation raise?
   ii. How did you deal with the names of any institutions or offices that the advice page mentions?

OR

B. Go to Liverpool's Community Advice page or select the Advice page of a different local authority of your choice. If the page is available in more than one language that you know, compare the versions.
   i. You may be completely happy with the versions; but if you are not, why not?
   ii. How do the different versions deal with the names of institutions and offices that they mention?

2.1.4 Instructions for Use

Instructions for the installation and use of various products are, as Olohan (2016: 51) points out, frequently available in many languages. Olohan mentions instruction manuals, user guides and operating and installation instructions; however, texts related to hobbies like gardening, fishing, car maintenance, decorating, playing musical instruments, and playing games share many of the features displayed by these genres, and are equally frequently provided in many languages. As Olohan (2016: 55) further remarks, instruction texts come in many forms, from short leaflets to substantial manuals and handbooks, and may consist of various sections. The key criterion for the success of a set of instructions for use is usability, since the point of the instructions is to enable the user to perform the task that the documentation explains and instructs the reader to undertake (Olohan 2016: 51). This obviously requires the reader to understand the instructions, and in the case of instructions for use which include written text (some sets of instructions contain only pictures), comprehension depends at least to some degree on the readability of the text. Text readability is defined by Crossley, Skalicky and Dascalu (2019: 543) as 'the ease with which a text can be read and understood in terms of the linguistic features found within a text'. Linguistic features that affect readability include lexical sophistication, syntactic complexity, discourse structures (Crossley et al. 2019: 554, referring to Just and Carpenter 1980) and narrative complexity, 'the more or less linear way a story is presented' (Perego, Del Missier and Stragà 2018: 142).

Lexical sophistication depends on sound and spelling relationships between words, word familiarity, word frequency, word imageability, word concreteness and word meaning (Crossley et al. 2019: 544, referring to Juel and Solso 1981; Mesmer 2005; Howes and Solomon 1951; Richardson 1975 and Mesmer, Cunningham and Hieber 2012). Sets of instructions for the assembly and use of items often contain terms that may not be in common use in everyday language, so it is helpful if there are accompanying pictures of the items. When translating texts that include images, it is important to locate the translated text parts in such a way that it is obvious which image each text part belongs with.

Text complexity depends in part on the number of words or morphemes per sentence in a text and on the ease with which readers can understand the connection between the clauses and sentences of the text (Grimes 1975). A sentence may consist of a main clause and any dependent clauses that accompany it, or several main clauses conjoined. In general, texts are more easily understood the less sophisticated the words they contain are, and the fewer verbs, three-word phrases and proper nouns they contain per sentence (Crossley et al. 2019: 546). However, as Liu, Zheng and Zhou (2019: 260) point out, a reader's background knowledge and prior experience of reading can play a significant role in how difficult a particular text is for them to read.

Of course, most sets of instructions do not contain especially long sentences or stretches of text, but it is worth remembering when translating that raising the register of a text (e.g. using more 'formal' vocabulary and more complex syntax) may make the text more difficult to understand; that increasing sentence length may not facilitate reading; and that complicating syntactic structures will not do so either. Conversely, doing the opposite may ease reading, and this may be important if the set of instructions that is being translated is intended for an audience that can be expected to be less literate or less expert in the text's topic, or in similar topics, than the first-written text's intended reader. However, certain sections of user instructions, such as liability statements (in which a producer or company declares, for example, that they shall not be held responsible for accidents arising from misuse of the product) need to employ relevant features of legal language (Olohan 2016: 66).

Formality is, in any case, language specific. Consider an instruction manual that accompanies a child's car seat sold by a UK manufacturer. The instruction manual runs to three volumes, giving instructions in fourteen languages. Since the seat is made by a British manufacturer, I shall assume that English is the first-written language of the manual, but this is not important for the illustration it provides of the complex nature of formality considered cross-culturally and cross-linguistically.

The English version of the brochure begins, 'Congratulations. You have purchased a high quality, fully certified child safety child restraint.' For any translator working into a language that, unlike English, distinguishes in its pronoun system between formal and informal address, this innocent-looking opening poses a question with scope over the entire manual, namely the question of which mode of reader address to select. The Danish version selects the informal 'du' (as opposed to the formal 'De'); the German selects the formal 'Sie' (as opposed to the informal 'du'). This arguably makes for a different relationship between the reader and the addresser in the three versions. In the English version, the relationship is a neutral one of knower (the addresser) and non-knower (the addressee). In Danish and German, in contrast, this relationship is overlaid by another relationship indicator, namely an impression of equal status of both parties (Danish) versus an impression of a hint of respectfulness, not to say subservience of the addresser vis-à-vis the addressee (German). But it is very common in Danish texts of this type, and many other types for that matter, including information for citizens found on webpages like that of the Danish tax authorities and of the railways, for example, to use the informal mode of address, whereas in German it is most common to use the formal mode of address. Therefore, these choices arguably constitute normal usage in the two languages/cultures respectively, and it would be odd or unnatural not to adhere to this normal usage. Therefore, a translator translating between the three languages in question might consider conforming to the apparent norms in each language, regardless of the source text's choices. That is, when translating into English, there is no choice to make; but when translating into Danish, it may be most natural to use the informal form of reader address, regardless of the first-written text's choice, whereas when translating into German, using the formal term of address may be most natural. In Danish, using the formal mode of address would seem stilted; in German, using the informal mode of address might appear overly familiar. Neither would reflect the addresser–addressee relationship that the manufacturer of the car seat is likely to want to establish with its customers.

Exercise 2.5 Translating instructions for use (emphasis on text structure, illustration and specialist terminology)

This exercise focuses on the translation of instructions for use. It is intended to consolidate your awareness of the relationships in such texts between text structure and illustrations, adding a focus on specialist terminology.

A. Select a set of instructions for use. If your set of instructions is a substantial stretch of text, for example a manual of use, describe its structure. If your set of instructions is illustrated, are the illustrations helpful? How do they relate to the text? Does your set of instructions use specialized terminology? Is your set of instructions available in different language versions?
B. If the set of instructions you have chosen is monolingual, translate it. Discuss any difficulties you encountered.
C. If the set of instructions you have chosen is multilingual, compare the versions and discuss the relationships you identify between them.

2.1.5 Legal Texts

As Cao (2007: 114) points out, the basic function of law is to regulate human behaviour. For that reason, the illocutionary force of any speech act performed by a sentence in a legal text is arguably among its most important facets. A theory of speech as action was developed by the philosopher J. R. Austin in the 1930s and has formed an important part of the discipline of discourse pragmatics – roughly, the study of language in use – since Austin published his theory in the early 1960s (Austin 1962). According to Austin (1962: 94–108 and *passim*), every utterance performs three acts simultaneously: (i) a locutionary act (saying something in the full, normal sense of uttering certain noises that form words that together have certain meanings in a language), (ii) an illocutionary act, such as asking, answering, informing, giving a verdict, and so on, and (iii) a perlocutionary act, which relates to the consequences, intentional or unintentional, of the act. This framework is easily applied to written texts too; in fact, one of Austin's own examples of a speech act is '"I give and bequeath my watch to my brother" – as occurring in a will' (Austin 1962: 5); although in writing, the speech act will obviously be realized by marks on a surface rather than noises in the air.

Every utterance has an illocutionary force which can be identified by way of the so-called speech-act verb which is either present in the utterance, or which could appropriately be added to the utterance to make it explicit which act the utterance is performing, simply in being made, in the here and now. For example, 'I order you to go' makes it explicit that the utterance is an order by way of containing the term 'order'. The simple utterance 'Go' is likely to be understood as an order too by speakers of English, and it could in theory be prefaced by the words 'I hereby order you to . . .', in which, again, the speech act being performed (order) is mentioned. In fact, what distinguishes speech-act verbs from other verbs is that if 'I hereby . . .' is prefaced to them, a functional utterance is made, whereas for non-speech-act verbs, this is not the case. For example, it makes perfect sense to say 'I hereby offer/promise/declare . . .' (although it is a little stilted), but it would not make sense to say 'I hereby sit/walk/drive.' However, although not every verb is a speech-act verb, every utterance is a speech act. We see that this is so when we note that it is possible to begin any declarative utterance with 'I hereby state that . . .'. Given that every utterance is therefore a speech act, every utterance has an illocutionary force. There are clearly as many illocutionary forces as there are speech-act verbs but, according to Austin, speech acts with their illocutionary forces can be divided into five broad classes: (i) verdictives (giving verdicts, judgements, estimates, reckonings or appraisals, findings in general); (ii) excercitives (exercising powers, rights or influence, for example to appoint, vote, order, urge, advise, warn); (iii) commissives (committing oneself as in the case of promising, declaring, announcing intentions); (iv) behabitives (which have to do with social behaviour and include apologizing, congratulating, commending, condoling, cursing and challenging); and (v) expositives (which show how an utterance fits into the ongoing discourse, as in 'I reply/concede/assume/postulate') (Austin 1962: 150–152). Certain rules govern the use of these classes of speech acts, and if these rules are not adhered to, the act will either not be achieved, or the language will have been abused. For example, although anyone can utter the words 'I hereby declare you husband and wife', there are restrictions on whose utterance of these words can actually bring about a marriage. If the person uttering the words is not a person with the authority to marry people, then no marriage will have been achieved. Further, there is usually more to a marriage ceremony than the uttering of words; there may, for example, be papers to sign, with witnesses adding their signatures too. Similarly, if I say to you 'I promise' without having any intention of doing whatever it is that I promise, then I am abusing the speech act of promising (see further Austin 1962: Chapter II). The relevance of all this to legal translation is that a legislative text is a speech act with an illocutionary force (typically a text includes several speech acts) and which has a perlocutionary effect that arises from the perlocutionary force of the utterance, and 'it can be said that the translator's task is to put language into action to achieve the intended legal effects, i.e., to achieve legal equivalence' (Šarčević 2006: 28). However, 'languages differ considerably in how [they] express obligation, permission and prohibition' (Cao 2007: 115). In addition, as Cao (23ff) points out, legal texts and legal language are tied to national legal systems and these differ between nations. For instance, the so-called common law that operates in Britain is unwritten and based on legal precedents, meaning that judgements made in the past by judicial authorities and public juries are consulted and can guide future action. In contrast, civil law, which is used in many Asian and continental European legal systems, is based on general principles.

Because of differences between legal systems, the legal concepts that operate in one nation may have no counterpart and therefore no terms to express them in the language of another nation's legal system. Šarčević (2006: 27) gives the example of the concept of 'décision' in French law. In German law, no single concept corresponds exactly to this French concept. Rather, two concepts, denoted by the terms 'Entscheidung' and 'Beschluss', are used (although both terms are nouns, it may be suggested that the former connotes the mental process of deciding that has led to the decision; the latter connotes the decision itself). Dutch law, she continues, employs three concepts and terms, 'Beschikking','Besluit' and 'Beslissing'. Of course, other, more general differences between concepts and hence terms in different languages also affect legal texts.

Cao (2007: 9–10) identifies four major types of written legal texts:

> (1) legislative texts, e.g. domestic statutes and subordinate laws, international treaties and multilingual laws, and other laws produced by lawmaking authorities; (2) judicial texts produced in the judicial process by judicial officers and other legal authorities; (3) legal scholarly texts produced by academic lawyers or legal scholars in scholarly works and commentaries whose legal status depends on the legal systems in different jurisdictions; and (4) private legal texts written by lawyers, e.g. contracts, leases, wills and litigation documents, and also texts written by non-lawyers and used in litigation and other legal situations.

These may be translated for one of three main purposes (Cao 2007: 10–11). Normative purposes are served in bi- and multilingual situations when it is necessary for the law to be available in more than one language. In such situations, the different language versions have equal status. This is the case, for example, in the European Union and in the United Nations, where a text that is law is law in any of the languages it exists in. Secondly, texts like statutes, court judgements, and scholarly works about law may be translated for informative purposes; these texts will not themselves have legal status. Finally, legal texts can be translated for information (e.g. for use as documentary evidence in court proceedings).

There are several lexical, syntactic, textual and pragmatic linguistic features peculiar to legal language (Cao 2007: 18), but these are not the same across languages. For example, Cao (2007: 21–22) mentions that while much legal vocabulary in English is archaic and ritualistic and used with meanings that differ from the meanings the terms have in everyday language, Chinese legal language uses normal terms that have special, legal meanings. In English, for example, 'whereas', when used in legal agreements, means 'given the fact that', whereas in everyday usage it functions as I have just used it, to indicate contrast (Cao 2007: 86).

Sentences in English legal language tend to be long and complex with extensive use of conditions, qualifications and exceptions; the passive voice is often used, as are multiple negations. Often, there are so-called word-strings, which are used to cover all eventualities in contracts (Cao 2007: 88–89); for example (word-strings with my underlining) 'risks for any liabilities, expenses, losses, damages and costs'; and 'it is their intention to hereby fully, finally, absolutely and forever settle . . .'. As Cao (2007: 90) points out, since the words in word-strings mean more or less the same as one another, it is easy to assume that if similar lists are not used in another language, the translator can select just one word for use in a translation. However, she continues,

> In law, sometimes each and every word may carry different legal meanings and legal consequences. When disputes arise, courts may be asked to interpret each such individual word, and give them different meanings. Thus, for the translator, it is not always possible or advisable to combine the synonyms into one word.

Biel (2014/2016: 178–182) identifies several phraseological patterns characteristic of legal language. These include text-organizing patterns, grammatical patterns, term-forming patterns and term-embedding collocations.

A typical text-organizing pattern in EU directives is that a title is followed by several chapters, each with several sections, each with several articles (an article in a legal document is a rule or stipulation). Further, there are usually several annexes at the end of the document.

Grammatical patterns in legal texts include (i) patterns that express deontic modality (dealing with what must or may be done) which (in English) employ modal verbs like *may, must, shall, should,* and (ii) patterns that express conditions, using adverbials like *if, in case, unless, provided that.* The passive voice and other impersonal structures (structures that do not identify agents, e.g. 'have been reviewed', 'it is appropriate') are often used.

Term-forming patterns in legal texts are composed of several words like 'legislative framework for' and 'essential requirements for' (from Directive 2008/98/EC of the European Parliament and of the Council of 19 November 2008 on waste and repealing certain Directives (Text with EEA relevance)). The matching expressions in the corresponding Danish text are 'retlige rammer for' and 'grundlæggende krav til', and those in the German text are 'Rechtsrahmen für' and 'grundlegende Anforderungen an'. Of particular note here are the prepositions, which are not direct translation equivalents of each other. The English text uses 'for' with both 'framework' and 'requirements', whereas the Danish text has 'for' in one case and 'til' ('to') in the other; the German text has 'für' ('for') and 'an' ('to'). Prepositions can be challenging for translators, but seeing them as parts of longer phrases, which can be focused on as wholes, can help build familiarity and make it easier to remember how and when to use them.

Biel's fourth and final phraseological pattern characteristic of legal language is term-embedding collocations. A term-embedding collocation is a collocation between a specialist term and an item or items in general use.

The notion of the collocation derives from the work of J. R. Firth (1957), who understands the notion in terms of the company a word keeps (1957: 11). This is still the basic concept of collocation, but because the advent of large corpora of electronically storable and searchable texts has made it possible to be very precise about whether terms go together more regularly than chance would predict, the definition has been refined to read 'the statistical tendency of words to co-occur' (Hunston 2002: 12). For example, *shares* (as a noun in the plural) collocates strongly with *hold* (rather than with e.g. *own*); *the right to vote* collocates strongly with *conferring* (rather than with e.g. *giving*); and *right* collocates strongly with *to vote* (rather than with e.g. *permission* to vote).

The European Union provides a large number of legal texts in each language of the Union on its EUR-lex website.

Exercise 2.6 Analysis of legal documents in two or more languages (emphasis on speech-act verbs, prepositions and collocations)

This exercise is intended to highlight the use of speech-act verbs, prepositions and collocations in legal documents in different languages. The European Union's website is a useful source of documents like this, so the exercise suggests you source the documents you need in order to undertake the exercise from there.

A. Visit EUR-lex (https://eur-lex.europa.eu/homepage.html), the official website of the European Union and select two or more language versions of a legal document.
   i. Compare them to see (a) how they use speech-act verbs, (b) which prepositions they use, and (c) how they are structured.
   ii. Make a note of any collocations that you think are specific to legal language and legal documents and identify their nearest everyday language equivalents. Notice that collocational patterns, like the choice of prepositions, very often differ markedly between languages.

2.1.6 Medical Texts

It has been said that one of the oldest types of translation is that which deals with topics related to medicine (see e.g. Muñoz-Miquel 2018: 25; Montalt Resurrecció 2010: 72), and it is perhaps not surprising, given the life versus death issues that may arise in this context, that the question of subject-matter expertise versus translation expertise is often raised in connection with the translation of medical texts (Fischbach 1998: 4; Muñoz-Miquel 2018: 26). Many translators of medical texts (37% of the participants in Muñoz-Miquel's 2018 study; see Muñoz-Miquel 2018: 44) collaborate with colleagues or experts in medicine, and Muñoz-Miquel (2018: 47) recommends the provision of specialized postgraduate courses in medical translation.

Medical texts may be divided into two very general groups, namely texts to be shared among medical professionals and texts meant for the general public, though there is some overlap between the two groups. For example, a medical student or a doctor and a lay person might both own or consult anatomical atlases, instruction manuals on the use of medical devices, websites dealing with diseases or health complaints, and market research documents relating to medicine or health-related habits.

Texts aimed primarily at medical professionals include case reports, medical records, medical reports, medical textbooks, medical research articles, clinical trial reports, clinical guidelines, summaries of product characteristics and applications for new drug releases. Medical research articles typically appear in medical journals which, like other journals, will have guidelines for authors to follow. And translators of medical articles will, in turn, need to ensure that the texts they translate comply with the norms for medical articles in the language being translated into and with the house style of the journal in which a translated article is to be published. Like most journals, *The British Medical Journal*, for example, provides guidelines for authors on its website.

Medical texts aimed at lay readers include advertising material, press releases, documentaries, patient information brochures, leaflets, fact sheets, informed consent forms, medical questionnaires, packet leaflets with information for the user of the medicine in the packet and summaries of various kinds for patients.

Like all specialized texts, medical texts are characterized by terms referring to their subject matter, but some medical texts also tend to employ:

> a passive and impersonal style that focuses on objective, measurable phenomena rather than concrete actions. This style is attained through heavy noun phrases (with nominalized actions), passive clauses, and a preference for third-person pronouns rather than first-person ones. (Zethsen and Askehave 2006: 646)

The following information about aspirin, from *The British Medical Journal*, illustrates 'heavy' noun phrases (noun phrases underlined; head nouns in bold; my underlining and emphasis).

Aspirin

Daily, low dose **aspirin** is not associated with a significant **reduction** in death, dementia, or persistent physical disability in healthy people aged 70 or over, a randomised **trial** that also found increased risk of major haemorrhage has shown.

'The **results** provide the most reliable **evidence** on the balance of risk and benefit of starting aspirin after the age of 70 in healthy people', said **Peter Rothwell**, **professor** of neurology and **head** of the Centre for the Prevention of Stroke and Dementia at the University of Oxford. **He** added, 'There were too few **people** in the over 70 age group in previous **trials** to draw reliable **conclusions**.' Several **studies** have shown the **benefits** of low dose aspirin for **people** with a history of coronary heart disease, but the **evidence** for primary prevention in healthy older people has been inconclusive. **Guidelines** do not recommend this **treatment** even though **it** is widely used by elderly **people**.

The British Medical Journal

The first noun phrase is the grammatical subject of the first sentence and is related by the agentless negative verb phrase, in the passive voice, to the second, longer noun phrase which reports the information that has just been presented. A similar structure is displayed in the second sentence, where a brief reference to the subject of the sentence, the results, is related by way of the verb 'provide' to the following very long noun phrase. The information concerned is then attributed to its source, Peter Rothwell, and his status is provided in a further very long noun phrase, before we are told what else he has said, again by way of a long noun phrase that follows a brief verb phrase, 'he added'. This structuring is typical of text in which it is important to be specific about who or what is affected by whom or what; but it may be difficult to attribute agency and effect in structures like this, and the style and structure used in medically related text aimed at lay readers needs to be simpler in structure and syntax. In Chapter 3, Section 3.3.2.8, we examine a packet insert for a widely used medicine known in English as Aspirin, noting the differences between the English, Danish, German and French language versions.

However, structure and lexis are not the only aspects of medical texts that may be challenging for translators. For example, as Taibi and Ozolins (2016: 43) point out, 'the translation of medical informed consent forms into "minority" languages is a prototypical case of the sociocultural challenges and the professional and ethical dilemmas facing community translators'. Medical informed consent forms may contain sensitive personal information which patients may be reluctant to share, especially, perhaps, with persons of the opposite gender, or persons younger than the patient, especially non-medically trained persons like translators. A medical consent form gives information about a person's state of health and medical condition, about their treatment or their proposed treatment and about any risks associated with the treatment. Because a medical consent form is a legal document, its precise structure and the information it contains are in part determined by aspects of the legal system in its country of use (Taibi and Ozolins 2016: 44), and it has to be signed by the patient, or by their legal representative, who in signing it declares that they have understood the information it contains. Therefore, translation is crucial in cases where the person signing does not understand the language of the form; and since the form may contain complex information about a health condition, using the associated medical terminology, a translator will need to understand and be able to use appropriately such terminology in both relevant languages. It is especially important in the case of medical consent forms that translators do not raise the register or complicate the sentence structure of the original.

Samples of medical consent form templates in English can be accessed on the internet.

Exercise 2.7 Analysis of medical texts and translation considerations

This exercise is intended to heighten your awareness of the requirement for specialist understanding and specialist terminology in the translation of medical texts. (This exercise does not ask for a translation given the nature of the text and the requirement for specific terminology when translating medical texts.)

A. Select a medical text of any type. Would you be confident about being able to translate it accurately (in such a way that it represents the meaning of the first-written text)? and appropriately (in such a way that it sounds 'natural' in the language it is being translated into)? What problems would you need to solve? How would you go about solving them?

2.1.7 Official Documents

Examples of official documents include contracts, refugee statements, driving licences, statutory declarations, and certificates of birth, baptism, education, employment, marriage and death. Certificates of birth and baptism tend to be translated to establish a person's identity and may be required by various kinds of official body. In the UK, these might include the Home Office, the Courts, the Passport Office, the National Academic Recognition Information Centre (NARIC) and academic institutions. Academic institutions and many prospective employers will also need to see applicants' certificates of education. Certificates of education usually include lists of subjects and grades from institutions an individual has attended, and it is helpful for (and often required by) the person or institution who needs to see a translation of such a certificate if the translation is accompanied by information about the grading system used by the issuer, the relevant country's education system, the level within this system of the institution that has issued the certificate, and so on. If such information is not available on or with the certificate, it may be difficult for a translator to supply it. And it is not really the translator's job to do so, although they might advise the customer or client that certain supporting documentation may be required by the person or institution that is going to use the translation – provided, of course, that the translator knows who that is. Graduates of universities in countries taking part in the Bologna Process within the European Higher Education Area (EHEA) have the right to receive a Diploma Supplement, which explains the learning outcomes of the programme studied, the European Credit Transfer and Accumulation System (ECTS), and the relevant national qualification system. The supplement is available to graduates free of charge in any major European language from the EU website along with a copy of the Diploma Supplement form.

2.1.8 Scientific Translation

Scientific texts typically make claims about the world, which have implications for how we interact with the world, and which can be tested against the world (Chalmers: 1978/1999: 248). Therefore, they aim for factuality or at least hypotheses about what is factual; they report the views of their authors but also, importantly, the views of the authors of other articles expressing other, often contrasting, views. Although an author's stance vis-à-vis various opinions may be signalled explicitly ('I disagree with the view expressed by X'), authors often resort to more subtle ways of indicating their opinions of views that conflict to a greater or lesser degree with their own ('I will address the surprising/provocative/extraordinary/controversial/etc. claim made by X that . . .'). In addition, authors often express tentativeness of confidence in their own views, prefacing the expression of these views with markers like 'in my opinion' (Labinaz and Sbisà 2014: 50). The expression of a lack of total conviction is known as hedging (Hyland 1994; Salaga-Meyer 1997) or mitigation of certainty (Labinaz and Sbisà 2014: 41) and in English it is typically expressed

> through use of modal auxiliary verbs such as *may, might* and *could,* adjectival, adverbial and nominal modal expressions (*possible, perhaps, probably*), modal lexical verbs (*believe, assume*), IF-clauses, question forms, passivization, impersonal phrases, and time reference. (Hyland 1994: 240)

To this taxonomy, Salaga-Meyer (1997: 110) adds approximators of degree, quantity, frequency and time, such as *approximately, roughly, about, often, occasionally, generally, usually, somewhat, somehow, a lot of*; introductory phrases like *I believe, to our knowledge, it is our view that, we feel that*; and if-clauses like *if true* and *if anything*. In Salaga-Meyer's view (1997: abstract), hedging conveys 'the fundamental characteristic of science of doubt and skepticism'.

It is important to convey hedging accurately in translation to enable the reader to judge the writer's stance vis-à-vis the content of a text, but hedging mechanisms differ considerably between languages. In fact, they can differ between different versions of the same language according to Hennecke (2017), who writes on the use of 'comme' and 'genre' in Canadian and European spoken French. Similarly, Beeching (2011: Discussion) highlights difficulties of conveying hedging cross-linguistically:

> As there is no direct equivalent for *well* in Swedish which captures all of its meaning, there is inevitably either under- or over-translation – part of the meaning is either lost or made more explicit in the translation.... There is no translation equivalent in English for the 'stage-marking' use of *bon* though *well ... but* captures *bon ... mais* almost perfectly. Equally, there is no real equivalent [in French] for English *well* as a dispreferred response marker – *c'est-à-dire que* may be pressed into service here (but it is less firmly coded in French in this function and is probably still a contextual implicature, rather than a fully-fledged and coded meaning of the term). There is no real one-word English equivalent for the synthesizing sense of [the French] *enfin* whereby, as Hansen (2005: 155) says, 'it marks (a part of) an utterance that sums up the previous discourse, formulates it more pithily, or draws a conclusion from it'. 'In short' is the closest equivalent and makes explicit what is implicit in *enfin*.

Exercise 2.8 Translating scientific texts (emphasis on hedging)

This exercise is intended to enhance your familiarity with hedging expressions typically found in scientific discourse and to help you consider how you might translate them into another language or other languages.

A. Select a scientific text of any type. Identify the hedging terms and expressions it contains and try to translate the text into another language of your choice. Write a commentary highlighting the difficulties you encountered in translating the hedging terms and expressions, stressing especially any changes in indications of writer attitudes which were implied by means of hedging but not stated directly in the first-written text.

2.1.9 News Translation

As Conboy (2007: 5) puts it, 'The language of the news plays a major part in the construction of what Berger and Luckman have referred to as the "social construction of reality (1976)".' Language plays this role whether in a first-written text or in translation, although in a pair or set of a first-written text and its translation(s), it may seem that not exactly the same reality is constructed in each. A similar phenomenon is evident in comparisons between different newspapers' reportage of one news story, even in the same language, as often illustrated in work on journalistic language and on critical linguistics (see e.g. Fowler et al. 1979; Fowler 1991). For example, by using the present progressive form, 'are dying', the British newspaper *The Guardian* of 30 April 2020 presents the situation of patients in British hospitals with Covid-19 as a continuous process; in contrast, the British newspaper *The Times* for the same day uses the past perfect, 'have died', thus focusing on what is in the past. In both papers, stark figures are followed by what looks like a direct quotation, presented between quotation marks, from Professor Calum Semple. Here, *The Guardian* has

> 'People need to hear this and get it into their heads,' Semple added. 'The reason the government is keen to keep people to stay at home until the outbreak is quietening down is because this is an incredibly dangerous disease.'

The Times has

> 'People need to get it into their heads: the reason the government is keen to keep people at home is that this is an incredibly dangerous disease.'

Clearly the differences here are not material to the general meaning of the quotation; however, it is obvious that it is not possible for both stretches of text that are placed between quotation marks to be verbatim quotations, given that they differ in detail. Perhaps the quotation in *The Times* is a shortened version, and perhaps there is a misprint in the version in *The Guardian*. Given that apparently verbatim written reports of what someone has said can vary like this within one language, it is not surprising that translations of someone's speech can be subject to variation too. For example, on 3 May 2020, the e-newspaper *Finans DK* reports

> 'Takket være en konstruktiv dialog og forhandlinger med obligationsejere og andre parter kan jeg med glæde bekræfte, at vi er nået til enighed med obligationsejerne' siger adm. direktør i Norwegian, Jacob Schram, i en meddelelse. https://finans.dk/erhverv/ECE12115556/norwegians-aktionaerer-skal-godkende-redningsplan-mandag/?ctxref=ext (accessed 24 January 2024)
>
> 'Thanks to a constructive dialogue and negotiations with bondholders and other parties, I am pleased to be able to confirm that we have reached an agreement with the bondholders' says CEO of Norwegian, Jacob Schram, in a message).
>
> This is rendered on *Global Domain News* as
>
> – I am happy to announce that we have reached an agreement with our bondholders,' says Jacob Schram, CEO in Norwegian, in the message.

www.globaldomainsnews.com/norwegian-takes-first-step-in-approval-of-the-rescue-plan (accessed 03.05.2020)

Clearly, Mr Schram's full statement is not provided in its totality in the translation quoted here. In fact, news translation is often intermixed with a good deal of editing, so that it is difficult to divorce the effects of editing from the effects of translation per se (Van Doorslaer 2009: 85). To overcome this difficulty Matsushita (2019) focuses on the translation (into Japanese) of direct quotations of public speeches made by especially important people. As she points out, 'direct quotations of public speeches by high-level officials are expected to be the most accurate and complete translation that a journalator [a journalist who translates; see Van Doorslaer (2012)] can produce' (Matsushita 2019: 15), something that is indeed stressed in guides to translation issued by Reuters, the *New York Times*, and the Associated Press (Matsushita 2019: 24). Of course, the translation of speech events faces the difficulty of having to represent speech in writing, even though the two forms of communication differ in nature (see below). A factor that may mitigate these differences to a certain, though limited, extent is present when, as often happens, a public speech is written down and read out.

Time pressure is very often at play in news translation (who wants to read yesterday's news?), and Matsushita (2019: 102ff) finds that omission, which we met in the translation of Jacob Schram's statement quoted above, is the predominant type of non-literalness found in translations into Japanese of former US president Obama's victory speech (given on 7 November 2012). The next most frequent types of non-literalness are substitution and addition. Omissions tended to be of adjectival noun modifiers and names of American locations, which might not be familiar to the readers; additions and substitutions tended to be explicitating, that is, they tended to provide information that the readers in the language of the translation might not have but which was important to enhance their understanding of the speech. Overall, Matsushita's analysis clearly shows significant deviation from the closest possible translation, 'despite the fact that direct quotations are supposed to be faithful reproductions of the original speech' (2019: 119). The instances of non-faithfulness Matsushita identifies seem to be made with a strong reader orientation in mind, although Matsushita's own explanation is provided in terms of Pym's concept of risk management (Pym 2015, 2016; Pym and Matsushita 2018). Finally, the written records of press briefings, which, like written records of public speeches, resemble subtitles in representing speech in writing, may also be translated. Choi (2022) examines a corpus consisting of ninety-two complete Korean language press briefings (c. 200,000 running words) and their translations into English provided on the Korean Ministry of Foreign Affairs website, focusing on briefings given to the press by the Korean government's spokesperson. Generally, these consist of two sections. The first section is the speaker's announcement, and the second consists of questions asked by the press and answers given by the spokesperson. The translation is usually published on the day the briefing took place and will therefore, like other types of news translation, be subject to time pressure. However, unlike many other types of news translation, which, as mentioned above, is often carried out by journalists, the translated briefings examined by Choi were made by in-house translators employed by the Ministry. The translators, as well as the revisers of the translations, were native speakers of Korean, but some of their higher education had typically taken place in an English-speaking country. The English translations of the press briefings are remarkable in what they omit, namely 'negative comments about the government and diplomatically sensitive and provocative issues pertaining to Japan, China, and North Korea'. Clearly these comments were omitted deliberately to avoid diplomatic difficulties and offence. Not so much lost, then, as manipulated away in translation.

Exercise 2.9 News translation (emphasis on the translation of spoken text into a written version)

This exercise is intended to heighten your awareness of the differences between speech and writing and the implications of these for translations of written accounts of speech.

A. Compare translations in local newspapers of news provided by Reuters or another large international multimedia news provider. How do they differ?
B. Listen to a recording of a press statement made by a politician or other important or famous person. Compare it to written accounts published in one or more languages. How do they differ?

2.1.10 Subtitles

Subtitling in the same language as the language being spoken on screen can be used for the benefit of viewers of films or TV programmes who are deaf or hard of hearing. Subtitles in a language other than that spoken on screen are mainly provided for the benefit of viewers who do not know the language being spoken by the actors or by a commentator. Both types may also, incidentally, aid foreign language learning. A number of constraints on subtitling apply whether or not translating is involved.

The focus in this section is going to be on providing subtitles in a language other than that used in the film or TV programme that is being subtitled. In such cases, subtitling stands between interpreting and translating insofar as its basis is in speech but its realization is in writing. So, rather than a first-written text, the translator is presented with spoken language, which must be rendered into written language. Of course, the dialogues in film and many TV programmes are likely to be pre-scripted, and pre-scripted speech is not a completely true representation of naturally occurring discourse. For example, Díaz Cintas and Remael (2007: 63) point out that 'Film dialogue does not render all the hesitations and false starts or requests for confirmation that are typical of conversation or speech in general.' Furthermore, dialogue in film has the dual function of, on the one hand, representing dialogue between the characters, while, on the other hand, informing viewers about aspects of those characters and their lives and concerns. So unlike most naturally occurring speech, TV and film conversations are designed for the benefit of a set of overhearers constituted by the viewers, just as the narration accompanying a nature programme, for example, is. Nevertheless, dialogue on screen obviously differs from writing in being delivered orally, and it is usually designed to emulate naturally occurring speech.

Providing a reflection of speech in writing is difficult because the media of speech and writing are different from each other and follow different sets of norms, so that what seems perfectly natural in speech may appear impossibly informal in writing, and vice versa. For example, Cook (2004: 39–40) points out that terms like 'footway', 'oncoming vehicles', 'unfounded' and 'allayed' are more likely to occur in writing than in speech, whereas terms like 'thingy' and 'loo' are more characteristic of speech than of writing. In addition, as Abercrombie (1965: 36) points out, 'the aim of writing is not, usually, to represent actual spoken utterances which have occurred'. In this respect subtitles differ from most writing, given that subtitles typically represent spoken utterances occurring in the programme that is being subtitled. They do mirror other forms of writing, however, in generally eschewing non-standard language (Gottlieb 2004: 21).

Cornbleet and Carter (2001: 10–11) consider the salient features of writing and speech, respectively, to be that, unlike speech, writing is a process which results in a permanent trace, which is most often to be used by individuals who are distant from each other. Further, an individual often engages in a degree of planning when needing to write, and situations that require writing are often formal. Writing in its finished form is linear, and is the result of a process of thinking, planning and making the relevant marks on material, usually paper. Speaking, in contrast, is (Cornbleet and Carter 2001: 18–21) composed of sounds, which are by nature impermanent (although of course there are means of recording them); speech is rhythmical, and reliant on pitch (loudness versus softness) for parts of its meaning. These features cannot be conveyed easily in subtitles; yet Cornbleet and Carter's example (2001: 19) of the contrast between 'WHAT did you say' and 'What did you SAY' (where capitals in my rendering indicate stress) clearly illustrates the kinds of variations in meaning that these features can engender. Of course, the soundtrack will be available for hearing users of subtitles, and this, along with the characters' general demeanour, can guide the viewer. Halliday (1989: 30) lists the following aspects of speech that have no counterpart in writing:

> Rhythm, intonation, degrees of loudness, variation in voice quality (tamber), pausing and phrasing – as well as indexical features by which we recognize that it is Mary talking and not Jane, the individual characteristics of a particular person's speech.

Clearly, there are ways in which writing can be made to indicate these so-called prosodic and paralinguistic features (as when I used capitals above to indicate which syllable in a stretch of speech was stressed), but in subtitling, these tend not to be used. Halliday (1989: 97) also stresses the dynamic nature of speech and the dynamic view that it presents of the world, as opposed to the synoptic, product-like view of the world provided by writing. As he points out, writing is not presented to us, typically, with all the false starts, hesitations and changes of mind that speech reveals, because these have been edited out before the written text is let loose on the world; in subtitling, they are usually edited out also to save space and allot reading time to the content of what is said rather than to the manner in which it is said, unless the latter is particularly important – more important than it is in the normal course of events. Obviously, because of the presence of the visuals in TV and film, the dynamics of speech in the immediate context of the speakers and their action make up for this loss to an extent; but it remains a loss, nevertheless.

Punctuation, which is used in subtitles, obviously does not occur in speech; and although punctuation was originally intended as an aid to reading aloud (Cook 2004: 101), there is not a clear correspondence between punctuation marks and features of speech such as pauses and intonation, and other means that speakers can use to augment their speech, such as gestures and facial expressions. There is, rather, 'some functional overlap', as Nunberg (1990: 6) puts it. The comma, for example, has two main functions, namely as a delimiter and as a separator (Nunberg 1990: 36). In addition, Nunberg remarks (37, Note 17), 'there is probably a third type of comma' which 'separates elements of different syntactic types', and which is sometimes 'used to avoid a parsing difficulty or an ambiguity'. Nunberg gives the following examples:

1. Those students who can, contribute to the United Fund.
2. Such women as you, are seldom troubled with remorse.

In a situation of subtitle reading, where the reader's attention is already split between picture and subtitle, it is important not to burden the reader with so-called garden path constructions (see Bever 1970; Sanz, Laka and Tannenhaus 2013) (constructions that 'mislead comprehenders to initially pursue an analysis that turns out to be incorrect, as if taking the wrong turn while walking through a maze in a garden' (Sanz et al. 2013: 85)). Without the commas, the two examples above would point the reader towards one interpretation until about halfway through, when they would need to go back and reinterpret because this initial interpretation had proved to be incorrect. Thus, a reader is likely to read 'contribute' in the first sentence as being a main verb preceded by the auxiliary verb 'can': 'The students who can contribute (should do so)'; and in the second sentence a reader is likely to read 'you' and 'are' as subject and predicator: 'Such women as you are (have all the fun)'.

One of Nunberg's two main types of comma is the separator comma, which is placed between 'conjoined elements, sometimes without an explicit conjunction, and sometimes with one' (Nunberg 1990: 37). This is the comma used in lists like '(I bought) meat, fish, fruit, bread and wine.' The second type of comma is the delimiter comma, which is used to show where an item of a certain grammatical category begins and ends, bracketing it off, effectively. Nunberg (1990: 38) gives the following examples, among others:

3. The key, obviously, has been lost.
4. The key, which I did not have duplicated, has been lost.
5. The key, Mother, has been lost.

Delimiter commas can also occur singly, as in 'Obviously, the key has been lost' and 'Mother, the key has been lost.' The importance, when subtitling, of placing them appropriately to what is being said and meant in a film or TV programme is especially clear in cases like 4 above, which would be ambiguous if the commas were omitted (it could then refer either to one of several keys, namely the one that the speaker did not have duplicated, that was lost, or to only one key; with the commas, only one key is possible).

In addition to commas, punctuation marks in English include full stops, which indicate sentence boundaries, colons, semicolons, dashes, hyphens, parentheses, apostrophes, quotation marks, question marks and exclamation marks. Punctuation marks can indicate which speech act (Austin 1962; see Section 2.1.5) is being performed (e.g. question, statement or order), whether what is written is being attributed to someone other than the writer (using quotation marks) and also the following relationships between parts of the written text:

(i) a relationship across space, indicated by a hyphen, which can be used to link parts of words that are split by a line break, or by a colon, which can be used to refer ahead to direct attention to what is to come just after the colon.
(ii) an appositional relationship, that is, a kind of parallelism, as between 'my husband' and 'David' in the expression 'my husband, David'
(iii) that a part of the written text is additional to the main discourse, as in the case of parentheses
(iv) place holding for a missing letter, for example, or to indicate the possessive in the case of the apostrophe (Halliday 1989: 33–34).

As illustrated in the examples above, punctuation often provides clarity about the relationship between units of language, and this relationship is crucial in the representation of relationships between the things and processes in the world that the language is about. For example, in the title of a book by Lynne Truss (2003), *Eats, Shoots and Leaves: The Zero Tolerance Approach to Punctuation*, the comma after 'Eats' indicates an expression that focuses on what someone does (eats, shoots and leaves (three verbs)). Had there not been a comma (*Eats Shoots and Leaves*) the expression would refer to what someone eats (shoots and leaves (two nouns)).

Generally, punctuation functions in the same way in subtitles as in other writing; but punctuation conventions differ between languages, and in subtitling, the conventions relevant to the language of the subtitles should obviously be employed.

Subtitling generally involves up to two lines of text consisting of between thirty-two and forty-one characters and spaces at a time (Díaz Cintas and Remael 2007: 9). Two lines with these characteristics are displayed for six seconds, and shorter stretches may be displayed for proportionally shorter periods (d'Ydewalle and De Bruycker 2007: 196). These space and time constraints often require the speech represented to be 'substantially condensed' relative to the speech produced (Pérez-González 2020: 97).

Another important consideration in subtitling is that the subtitle should appear when appropriate to what is happening visually; if the subtitle is a translation of speech, the subtitle should appear when the character is speaking, not just before or just afterwards – even though this might allow for more content to be represented in the subtitle – and it should disappear when the person stops talking (Díaz Cintas and

Remael 2007: 88). If two lines of subtitling of unequal length have to be used, placing the shortest line on top allows free view of more of the screen than placing the longest line on top (Carroll and Ivarsson 1998: 2), although the line break should respect the syntax of the speech (Díaz Cintas and Remael 2007: 87).

A particular difficulty that arises from the difference between the spoken and written medium is the indication in subtitling of non-standard dialect features and, especially, non-standard accents in the speech of characters and narrators. I mean by 'accent' a regionally or class-determined way of sounding one's utterances (for example dropping /h/ sounds at the beginning of words spelled with 'h' as the first letter, as in 'heaters', which may be pronounced 'eaters' and, often, conversely, adding an /h/ sound at the beginning of words that do not begin with an 'h', as in /hoil/ for 'oil'). My former colleague, Gillian Brown, mentioned (personal communication) a case in which someone pronounced the term denoting oil heaters as 'hoil eaters'. I mean by 'dialect' a regionally related version of a language that uses some lexis and some grammatical features in ways that differ in certain respects from those of the standard language; for example, in some midland dialects of English an off-licence (a shop selling alcohol for consumption elsewhere) is called an 'outdoor'; in some south-western English dialects, 'sausage' and 'chicken' are used as non-count nouns like 'sheep' ('how many sausage can you eat?'; 'How many chicken are there in that enclosure?'). A particular dialect is often associated with a particular accent; for example, the dialect known as Standard British English tends to be spoken with so-called received pronunciation, which is the accent many people associate with news readers and other journalists employed by the British Broadcasting Corporation (BBC) – although an increasing number of regional accents can be heard on the BBC as well as on other broadcasting outlets. In contrast, it is very rare to come across non-standard dialect on the BBC and on other broadcasting outlets, unless this is required or is present because of the nature of the programme (e.g. plays or programmes about language or which focus on or are set in different regions of the country; certain programmes with specific regional content may also use presenters who use the relevant dialect). Such features can be important in characterization and in setting the tone of a film or other type of programme, but they are difficult to deal with in writing in general, let alone in translation. In addition, not all language systems are equally welcoming of the use of non-standard spelling and grammar for any reason. For example, in translations into Turkish, 'dialects, sociolects, ethnolects and other varieties of language in numerous source texts have been systematically translated into perfect standard Turkish' to protect the Turkish language (Erkazanci-Durmuş 2011: 27). In addition, a reluctance to replicate features like swearing and blasphemy in writing, including in subtitles, even when they appear in speech, characterizes many languages. For example, Ghassempur (2011) shows that two translations into German of Roddy Doyle's *The Commitments* standardize the characters' language 'to a universal colloquial form of German and loses part of its original quality in the translation' (53). In any case, a subtitler may not wish to introduce the complications of, for example, non-standard spelling into a subtitle that stays on the screen only briefly, in case it disturbs the audience's reading.

Exercise 2.10 Subtitling (emphasis as in Exercise 2.9 but with time and space limitations added)

This exercise retains the focus on speech versus writing introduced in Exercise 2.9. Here, though, we introduce the further complication of screen space and reading time limitations that arise when speech is subtitled.

A. Try to create a suitable subtitle for a clip of film, for example part of a trailer available on your cinema listings. For example, the trailer for Ken Loach's film *Sorry We Missed You* contains the lines 'How does a company get away with this? This is my family and I'm telling you now, nobody messes with my family.' It takes approximately seven seconds for the actor to speak these words, and in writing they contain 110 characters and spaces. How would you distil them into no more than 82 characters and spaces arranged logically across two lines, in English? And in another language?

A number of free subtitling programs are available on the internet, and the *Code of Good Subtitling Practice*, authored by Mary Carroll and Jan Ivarsson and endorsed by the European Association for Studies in Screen Translation in 1998, is also available.

2.1.11 Localization

Localization is 'the complete adaptation of a product such as a website, product marketing kit, software program or advertising campaign into another language' (McKay 2006: 26) or, as Pym (2004: 1) has it, 'for a particular reception situation'. An example of this strategy was used in Chapter 1 to illustrate the adaptation of an advertisement for a skin cream for use by animals or by humans. An instructive illustration of adaptation to a different physical setting is found in Mousten's work (2008), which gives a thorough account of differences between the Danish and the British VELUX websites at a particular point in time. Localization of software is a particularly vibrant industry, because of the increasing technicalization of life and living. Unlike the localization of finalized texts, 'software localization projects are usually undertaken while the source product is still in development so as to have simultaneous shipment of all language versions' (Chan 2013: 347). If a website is associated with the software, which is normally the case, then it, too, will be adapted for different user locales, a process known as web localization. When you localize a project so that it is suitable for many locales in different countries and continents, internationalization and, ultimately, globalization may be claimed. Many software localization tools are available, and the website of the Globalization and Localization Association provides information about the industry, resources, membership, conferences and events.

2.2 Translations and Their Customers

In this section, we will focus on the actors who pay translators, be they individuals, businesses, public services, translation agencies or larger institutions. These are not usually the only or main audience for the translations, that is, the translations' prospective readers; I will discuss readers of translations in Section 2.3. The people and agencies to be discussed here are, rather, the people and agencies who want someone else to read the translation and who pay translators to facilitate this. These paymasters are often referred to as 'clients' or 'commissioners' (Taibi and Ozolins 2016: 72), and Byrne (2010: 120) uses the term 'Translation Initiator', reserving the term 'User' for the people who are going to use and therefore read the translation (Byrne 2010: 14).

Many translators work on a so-called freelance or self-employed basis; others are employed by an agency, company, corporation or institution. A self-employed person does not have a contract of employment that guarantees regular payment of a salary; self-employed translators take on any risks associated with a translation task and are liable for anything that may go wrong in connection with a translation task (though they can take out indemnity insurance). They generally provide their own equipment, although some clients will provide client-specific software and other facilities, including temporary work accommodation on their premises. Freelancers usually accept work from different commissioners, and these may in principle range from large companies and organizations to much smaller businesses or individuals. Many freelancers build up close relationships with a few, repeat clients, and many develop their own specialisms over the years, or may, indeed, have set out with a particular specialism from the beginning of their career, often related to a personal interest like gardening, cooking, travel, model airplanes, or just about anything at all, or to a subject they have studied. In principle, freelancers can decide their own working pattern and work–life balance, though clearly the need to make a living will influence their decisions. A freelancer needs self-motivation and self-discipline, and they must be sufficiently organized and focused to advertise their own services and run their own business; they must also be able to interact in a professional way with their clients and have the confidence and knowledge required to set charges that will not put clients off, while ensuring a decent standard of living. Importantly, they must also resist any temptation to take on work for which they are not qualified.

Working for a translation agency relieves some of the pressures of working freelance, in particular, the need to advertise one's services and negotiate with clients about fees and about quality. Working for a translation agency will enable a translator to spend more time translating; however, the agency will take a cut of the price the customer pays for the translation.

Some companies, corporations and institutions also employ translators on a full- or part-time basis, sometimes alongside freelancers. Typically, companies that employ their own in-house translators are those that need frequent document translation, perhaps between several language pairs. They may rely on cooperation between their translators and between their translators and other employees – for example those who author the texts to be translated. Many companies will ask people employed mainly as translators to undertake other tasks too. The following is a list of tasks that are regularly mentioned in translator job advertisement in the UK:

- translating a variety of text types on a variety of topics
- transcreating (adapting the message to suit different locales)
- reviewing colleagues' translations
- editing machine translations
- researching terminology
- creating and maintaining translation memories
- creating and maintaining style guides
- meeting and visiting clients
- project managing.

International organizations like the United Nations (UN) and the European Union (EU) also employ in-house translators. UN translators are appointed following success in an examination process, the details of which are available on the UN's website. The official languages of the UN are Arabic, Chinese, English, French, Russian and Spanish; some documents are also translated into German. EU translators need to succeed in a competition that includes a test of reasoning skills as well as a translation test. Sample tests are available on the EU website. The EU also employs freelance translators. Other international organizations that employ translators include, among very many, the European Space Agency, the International Monetary Fund, the European Organization for Nuclear Research (CERN), the European Patent Office (EPO), The International Maritime Organization (IMO) and the World Health Organization (WHO). There are also many organizations that rely on volunteer translators. Ethical issues involved in this practice are discussed in Chapter 3, Section 3.1.

Exercise 2.11 Tests for employment by large organizations

This exercise invites you to attempt one of the European Union's tests for prospective translators so that you can consider how well prepared you might be to apply to the EU's translation sections and gain practice in attempting the kinds of test you might need to pass before gaining employment as a translator.

A. Visit the EU's careers website (https://eu-careers.europa.eu/en/selection-procedure/epso-tests) and take a test relevant to your languages. Afterwards, identify aspects of your translation practice that you feel you need to strengthen.

In the UK, the Institute of Translation and Interpreting (ITI) provides advice and other benefits for aspiring and practising freelance translators, and the American Translators Association (ATA) does the same in the United States. Most countries have similar web-based guidance to their translator institutes and organizations, and it is important for aspiring translators to become familiar with these websites, since they tend to contain information that is both helpful and important for someone seeking to succeed in the profession as a freelancer.

Díaz Cintas and Remael (2007: 36) list subtitling companies, production and distribution companies dealing with film, DVD, VHS and corporate videos, film festivals, TV stations, publicity companies and the software industry as commissioners of subtitlers.

Translators of medical texts may be working, whether directly or via a translation agency, for research institutes, hospitals and other health services, pharmaceutical laboratories, publishers of medical texts, manufacturers of medical appliances, and health professionals (see further Montalt Resurrecció and Gonzáles-Davies 2007/2014: 26–27).

2.3 Translations and Their Readers

As Suojanen, Koskinen and Tuominen put it (2015: 1): 'most translators would like to prioritize the target readers and their needs when they make translational decisions'. To do this, however, translators need to know who their readers are and what these readers' needs are, and this information is not always available to them. Besides, some texts are aimed at a broad readership. For example, Zethsen and Montalt (2022) point out that 'information about health, medication etc. is often potentially aimed at the entire population of a country'. Still, some idea of the nature of the so-called implied or presumptive reader (Iser 1978: 34; Nunberg 1990: 109) (the reader whom the author of the first-written text may have had in mind) can often be found in a text, whether for translating or not; but there is the further complication in translational situations that the imagined readers or prospective audience or users of the translation may differ from those of the first-written text; indeed, in most cases they do differ in terms of aspects like location, nationality and language, with all that that implies.

Indications of what type of person the implied reader is can be found, for example, in the amount of explanation of concepts and terms a text contains. Usually, this will be more if the reader is believed to be less knowledgeable and less if the reader is believed to be more knowledgeable. However, there are times when knowing more can warrant more precise information. For example, in a trilingual tourist brochure (Danish, German, English) published by Opdag Jylland [Discover Jutland] (2018), the Danish text advises readers to take a boat trip 'på de smukke Silkeborgsøer med en Hjejle-båd fra Silkeborg, Ry eller Himmelbjerget' (on the beautiful Silkeborg lakes on a Hjejle-boat from Silkeborg, Ry or Himmelbjerget). The places and their names in this text are likely to be familiar to Danish visitors to the area around Silkeborg, and many will understand that a Hjejle-boat is named after the bird which is called a golden plover in English and 'hjejle' in Danish. There are eight boats sailing from Silkeborg to the other towns along Gudenåen mentioned in the text, and seven of these boats are named after a type of bird that lives by the river (Hjejlen, Hejren, Mågen, Rylen, Tranen, Ternen, and Falken – The Golden Plover, The Heron, The Gull, The Stint, The Crane, The Tern, and The Falcon); the eighth boat is rather oddly called Turisten (The Tourist). These boats are iconic, and the area is a popular mid-Jutland destination for a day out for Danes. Silkeborg is famous as a town formed around its paper mill, established in 1899, and the river, Gudenåen, on which the town stands, is the longest in Denmark (149 km) and runs through seven towns. It is popular with sports fishers, and dwellings along the river are highly desirable. Himmelbjerget (The Sky/Heaven Mountain), at 147 metres, is one of the highest points in Denmark. For all these reasons, most Danes will have something more than a fleeting familiarity with the area, if only from their school lessons in Danish history and geography.

In contrast, the German and English texts confine themselves to advising tourists to take a boat trip 'auf dem Gudenå oder den Silkeborg Seen' (on the Gudenå or the Silkeborg lakes) and 'with one of the nostalgic tour boats on the beautiful lakes', respectively. No need to dwell on the name of the boat, nor, in the English text, on the difficult Danish place names, since these would either simply get in the way of understanding or require too much added information in a small brochure aimed at introducing twenty-five attractions in Jutland quickly and concisely.

It is easy to jump to the conclusion that people who need a translation reside in a different country from the one in which the first-written text was made and used; however, in modern, multicultural societies and in the context of significant movement of people between countries on a more or less permanent basis, so-called community translation, also known as public service translation, is common. Community translation (see also Section 2.1) is translation done to enable every resident in an area or belonging to a subculture, whether formally a citizen or not, to participate fully in the society in which they live (cf. Taibi and Ozolins 2016: 7). Translation between the languages of co-located communities does not differ essentially from translation between communities that live apart, except that, as mentioned in Section 2.1, in the case of co-located communities, there is often no need to translate the names of public bodies, institutions and organizations; indeed to translate these names might be unhelpful and hinder understanding, since their names are often signposts to the identification of their locations, both physical and virtual, and therefore essential for access to translated information about them. Instead, a translator might add an explanation of what the names mean and what the body's or institution's remit is.

Finally, it is important to remember that there are many sets of readers, or individual readers, of a translation beyond the end user. Mossop (2009: 246) lists the following potential readers in corporate or government settings: revisers, proofreaders, page designers, style editors, subject-matter experts, marketers, clerks, messengers, the commissioner, the writer of the source text, and, lastly, the final users. Clearly, in other settings, the various agents will be fewer, but it is important to keep in mind as a translator that there may be many people examining one's text and making comments and suggestions. Tolerance of other people's views is paramount, though it can be very difficult to attain, especially when one is working for clients who are less well organized than Mossop's scenario suggests, or clients who have not requested translations very often, if at all, in the past, especially if they have knowledge of the language the text has to be translated into but not, perhaps, of particular genre conventions which demand deviations from close translation and from mirroring the structure of the first-written text.

Exercise 2.12 Translating for different readership groups

Not all prospective readers for a translation will be equally well prepared to understand it, and translators often need to make assumptions about the kinds of background information different potential readership groups might bring to their reading of a translated text. This exercise is intended to raise your awareness of such potential readership group differences and to help you think about how you might accommodate them in your translation work.

A. Select a text and make translations of it into another language for more than one set of readers.
B. Comment on how the different readerships have influenced your translations and on how the differences between them affect the general meaning of the translations (if at all).

Summary

We began this chapter by considering the concept of genre and a number of examples of genres, noting that the same genre in different cultures may display radically different structures and linguistic realizations. We emphasized the need for translators to understand the locales for their translation in terms of genre-related subject knowledge, something that is especially acute in genres where lack of understanding of the subject matter on a translator's part can lead to serious mistranslations that may in turn have serious consequences for the users of translations. Next, we addressed the relationships between translators and their customers, noting that translators may be employed full-time in companies or may work freelance. We addressed the advantages and disadvantages of each mode of employment. Finally, we noted the need for translators to understand their projected readership's culture and probable background understanding of matters related to a given text so that these features of the readership for a translation can be considered when the translation is being prepared.

Further Reading

On subtitling:

Díaz Cintas, J. and Remael, A. (2007). *Audiovisual Translation: Subtitling*. London: Routledge.

This book provides an overview of the practice of subtitling across eight chapters covering the activity itself, the working environment in which subtitling takes place, and the kinds of linguistic and technical considerations that need to be taken into consideration.

On scientific and technical translation:

McKay, C. (2015). *How to Succeed as a Freelance Translator* (3rd edition). Colorado: Two Rats Press.

This book features fourteen chapters which cover the practicalities of setting up as a freelance translator, an overview of the translation business, marketing, translation technology, translation techniques, and the importance of a web presence. Repeat editions of this work testify to its enduring relevance, despite the inevitability of web developments having overtaken some information provided.

Olohan, M. (2016). *Scientific and Technical Translation.* London: Routledge.

This book contains eight chapters that explain the professional activity of scientific and technical translation and the resources required by that activity. Genres in particular focus are technical instructions, technical data sheets and brochures, patents, and professional and popular science.

On the practicalities of working freelance:

You can find medical consent form templates in English by searching for "medical consent form", and in French by searching for "French medical consent forms".

CHAPTER 3

Where Translation Happens

Preview

Languages tend to be closely related to societies; not in a one-to-one manner because of many factors, including migration and colonization and other forms of socio-political dominance, but most people who form social or even political groupings for reasons of perceived commonalities tend to share one or more languages to which they are emotionally and politically committed. Therefore, many international organizations are at pains to ensure parity among all the speaker groups of which they are formed, and this, in turn, leads to the need for translation between the languages preferred by the different social groupings involved. Other reasons for translating between languages include the desire by peoples to learn about each other's literatures, histories, sciences and cultures, and by groups with shared interests to interact on various social media platforms. In this chapter, we explore translation within different linguistic, political and cultural groupings and also the relationships translators may have with their work.

3.1 Translations and Their Societies

According to Li Wei (2006: 1), a third of the world's population (individuals) use more than one language regularly in their everyday lives, and still more people use several languages occasionally for special purposes. This fact, along with numerous other features of the life of the world, has consequences that impinge radically on societies, including on the translation activities that are engaged in within, beyond and between them.

Translations and the translating activity are bound up with societal conditions in several ways. Most obviously, population shifts occurring as a result of political and cultural conflicts have created needs for so-called community translation, which Taibi and Ozolins (2016: 10) define as 'written language services needed in a variety of situations to facilitate communication between public services and readers of non-mainstream languages'. We discussed community translation in Chapter 2, Section 2.1.

More than 7,000 languages are spoken in the world. The exact number is in constant flux, and approximately 40 per cent of the existent languages are endangered, having fewer than 1,000 speakers. More than half of the world's population is served by one of twenty-three languages, the top ten most spoken languages being, with the most spoken mentioned first, English, Mandarin Chinese, Hindi, Spanish, French, Standard Arabic, Bengali, Russian, Portuguese, and Urdu (Ethnologue Languages of the World; www.ethnologue.com/).

The United Nations (UN) counts 195 countries as members or observer states, so it is clear that languages do not correspond one-to-one to countries, either at the upper or lower estimated number of languages spoken in the world. On the one hand, some languages are spoken in more than one country, and on the other, many countries are either officially or unofficially multilingual, having more than one language used within them. This does not necessarily, or even usually, mean that the whole population of a country uses several languages or that more than one language is recognized as an official language of the country, and it is also important to distinguish, as is done in bilingualism theory, between societal and individual bilingualism (see e.g. C. Baker 2010). In particular, it is important to note that if a country is officially bilingual, it tends to be possible for individuals living there to use only one of the official languages (except perhaps in school language lessons), because an officially bilingual country tends to make all information available in both or all of its official languages. For example, the Canadian parliament's *Hansard* is published in both English and French, and roads in Wales are regularly adorned with the message 'Slow Araf', inviting people to drive slowly, in both English and Welsh (and not, as a quite young person of my acquaintance once suggested, encouraging a person named Araf, well known for speeding, to slow down).

So, on the one hand, translation is widespread within officially bilingual countries like Canada, or within bilingual parts of countries (Wales, for example, is part of the United Kingdom) because the several populations may not speak all of the languages that operate in their country, meaning that much information is made available in the languages used within them. On the other hand, translation is used to enable people in different countries in which different languages are spoken to communicate.

Baumgarten and Cornellà-Detrell (2019: 13) note, quoting Jacquemond (1992: 27), that 'the global translation flux is predominantly North–North, while South–South translation is almost non-existent and North–South translation is unequal: cultural hegemony confirms, to a greater extent, economic hegemony'. In other words, it is much more common for economically secure cultures to translate between one another and for their texts to be translated into the languages of poorer nations than it is for texts that originate in poor economies to be translated into the languages of other poor economies or into the languages of rich economies.

The availability of online social media has, however, enabled and empowered especially determined groups that have access to these media within societies to mobilize against what they see as injustice and inaccuracy. For example, Desjardins (2017: 11; note 2) cites the *printemps érable* (Maple Spring) movement in Quebec, which was formed 'in response to proposed post-secondary tuition hikes and changes to post-secondary bursary and funding programmes in the spring of 2012'. According to Desjardins, when the anglophone media seemed to mistranslate the French language coverage, members of the movement 'sought to provide "better" and "more adequate" translations of the original French-language press articles'. These alternative translations were presumably not remunerated. The concept of unpaid, volunteer translating raises questions which have been addressed by several scholars in various outlets (see McDonough Dolmaya 2011). Some translators and scholars consider volunteering a valuable way for those fairly new to the profession to gain experience; others consider it both exploitative and a threat to the industry, because if translations can be sourced gratis, translators who charge for their services are clearly placed at a disadvantage. Arguably, both points of view highlight elements of truth. In addition, in the case of translation of specialist genres, especially those related to entertainment, an element of interest and enjoyment on the part of the unpaid translators often plays a part too. Ultimately, each translator must make up their own mind about whether to participate in volunteer, unpaid translating activities or not. In any case, serious publishers of potentially valuable, income-generating texts are unlikely to risk compromising the quality of translations by trusting these to amateurs, while enthusiast participants in genre or interest-focused online activity are likely to continue to want to participate in translating events that are relevant to that activity.

Exercise 3.1 Volunteer translation activities

This exercise is intended to heighten your awareness of the issues raised by volunteer translating activities.

A. In groups, if possible, discuss the advantages and disadvantages of volunteer translation (translating without remuneration). You may, for example, take into consideration factors like the nature of the organization you might be volunteer translating for, and the possible benefits and disadvantages (for translators, for organizations, for readers) of relatively inexperienced translators using this avenue to gain experience.

3.1.1 Translator Associations and Networks

In many countries, there are professional associations of translators. There may be tests to be passed before a translator can become a member of such an association, or an amount of translating experience along with certain formal educational qualifications may be conditions of membership. As McDonough Dolmaya (2022: 199) points out, these formal associations can be distinguished from less formal translator networks:

While all associations are networks, not all networks are associations. To qualify as a network, a grouping need only be comprised of a set of actors, such as translators, connected to one another through a set of ties, such as interactions in an online forum. By contrast, as Pym (2014: 467) notes in his study of 217 translator associations, a legal framework of some kind regulates professional associations, which may also use terms such as 'order' or 'union' to refer to themselves.

McDonough (2007) and McDonough Dolmaya (2022) divide networks into four main types depending on whether they are largely focused on translation as a professional activity, on practical aspects of translation, on translator education, or on research related to translation. A profession-oriented translation network will seek to defend the rights of translators, improve their working conditions and enhance their social status, in some cases by providing professional development and networking events and by setting professional certification exams (McDonough 2007: 796) like those provided by the Chartered Institute of Linguists in the United Kingdom and by the American Translators Association in the United States. Practice-oriented networks tend to focus primarily on aspects of performance and on activity related to marketing and contracts; and members of education-oriented networks focus on translation pedagogy (McDonough 2007: 797). Finally, research-oriented networks seek to enhance our understanding of any aspect of translation, including its relationships with other areas of study or practice. Their members do this through concentrated, focused investigation.

Exercise 3.2 Translators associations and networks

This exercise is intended to raise your awareness of the associations and networks of translators that are present in your country of residence or origin and in other countries, and of the qualifications, if any, required for membership of them.

A. Explore associations and networks of translators in your country of residence or your country of origin. You can search for them on the internet.
B. Is it necessary to have formal qualifications to become a member of these associations and networks? If so, must these qualifications be translation qualifications?
C. Is it necessary to have translating experience to become a member of these associations and networks? If so, how, if at all, do they provide for novice translators?

3.1.2 Codes of Conduct for Translators

Both translator associations and less formal networks may adhere to codes of conduct, which express the principles and standards of behaviour that members are expected to respect and uphold. For example, the code of professional conduct of the United Kingdom's Chartered Institute of Linguists (CIOL) sets out the conduct that clients, employers, colleagues, the professional body itself and society at large are entitled to expect of a professional linguist (www.ciol.org.uk/code). The CIOL Professional Code of Conduct:

1. defines standards for best practice by members/chartered linguists
2. provides members/chartered linguists with a framework for making decisions on ethical, professional and business conduct
3. fosters good professional relationships between members/chartered linguists, between members/chartered linguists and their clients/employers, and between members/chartered linguists and other professionals
4. protects members/chartered linguists against undue pressure from clients/employers or fellow professionals in relation to professional conduct
5. in conjunction with the CIOL's Investigation and Conduct Procedures, upholds the integrity and reputation of the language professions.

Eight principles of professional conduct underpin the framework for ethical conduct by language professionals. These are:

1. Professional judgement
   This relates to point 4 above. You can refer to the code if clients or employers ask you to undertake work you feel unqualified for or which you think will place you in breach of the code.
2. Linguistic competence
   Members are encouraged to offer services only in those language pairs which are registered by the CIOL as that member's working languages. More generally, though, the principle is that you should only work within your linguistic competence. In this context, linguistic competence is defined as a person's 'spoken and/or written command of the language(s) concerned, their awareness of dialects and other language variants, and their knowledge of the cultural, social and political features of the country or countries concerned' (p. 4). It is very important to note the emphasis here on 'the cultural, social and political features' of the relevant countries. Linguistic fluency alone is far from sufficient to guarantee successful translation, and cultural, political and social understanding are important additional elements in the production of an appropriate translation.
3. Subject competence
   We discussed the question of subject competence in Chapter 2, Section 2.1. As mentioned there, few would deny that translators of specialist texts benefit from an understanding of the topics of the texts, but that translators often need to use their capacity to transfer skills between topics. The CIOL, however, requires members to work 'only within their subject competence', which means only with texts concerning topics or specialist fields that they are familiar with, whether 'through formal qualifications, experience, research, self-guided learning or training (informal and formal)' (p. 4).
4. Professional competence
   The specification of this principle states that 'Members will work only in areas of professional practice for which they have the necessary technological, practical and theoretical knowledge and skills' (p. 4).

5. Continuing Professional Development
   It is crucial for people in any professional field to keep themselves informed about new legislation and new developments. This is why considerable emphasis is placed in industry and business as well as in education on continuing professional development (CPD). Translators, for example, need to keep abreast of new technology, and to understand legislation relevant to their work. CPD courses may also focus on aspects such as professional indemnity insurance, which is a type of insurance policy designed to protect you in case a client claims that your service is inadequate, or they may introduce you to any new qualifications that are proposed or become validated by relevant professional or government bodies. The CIOL makes CPD a condition of initial and continuing registration (p. 5).
6. Responsibilities to clients/employers
   These are listed as follows (pp. 4–5):
   6.1 'Members/Chartered Linguists will take responsibility for their work and for its quality, even where part or all of the work is sub-contracted'. So even if you ask a colleague to undertake part of a translation for you, if the client's contract is with you, you are responsible for the work.
   6.2 'CIOL recommends that Members/Chartered Linguists make every effort to secure a briefing from clients/employers regarding the requirements for each job and to keep a record of this information' (p. 5). This recommendation highlights the importance of knowing exactly what it is that the client expects of you. In the case of translation work, it is often the case that the client in fact does not know exactly what they need because they may not know the norms and regulations governing text organization, terminology use and so on in the language and culture being translated into for them. But as a translator, you can use your expertise to assist clients to ensure that they have a good chance of obtaining whatever their goal is by means of the text you are creating. The importance of the brief will be further discussed in Section 3.3.1.
   6.3 'Members/Chartered Linguists will carry out all work impartially'. In other words, you must not allow any interests, aversions or preferences you may have vis-à-vis a text topic, a translation purpose, a client or any other party to influence the quality of the translation you deliver. If you feel uncomfortable about making a particular translation for any reason, then you should not accept the translation commission. Clearly, this stipulation can cause difficulties if you work as an in-house translator; in that case, each individual instance will need to be discussed with your employer.
   6.4 'Members/Chartered Linguists will take all reasonable precautions to keep information and material provided by clients/employers confidential and secure (except where disclosure is required by law).' Disclosure may be required by law where public safety is at stake. For example, in the UK, people who drive cars are legally bound to inform the Driver and Vehicle Licensing Agency (DVLA) if they become unfit to drive. Should they refuse to do so, then a doctor should contact the DVLA and disclose the information (having informed the patient that they are going to do so) (Medical

Protection Society). Other circumstances in which disclosure may be required involve terrorism prevention, for example.

6.5 'Members/Chartered Linguists will not use information acquired during their work to gain unfair advantage or to disadvantage their client/employer.' For example, you must not solicit work directly from a client for whom you have previously worked through an agency.

7. Responsibilities to fellow language professionals and to the Chartered Institute of Linguists
These responsibilities commit members/chartered linguists to not bring colleagues, the Institute or the language professions into disrepute, as they might do by acting in ways other than outlined in the rest of paragraph 7, namely to be courteous, honest and act with integrity; to adopt a professional tone when communicating in public and through social media; to do their best to contribute to a professional community of practice; and to engage with any investigations that might arise as a result of complaints raised against them for an alleged breach of the code (p. 6).
8. Responsibilities to other agencies, public bodies and society
These include complying 'with all statutory requirements and keep[ing] all records required by official agencies'. The CIOL also strongly recommends that translators take out professional indemnity insurance cover. Further, the responsibilities outlined in the code include not to undertake work that you know 'might expose [you] to criminal prosecution or civil liability or in relation to which [you] have a duty of disclosure to an official agency'; and to 'not accept or carry out work that may result in discrimination of any kind against another individual/group except where rendering such material falls under the professional obligation to provide accurate translation or interpretation of specific content e.g. interpretation of discriminatory comments in a court case or translation of some political/religious material' (p. 6).

Exercise 3.3 Professional codes of conduct

This exercise is intended to enhance your awareness of the nature of professional codes of conduct, especially those that pertain to translators.

I have used the CIOL's code as a detailed example of a professional code of conduct. You can access the original and full version on the CIOL's website (www.ciol.org.uk/code; accessed 20 November 2024).

A. Compare the two codes. How do they differ? Discuss the relative merits of each.
B. Try to identify other translation organizations' codes and compare them.
C. Write your own code. Justify your choice of content.

Other, less formal translator communities, often virtual, exist mainly for members to learn from one another and share knowledge (Risku and Dickinson 2009: 51).

Members of these tend to share a common purpose or interest (Risku and Dickinson 2009: 53), and whereas codes as such do not guide these communities, a set of rules of etiquette that regulate members' behaviour vis-à-vis one another is often observed (2009: 55). One such community is ProZ.com, which offers a selection of free services along with paid standard membership or plus membership which offer further services. Members must register and agree to a set of rules of usage as set out in the user agreement available on the ProZ.com website:

1. You may not misrepresent yourself or your firm.
2. Projects should be specified in detail. The more detailed a project description, the higher the chances of getting the right person, and completing the job smoothly.
3. Do your best work. As a freelancer, take pride in quality and deadlines. As an outsourcer, take pride in prompt payments. Do whatever you can to keep your promises.
4. Inform ProZ's staff if you see something improper taking place. (The staff may not be able to do anything about it, but inform them anyway.)

Exercise 3.4 Codes of conduct versus rules of etiquette

This exercise is intended to raise your awareness of codes of conduct versus rules of etiquette.

A. Compare a professional translator code of conduct with a set of translator rules of etiquette, preferably both from the same country.
B. What are the main differences between them?

3.1.3 Collaborative Translating

On social media, as Desjardins (2017: 17) puts it, 'translation is not reserved to a special workforce ... *everyone* can, ostensibly, translate', and it is not necessary to belong to either a formal or a less formal association or network. In addition, the availability of the internet has made collaborative translation, formal or informal, easier, or at least more convenient to pursue than it was in the past, insofar as there is no need for the translators to meet in person and insofar as it is possible to share and co-work on texts electronically from different locations. For example, Henkel and Lacour (2021) describe the free open source, web-based collaborative environment for computer-assisted translation, TraduXio, which is not only collaborative but multilingual, and whose basic premise is that users do not only translate between a source language and a target language, 'but rather from a singular text to many others' (Henkel and Lacour 2021: 154). Among its advantages is that 'language students can ... use the platform to propose multilingual translations of assigned texts, either individually or as a group' (155).

Exercise 3.5 Co-translation

This exercise encourages you to explore TraduXio and to practise co-translation. It draws on an exercise described by Henkel and Lacour (2021: 158–160).

A. Organize yourselves into groups of three or four people who share a language pair. In each group, agree on a text of about 1,000 words to translate.
B. Upload the texts to TraduXio. Each member of each group should now translate the text and upload their translation proposals to a new TraduXio column shared by the other members of the group.
C. Leave comments for one another on the translations until you reach a consensus on a final translation of each text.
D. Submit the text to your teacher for comments and subsequent discussion within your group.

3.2 Translations and Their Languages

It follows from the hegemony that exists in terms of translation directions mentioned at the beginning of Section 3.1 that more translations are made from texts written in languages of economically powerful nations, like English, French, German and Spanish, than from languages of smaller or less economically and politically powerful nations. Organizations like the European Union (EU) and the United Nations (UN) strive for linguistic equality as far as translating is concerned, but the fact remains that in 2023, of the 2,597,178 pages translated by the translation service of the European Commission, for example, 2,355,021 pages were translated from English. French was the most translated-into language, at 164,127 pages. The second most translated-into language was German, followed by English, Spanish, Italian, Polish and Dutch. The full set of figures for the twenty-four languages of the Union (plus a section for 'others') for 2023 is available on the European Commission's publications website (European Union Publications Office 2023).

Translation activity in the United Nations between 2016 and 2021 is documented in Report A/77/91 of the United Nations General Assembly (17 June 2022), 'Patterns of Conferences', section III, 'Documents management'. The UN accounts for its translation activity in terms of words rather than pages, and in 2021, the total number of words submitted for translation across its offices in New York, Geneva, Vienna and Nairobi was 219 million. Assuming a number count per page of 330, that makes 663,636 pages. The UN has six official languages, Arabic, Chinese, English, French, Russian and Spanish, and Chapter XIX, Article 111, of the Charter of the United Nations specifies that the versions of the Charter in each of these languages are equally authentic. Some documents are also translated into German. Data on the breakdown of the volume of translation between different language pairs is not available in the UN's reports of its translating activity.

3.2.1 Translations of Translations

As Dollerup (2000: 18) points out, it often happens that a translation is 'not based on the text of the original in the source language, but on realisations of the original in yet other languages'. He refers to this situation as one of relay (2000: 24), though the term 'indirect translation' is also often used. Wenjie Li (2017) uses the term 'mediating texts' to refer to the text in the language first translated into, and which becomes the source for translations into subsequent languages. She refers especially to English translations of Danish texts by Hans Christian Andersen, which were used as the source texts for translations into Chinese. Indirect translation is, as the Society of Authors website explains, most likely to take place when a text in a relatively minor language (they suggest Finnish) is going to be translated into another relatively minor language (they suggest Korean). Because it may be difficult in such a situation to identify a translator between the two relatively minor languages, a translation into a major language may be used as the source text for the subsequent translation. In many cases, this raises issues of copyright; as the Society of Authors website has it,

> Translations have their own copyright – in addition to (not replacing) any copyright in the original work (and whether or not the original work is still in copyright). Copyright is infringed if the skill and labour which goes into creating a work (in this case the translated version) is relied on to a substantial degree by someone else. So – quite independently of needing permission from the copyright owner of the original work itself – if a new translator were to rely substantially on the English translation as the basis for their third-language translation, they would need permission; failing which the relay translation would be an infringement of the copyright in the English translation. (www2.societyofauthors.org/wp-content/uploads/2020/05/Guidance-on-Relay-Translations.pdf)

Obviously, this raises the question of how to assess the extent to which the skill and labour of the translator of the text into the major language is relied on by the translator into a minor language. It also raises a further issue, namely that it is likely that with every successive translation iteration of a text, the distance between it and the first-written text (which is in a sense the original for all of the iterations, even though each iteration is made from a new translation) becomes a little greater. Every successive translator will make personal choices and decisions about parts of the text that are challenging – and even about parts that they find unproblematic – and these items will of course become the sources for the further translation of the existing translation into yet another language, where the same will happen. An inspiring case study of relay translation, in this case from Danish via English, German or Japanese to Chinese, is Wenjie Li's (2017) account of the Chinese versions of Hans Christian Andersen's stories mentioned above. The first direct translations of these tales, from Danish into Chinese, was made by Ye Junjian from 1953 onwards, culminating in a complete translation in 1978 (Wenjie Li 2017: 159), but 'even after the appearance of three direct translations in 1958 … 1995 … and 2005 … various indirect translations … continued to appear' (Wenjie Li 2017: 242).

There are clearly risks associated with indirect translation. Most obviously, errors or outright manipulations in the mediating translation will tend to be inherited by further translations of it; on the other hand, as Wenjie Li remarks (2017: 250), 'sometimes an adequate and accurate mediating text is more reliable than a fallible direct translator'.

Exercise 3.6 Relay translation

This exercise is intended to raise your awareness of issues pertaining to relay or indirect translation. It requires at least two people to share each language involved in the exercise in addition to English.

A. Each person selects a short text or a text extract of no more than 250 words in a language of their choice other than English; this is called the A language text. Each person translates the A language text into English, e.g. texts in French, German, Chinese, Korean, Arabic ... are translated into English.
B. The English translations are used by other members of the group who speak the A language as source texts for translations from the English translations into the A languages.
C. Compare the translations into the A languages with the original A language texts and discuss your findings. You can expect to find stylistic, lexical and grammatical differences between the two A language texts; list these.
D. Do you also find differences in meaning? It is not surprising if you do, given the close connection between how something is expressed and how it is understood.

3.2.2 Translated Language

Some scholars have sought to identify features that might be specific to translated text irrespective of the source–target language pairs involved and irrespective of the genres of the texts. As Behrens (2022: 97) points out, 'A translation differs from other writings in that it is meant to communicate what somebody else has said or written', not in the sense of indirect speech or paraphrase, but 'as text transferred from one language into another "on behalf of" the author of the original text'. It is of course far from obvious why this should cause the language of translations to differ from the language of text that has not been translated; however, there has long existed evidence for a phenomenon which Blum-Kulka (1986: 17) refers to as explicitation in translation. Her 'explicitation hypothesis' postulates 'an observed cohesive explicitness from SL [source language] to TL [target language] texts regardless of the increase traceable to differences between the two linguistic and textual systems involved'. Because the increase in explicitness takes place irrespective of which language pairs are involved, Blum-Kulka views explicitation 'as inherent in the process of translation' (1986: 19). Øverås (1998), Olohan and Baker (2000) and Hansen-Schirra, Neuman and Steiner (2012) have confirmed the presence of explicitation in studies examining large electronically readable corpora (Behrens 2022: 102).

A second characteristic of translated text as opposed to non-translated text is that translations tend to make more use of features characteristic of the language translated into than texts in that same language which have not been translated. This phenomenon has been referred to as normalization. On the other hand, according to Toury's so-called law of interference, 'in translation, phenomena pertaining to the make-up of the source text tend to be transferred to the target text' (Toury 1995: 275). When both languages share a particular feature but that feature is more common in the source language (language A) than in the target language (language B), then, in a translation from language A to language B, the feature will be more frequent than in a non-translated text in language B. This phenomenon is often referred to as 'shining through' (Teich 1999).

Exercise 3.7 Aspects of translated language

This exercise is intended to familiarize you with the concepts of explicitation, normalization, interference and shining through.

A. Select a short text or a text extract of no more than 1,000 words in a language you know well. Select a translation of it into a language you also know well. Compare the two texts, looking for evidence of the four phenomena of explicitation, normalization, interference and shining through.
B. Discuss your findings. For example, where you found evidence of the four phenomena, do you think that the use of expressions which led to them appearing was necessary? Did their use distort the translation vis-à-vis the source text?

3.3 Translations and Their Makers

According to Maginot (2018), the market for translation in the US is buoyant, and 'the employment outlook for translators and interpreters is projected to grow by 29% through 2024'. However, the translation profession in that country, as in many others, is unregulated; as mentioned in Section 3.1.3, anyone can set themselves up as a translator. This means that competition for work can be fierce and that a translator's ability to argue for their translation choices and to convince clients of the value of their qualifications are of great importance, to freelance translators in particular, but also for translators seeking in-house positions.

Obviously, translators are essentially and centrally involved in the process of making translations, but several other agents take active parts in that process too. In Section 2.2, the people who pay translators, whether individuals, businesses, public services, translation agencies or larger institutions, were identified as translators' customers or clients; and these customers or clients are crucially involved in the process through which many translations come to exist, because they are the ones who ask for the translations to be made. Other important agents include revisers, checkers, editors, project managers, terminology managers and localizers – though these roles, or selections of them, can be embodied in one person. It is prudent, therefore, for someone entering the translation profession to be cognizant of all these roles and to have practised as many as possible. Section 4.3 is dedicated to editing translations. In addition, almost all translators regularly use translation technology, so technological tools can also be considered agents (albeit inanimate) involved in the translation process. We will discuss translators' potential roles in Section 3.3.2. Here, we will concentrate on translators' interaction with their clients or customers, as outlined by Vienne (1994) in an account of a training programme in which students are explicitly trained in client management and customer education within the context of the research that precedes, coincides with or follows translating.

3.3.1 The Translation Brief

Vienne is concerned to ensure that translation students are able to develop, or encourage their clients to develop, using Fraser's term (1996: 73), a translation brief. As Nord explains:

> the translator needs as much knowledge as possible about the communicative purposes the target text is supposed to achieve for the addressees in their communicative situation. These details are explicitly or implicitly defined in the translation brief. (Nord 2008: 46)

Fraser's own findings from two studies of twelve community translators (1993) and twenty-one commercial translators (1994) are that 'the brief for the translation and the nature of the readership are of considerable importance in professional translation, especially in choosing appropriate renderings when dealing with non-formulaic and non-technical texts. Even ... where translators were not given a brief, they often assumed one' (Fraser 1996: 73). In Vienne's account of the training programme he delivered at the University of Turku, Finland, the nature of the students' own efforts to develop a brief are described in detail.

The students first analyse what Vienne (1994: 55) refers to as the translational situation surrounding a given task. During this analysis, they list questions that they might ask the person who has requested the translation, such as who will be their contact in the client's organization, who wrote the text to be translated, and who the people are who will be using the translation to access information. In addition to these contact-focused questions, the students also contemplate the context in which the first-written text was used, who it was written for, its purpose and its format. A similar list of questions is formulated for the prospective translation (who needs it, what for, in which format). Having this information, the translator can define the translation product required and judge whether the first-written text they have been given can be used to generate the kind of translation required. This is not always the case. For example, if a very general product label were to be translated for a product that is to be marketed in a location where detailed lists of ingredients are mandatory, the translator will need to obtain the requisite information, from the client if they have it, or in some other way. If this is not possible, an adequate translation cannot be made. Assuming that all is well so far, though, the translator can ask the client for further useful information, such as whether the first-written text is to be or has been translated into other languages, and whether there are similar texts available in the target language so that the translator can check the format, structure and terminology used in these texts. There may also be helpful sources of further information such as books, magazines, brochures, catalogues, and so on (see Vienne 1994: 55) and, of course, documents available on the internet.

Exercise 3.8 The translation brief

This exercise is intended to heighten your awareness of the concept of a translation brief. It is based on the exercise outlined in Vienne (1994: 54). You can work either individually or, preferably, in groups.

A. Each participant selects a text or text extract of around 500 words to translate into a language of their choice.
B. For each text, participants (individually or in groups) identify questions they need to find answers to before they can translate the text. For the source text, these questions may focus on
   i. who wrote the text
   ii. who its intended readership was / might have been
   iii. its layout

   For the translation, the questions may focus on
   i. who its intended readership is / might be
   ii. its purpose (for information about something outside the text itself; simply for information about the source text; for publication; for gist ...)
   iii. the appropriate layout for such a text in the target culture/language.

Information about (iii) above for the translation can be gained by looking for texts of a similar type originally written in the target language or translated into the target language. Such texts are often known as parallel texts. So ...

   iv. Seek out parallel texts in the language you are going to translate the text into and use these as a guide to the layout of your own translation.
   v. What, if any, are the main differences between the layout conventions of the source text and the target text?
   vi. If working in a group, compare your findings with those of other members in your group. Are there any regularities of either similarity or difference or both?

C. Translate the text.

3.3.2 Types of Translators

In this section, we will discuss different ways in which translators work.

3.3.2.1 Freelance Translators

As mentioned in Chapter 2, Section 2.2, many translators work on a freelance basis, and are thus self-employed. Schäffner (2020: 63) points out that it is difficult to estimate the numbers of translators that are active in the market and the proportion of the profession who are self-employed; but at the time of writing, in 2024, many translation service providers suggested on their home pages that there are 640,000 translators in the world, of whom 75 per cent worked on a freelance basis; indeed, according to Drugan (2013: 3) 'The bedrock of the industry is the freelance translator.'

Freelance translators may have their own clients, or they may undertake translation tasks for translation companies or for other types of company that need translation services. Clearly, it is also possible to combine these two avenues of income.

Freelancers have a certain degree of freedom to organize their own work time, although clients often need translations in a hurry, which limits this freedom. Freelancers must source their own equipment, including, preferably, a translation workstation, and they need to make a concerted effort to remain up to date with developments in their industry, with translation-related resources, and with developments in their languages and the relevant cultures. They need to make themselves visible on the jobs market, which effectively requires them to maintain a website and to approach potential clients either in person at conferences, trade fairs or similar events, or by (e)mail-shot – although the latter can backfire; many people object to unsolicited approaches. It is in freelancers' interest to maintain a database of previous work and resources consulted, along with a terminology store, which also needs to be kept up to date; a translation workstation (TWS) will do this:

> When a translator translates a new document in a TWS, the segments are matched against those already present in the translation memory (TM), which can then be reused for informing the new translation. The translator can also update the TM with his own new translations. (Carl and Planas 2020: 362)

Freelancers can choose to work together on an ad hoc basis when offered jobs that require translation into several languages, for example, or which require large amounts of translation to be made within a short timeframe. In such a case, it is beneficial to have a member of the translation team reading through the finished translation to ensure consistency of, for example, style and terminology.

Obviously, the freedom a freelancer has to regulate their own working practices is inviting in many ways, but as Hinchliffe, Oliver and Schwartz (2014: 10) put it,

> a translator in private practice is also chief financial officer, bookkeeper, marketing manager, IT [information technology] director, production and QA [quality assurance] supervisor, PR [public relations] manager, cleaner and tea maker, all rolled into one.

Freelancers are also responsible for setting money aside for their retirement, if they want to live beyond the means provided for by a state pension.

3.3.2.2 Company Translators

Company translators work in-house for one company or organization (typically) and will undertake translation tasks as required by that company or by the company's clients if it is a translation company. Company translators may benefit from company resources available on the company's premises as well as digitally, and from work previously undertaken by other translators for the same company. They may be able to discuss their work with colleagues who have or are translating the relevant texts into other languages. In-house translators may also have the advantage of direct access to colleagues who have written the documentation they may be translating or who are familiar with the products that the translation relates to. Their employers may also operate a pension scheme.

3.3.2.3 Self-Translators

A different distinction to that which can be drawn between freelance and company translators can be drawn between translators who translate text written by other people and translators who translate text that they have authored themselves. Translators who translate text that they have authored themselves are known as self-translators. Self-translation is more common in the case of literary translation than in the case of translation of other text genres; however, Jung (2002) reports on a study of self-translation of eight texts, each on a social sciences topic, and classified by Jung as 'academic texts' (35). As she points out (2002: 20, 29), 'Self-translators are given the role both of translator and author's editor in their writing or re-writing'; they also function as both readers and requesters of their own translation. Further, 'they are perceived as performing a transformation of their original creative act rather than producing a text structure, which [for assessment purposes, if any] is then to be compared to the structure of the first text' (46). Self-translators have been shown to allow themselves to take liberties with the first-written text that a translator of someone else's text would be unlikely to engage in (Cordingly 2013: 2). For example, Krouwer (1981: 15) self-translates, or perhaps we should say 'reflects', her poem 'Verfangen' ('caught'), as shown below in the poem 'Involvement'. In the first-written text below, I have added English glosses of the German lines:

VERFANGEN
In den Hoelen des Selbst
    (In the caves of the self)
verfangen, entschwindet
    (caught, disappears)
der Blick in die Welt.
    (the view into the world)

Da sind andere Menschengeschichter,
    (there are other human faces)
Schiksale, Blumenbilder, da sind
    (fates, flower-pictures, there are)
Tiere und fremde Voelker . . .
    (animals and foreign peoples . . .)

Huegel, Wellen und Wind;
    (Hills, waves and wind;)
Feuer brennt im Haus der
    (fire burns in the house of)
Freunde und das Ich verschmilzt.
    (Friends and the I melds.)

INVOLVEMENT
Cavernous self entrapment
Where is the view of the world?
Too much self indulgence leads
Away from the universe.

There are other faces
Strangers: their fate
There are fragrant flowers
Paintings . . . foreign countries
Tribes.

Hillsides with deer
Grazing, wind . . . singing
Waves; there are fires
Burning in houses where
Friends welcome each other
And in the eager handshake the
Entrapped self will melt.

It is obvious that the poet has not translated her poem literally; nevertheless, the pair of poems share almost all of their concepts:

> entrapment; cave(s); (the view of) the world / the universe; faces; strangers; fate(s); flowers; paintings/pictures; foreignness; tribes/peoples; hills; deer/animals; wind; waves; fire; house(s); friends.

The concepts of self-indulgence, welcoming, an eager handshake, singing, and fragrance (of the flowers) in the English version of the poem do not occur in the German poem, although some readers may want to argue that they can be inferred there. The English poem also contains the explicit sentiment that 'too much self indulgence leads away from the universe', which adds an extra six or seven feet (depending on how you might read the line out loud) to the six feet of the first two lines in both versions (stressed syllables in bold; in some readings, 'leads' might be stressed, giving seven feet in the line):

> In den **Hoe**len des **Selbst** ver**fang**en, ent**schwin**det der **Blick** in die **Welt**
> **Ca**vernous **self** en**trap**ment **where** is the **view** of the **world**?
> **too** much **self** in**dul**gence leads a**way** from the **uni**verse

The poet's address (as given in the literary magazine in which the poems are printed) is in the United States, so it is unlikely that language difficulties have interfered in the relationships between the two poems, and we can assume that the differences are introduced by the poet for (an)other reason(s).

The study by Jung mentioned above is limited to eight text extracts self-translated by eight published authors and to three student seminar papers self-translated by the student authors; these were compared to non-self-translations made by other student translators. The study confirms, and the two poems reproduced above illustrate, that self-translators may indeed take liberties that other translators would be less likely to take. Probably, they are also less likely than other translators to be chastised for taking them. The writer Karen Blixen / Isak Dinesen explains in the foreword to her *Syv Fantastiske Fortællinger* (1935), which is her own translation of *Seven Gothic Tales* (1934; my translation)

> When I wrote this book in English, for my own pleasure, I never imagined that it would be of interest to Danish readers. But its fate has been to be translated into other languages; so it seemed right to enable it to be published in my native country too. But then I wanted it to be published in Denmark as an original Danish book and not in any translation, be it ever so well done.
>
> Throughout the book, Danish names of people and places, accounts of Danish history and quotations from Danish writers have been used very freely. A large part of 'Seven Gothic Tales' has been thought out, and some of it has been written, in Africa, and the places in my book that are about Denmark should be taken more as a Danish emigrant's fantasies around Danish themes than as an attempt at realism.

Despite this declaration by the author, the Danish version stays very close to the original English; so close that it is inconceivable that the author wrote it without looking to the English original as the narrative that she now wanted to create in Danish. Whether one wants to deny that this is a translation, then, is a moot point. Personally, I would be happy to class it as a translation, albeit certainly not a word-for-word rendering; but then, very few well-made literary translations for publication are word-for-word renderings. In any case, as Anselmi (2018: 3) points out, there are also self-translators who adhere more literally to their first-written texts.

The Canadian writer Daniel Gagnon prefers the term 'cross-writing' to 'self-translation'. He explains his own reasons for engaging in the activity as follows:

> In the 1980s, although my first language is French, I wrote two novels directly in English: *The Marriageable Daughter* (Coach House Press, 1989) and *My Husband the Doctor* (1984, unpublished). I subsequently translated both novels into French: *La fille à marier* (Leméac, 1985) for which I won the Prix Molson de l'Académie des lettres du Québec, and *Mon mari le docteur* (Leméac, 1986). My principal motivation at the time for writing in English, although I was far from bilingual, was to escape the intense sense of confinement I felt in the French language ... As a Québécois francophone writing in the 1970s, I was caught between the limitations of 'joual,' a spoken form of heavily anglicized Québécois French, or the alienating straight jacket of imperial, Parisian French. Switching into English was a creative safety valve, an opportunity to find new linguistic and literary freedom. (Gagnon 2015: 46)

Exercise 3.9 Self-translation

This exercise focuses on self-translation and the extent to which a self-translator might decide to deviate from their first-written text.

A. Select a text or text extract and a self-translation of it. Compare the two texts. Are there instances where the two texts deviate significantly from one another in terms of meaning and/or structure and where these deviations cannot be explained as a result of differences between the two languages involved?

When deviations between a text and its translation cannot be explained with reference to the differences between the language systems involved, but where it is still clear that one text closely resembles another in terms of content and structure, the term 'adaptation' is often used to refer to the relationship between the first-written text and the text that is based on it. In a sense, 'adaptation' is the literary register's equivalent of 'localization', the term that is used in business and industry contexts (see Chapter 2, Section 2.1). For example, in *Pacific Quarterly Moana* 5(1) January 1980, on pages 52, 80 and the back cover, under the title 'Four German songs in Maori version', the commentary explains:

> Inspired by Kiri Te Kanawa's rendering of three lyrics by Herman Hesse and one by Joseph von Eichendorff in the *Last Four Songs* of Richard Strauss on a CBS Masterworks recording (SBR 235960) and finding the imagery and tone similar to that in the traditional Maori *waiata*, Katerina Mataira created these four Maori version. They are versions rather than translations because specific details of season and aspects of nature referred to in the originals have been adjusted to the landscape of Aotearoa.

B. Is there a point when you would deem a version of a source text to deviate so far from it that you would consider it a different text altogether?

If working in groups with different text pairs, compare other groups' findings with your own.

3.3.2.4 Pseudotranslators

Pseudotranslators are people who publish work that they have written themselves as if they were translations. Often, these are well-known writers – Toury (2012: 49–50) mentions for example Horace Walpole – whose motives for presenting their own work as translations may be to introduce something new and perhaps controversial into a potentially reluctant culture without personal risk or censure, as in the case of the *Book of Mormon* (published by Joseph Smith in 1830), which was used to support the creation of a new variant of Christianity. Other motives include seeking to enhance the appeal of a work presented to a culture where foreign work is valued highly, or to support national heritage and tradition, as in the case of the poems published by James Macpherson (1765), which he claimed to be his own translations from Gaelic poems written by Ossian. Macpherson claimed that he had collected the poems during a visit to the Western Highlands and Isles of Scotland, but it remains unclear whether these poems were wholly invented by Macpherson, or whether his claims have a factual basis. Often, a pseudotranslator will introduce into their pseudotranslation features that are believed to characterize translations into the relevant language from the language that the non-existing source text is claimed to be composed in. Tirkkonen-Condit (2002) has shown that beliefs about linguistic features that characterize translations are largely incorrect; however, in the case of passing something off as a translation, perceptions of typical characteristics of such texts are more important than the facts of the matter.

3.3.2.5 Translators as Gatekeepers

Translators operate as gatekeepers in two main ways. First, they may, as Jones (2001: 263) remarks, carry out a gatekeeping role vis-à-vis the conveyance of information by agreeing to translate or by refusing to translate, thereby exercising 'power to decide which writers and which ideas can be heard in the target culture'.

Secondly, by forming associations with specific requirements for membership they may, as Pym (2014) indicates, seek to gatekeep access to their own profession and its sub-specialisms. For example, the association of German-speaking translators of literary and scientific works, Verband deutschsprachiger Übersetzer/Innen literarischer und wissenschaftlicher Werke (VdÜ), states on its website that it is a condition of membership that a person has made a translation of a book, play or similar work that has been published or which is contracted, and which the translator has not paid to have published himself or herself (see the section headed 'Mitglied im VdÜ werden' (becoming a member of the VdÜ). Whether or not the person works as a translator full-time or part-time does not matter:

> Voraussetzung für die Aufnahme in den VdÜ ist eine veröffentlichte oder vertraglich vereinbarte Literaturübersetzung, die nicht durch Einsatz eigener Geldmittel erkauft sein darf – Buch, Theaterstück, Hörspiel, Drehbuch etc. Ob Sie das literarische Übersetzen im Hauptberuf oder im Nebenberuf ausüben, spielt keine Rolle. (https://literaturuebersetzer.de/mitglied-im-vdue-werden/)

According to Fujii (1988), the use of the concept of gatekeeping in communication research derives from Lewin (1947), who 'formulates a gatekeeping model of news translation, and identifies four gatekeeping functions performed by news translators: controlling the quantity of the message, message transformation, message supplementation, and message reorganization'.

In Chapter 2, Section 2.1.9, on news translation, we saw the first of these functions enacted: the extract from Professor Calum Semple's statement about Covid-19 in the *Times* newspaper was significantly shorter than the extract published in *The Guardian*; there was also some, albeit small, difference in formulation of the two statements; that is, there was a degree of transformation of the message.

To see an example of message reorganization, we can compare a brochure entitled *Besøg Holstebro og oplev mere: Natur, kultur og shopping* (Visit Holstebro and experience more: Nature, culture and shopping) and its German-language counterpart, *Besuchen Sie Holstebro und erleben Sie mehr: Natur, Kultur und Shopping* – the latter also containing small inserts of English language text. In a section entitled 'Strandingsmuseum St. George fortæller en dramatisk historie' (Shipwreck Museum

St. George tells a dramatic story), the Danish text recounts the dramatic story of a shipwreck in its first sentence and explains where memorials to the lost sailors can be found in the last sentence of the text. The German version begins with the location of the memorials, and gives the dramatic story last. Curiously, since the dramatic story recounts the loss of nearly 1,400 British sailors, there is no English language text insert focusing on this museum and this event; instead, the relevant space is given over to promoting fishing and water sports. We cannot know in this instance whether this reorganization was decided on by the translator or by, for example, the editor or publisher of the brochure, or, indeed, by the paying client (the local tourism organization), but it is clear that editors can play important roles in determining the final version of a translation.

Supplementation is used in translation for example when information which is not included in the source text is considered necessary to enable the target text readers to understand the text fully or to act on it in the way that it is intended to be acted on. However, Choi (2022: 97), whose study of government translation in South Korea we discussed in Section 2.1.9, also shows that 'greetings such as "Good afternoon"' may be added to the written translated versions of press briefings provided by the Korean Ministry of Foreign Affairs and Trade.

It is possible to view gatekeeping in positive terms, as a question of inclusion, rather than, or instead of, keeping out. For example, Park (1922: 14) points out that the organizations formed by the immigrant populations that came to the United States early in the twentieth century performed this important function. He explains that the majority of the members of immigrant populations had 'never seen, in their own country, any . . . reading matter printed in the language they [were] accustomed to speak, the only one they fully [understood]' and if they had ever tried to have reading matter printed in their vernaculars, these efforts had been suppressed, so that 'a literary language [had] grown up that [was] the exclusive property of the dominant classes, and the press consequently had been unintelligible to the majority of the population'. When they came to America, however, these national groups would organize: 'They [became] socialists or nationalists, or members of fraternal organizations, and read papers, because practically every immigrant organization publishes some sort of paper' (Park 1922: 10). The reason immigrants needed to read the news in their new country was that 'News is a kind of urgent information that men use in making adjustments to a new environment, in changing old habits, and in forming new opinions' (Park 1922: 9).

Furthermore, Marling (2020: 229) discusses editors, translators and literary agents as gatekeepers in the positive sense of facilitators of the dissemination of world literature, for example through adjustments to the audience expectations and concepts of acceptability they consider to be at play in locales other than the one in which a text began its life.

In business settings, too, according to Moore, Lowe and Hwang (2007: 3), translators

> wield considerable power . . . as they interpret not only language, but culture, between different parties in cross-cultural management situations, and thus

> have the power, through this knowledge-management role, to define and shape business cultures and communities in the eyes of both outsiders and their own members.

Referring to Barley (1983), they further remind us that in anthropology, translators are crucial to the success of data gathering, particularly, of course, if an anthropologist does not understand the language of a culture being investigated (Moore et al. 2007: 5), but since a translator tends to be well versed in the culture of the languages that they work in, they can also be helpful in facilitating access to information sources and spokespeople in the cultures an anthropologist may be visiting.

3.3.2.6 Translators as Localizers

There are times when a translation needs to deviate from its source in specific ways. Most obviously, in some, though not all instances of news translation, the translated version may need to adjust indexical terms – terms that indicate where a speaker or writer is positioned geographically and temporally relative to what is being narrated. For example, in news reporting, 'today' in the original may become 'yesterday' by the time the report has been translated and published in its new locale. But localizing a translation also involves ensuring that a text conforms to local norms of grammar, punctuation and spelling, and that the presentation of dates, times, addresses, phone numbers and currencies does so too. In addition, graphics and cultural references should be adapted to local manners of presentation, and links to URLs should be to those URLs that will be most useful to the potential users (Angelone, Ehrensberger-Dow and Massey 2020: 393).

Mousten (2008) describes a localization project involving the 2005-version Danish and English language websites advertising VELUX windows and skylights, a Danish product which remains widely marketed internationally. She focuses on the extent to which content was shared between the Danish and English websites, and also on which elements were shared (Mousten 2008: 233). She found that although some text from the Danish website did 'travel' (her metaphor) to the English language website, a greater amount of text did not. Some of the text that did not travel referred to objects not available in the English locale, and some text that differed between the two web pages concerned 'differences in the locales, for instance the height of the profiles of roof tiles, which apparently is max. 90 mm in the Danish market, and max. 120 mm in the English locale' (Mousten 2008: 262). This is a good illustration of the need, when translating, to take into consideration matters well beyond language.

Another illustration of this point is to be found on the Lego company's websites in Danish, English and German, accessed in August 2022. Like VELUX, Lego is a Danish company, so the original or 'main' website is the Danish one. I shall concentrate on a page headed 'Lego House: Home of the Brick' in each of the three languages. The Danish original moves straight from the heading to a set of three photographs, whereas the English and German versions each have a paragraph beneath the heading which says, in the English version:

> **A safe experience**
> LEGO© House always follows the current restrictions set by the Danish authorities, and at the moment there are no COVID-19 related restrictions that you as a guest in LEGO House must be aware of. However, it is important to us that it must be a safe and secure experience to visit LEGO House – without compromising on the play experience. Therefore, we always monitor the number of guests to make sure that you can feel safe in LEGO House. And there are of course hand sanitisers all around the house.

The German version has

> **Ein umbekümmerten [sic] Besuch**
> LEGO© House befolgt jederzeit die geltenden behördlichen Einschränkungen. Derzeit gibt es keine COVID-19-Einschränkungen, die Sie als Gast im LEGO House beachten müssen. Uns ist es jedoch immer wichtig, Ihnen einen unbekümmerten und sicheren Besuch im LEGO House bieten zu können – ohne dabei Kompromisse beim Spielerlebnis eingehen zu müssen. Daher überwachen wir immer, wie viele Gäste gleichzeitig in die Erlebniszonen gelassen werden, damit Sie sich sicher fühlen können. Darüber hinaus wurden im ganzen Haus Handdesinfektionsmittelspender aufgestellt.

My translation of the German:

> **A worry-free visit [the German heading is misspelled; see 4th line of the main text, where the correct spelling is used].**
> LEGO© House always follows current relevant restrictions. At this time, there are no COVID-19 restrictions which you have to observe as a guest in the LEGO House. But it is always important to us to be able to offer you a worry free and safe visit to the LEGO house – without allowing this to compromise the play experience. So we always monitor the number of guests that we give access to the experience zone at any one time, so that you can feel safe. In addition, there are hand sanitizers available throughout the House.

The main difference between the two non-Danish language versions is that the English does, while the German does not, mention that it is the Danish authorities which have, or rather have not, set restrictions on entry to the Lego House. However, the main difference between the Danish and the non-Danish versions is that both the non-Danish versions mention that there are no restrictions on entering the Lego House, something which the Danish visitors will already know because Covid-related restrictions overall were by then lifted in Denmark. This is clearly not a matter of language but of knowledge of local legislation.

Another difference between the texts is that both the Danish original and the English translation advise online purchase of tickets to the House, which will not only secure a ticket but will save the purchaser 50 DKK. The German version mentions the saving in euros with the Danish equivalent price in brackets following: '6,5 EUR (50 DKK)'; neither Denmark nor Britain are members of the euro area, whereas Germany is. This, again, is a matter of extra-linguistic features of different locales.

Exercise 3.10 Localization

This exercise is intended to raise your awareness of the issue of localization.

A. Select a set of texts and their translations into languages of your choice (languages that you understand) and look for localized features of the translations.
B. Select a text of around 1,000–3,000 words that is local to a specific area. Translate it, localizing it to a different locale.

3.3.2.7 Translators as Project Managers

Project management can be crucial to translation projects, large or small, although the larger the project, the more helpful project management will be. Project management involves project planning, work assignment, communication planning, document scoping and 'other instruments that promote feedback, interpersonal interaction and the sharing of requisite skills' (Shreve 2020: 165). Many project management tasks can be undertaken by translation memory (TM) tools (see Van der Meer 2020).

For individual freelancers, Drugan (2013: 83) recommends the use of an Excel database or electronic calendar, or 'the basic project tracking function bundled as standard with some TM tools' to keep abreast of commitments, whereas in-house project managers 'need more sophisticated applications which handle multiple complex projects concurrently and automate support tasks'. These can be undertaken by translation software, including, for example, Across Language Server, SDL WorldServer, GlobalLink, TransPort or Smartling; some of these also offer terminology management features.

3.3.2.8 Translators as Terminology Managers

Terminologists are central to all efforts to ensure terminological consistency within an enterprise or an area of specialization more broadly. Terminology is defined by Bowker (2020: 261) as 'the discipline concerned with the collection, processing, description and presentation of terms, which are lexical items that belong to a specialized subject field (e.g. economics, law, and medicine)'. Its aim is to 'ensure that the key terms (for a project, organization, product, brand, etc.) are maintained in some accessible system, regularly updated and consistently used by all those involved in the process'. A translator needs to be aware of the terminology relevant to their field of specialization, and has to know where and how to search for terminology that they do not know already. It is a common misconception, however, that terminology is only relevant to specialized text types. In reality, terminology belonging to a specialized field such as those mentioned by Bowker may in principle appear in any text a translator may come across. In addition, almost any sphere that may be written about and which may require translating will have its own characteristic set of terms and even characteristic grammatical and discourse features. Medical packet inserts illustrate this commonality of content and structure especially clearly.

Patient information inserts generally include instructions for use of the medicine in question, as well as information about what the medicine contains, possible side effects, and warnings about circumstances in which people should not take the medicine; they address the user directly using second-person pronouns (in languages where second-person address is not indicated in the form of the verb, e.g. Spanish). The inserts typically include the name of the product and its trademark, if any; if the trademark is the best-known name of the product, then the trademark tends to take precedence over the chemical description. For example, the trademark Aspirin takes precedence over 'Tabletten mit 500 mg Acetylsalicylsäure' (German), '500 mg, tabletter Acetylsalicylsyre' (Danish), and 'Tablets with 500 mg acetylsalicylic acid' (English) on the packet inserts in packs of aspirin tablets in each of the three languages. The same is true for French and Spanish, where the trademarks are Aspro and Aspirina respectively. The trademark and description, including the chemical content, is followed by an instruction (Danish, German, Spanish) or request (English, French) to read the insert because it contains important information. In French, German, English and Spanish, the link between the encouragement to read and the reason why this is important is explicitly signalled using 'denn' (because) in German, 'as' in English, 'porque' (because) in Spanish, and 'car' in French, whereas in the Danish insert, there are two free clauses: 'Læs denne indlægsseddel grundigt. Den indeholder vigtige informationer' (Read this insert thoroughly. It contains important information). The German original is 'Lesen Sie die gesamte Packungsbeilage sorgfältig durch, bevor Sie mit der Einnahme dieses Arzneimittels beginnen, denn sie enthält wichtige Informationen' (Read all of the packet insert before you begin taking this medical remedy, because it contains important information), and the Spanish reader sees 'Les todo el prospecto detinidamente porque contiene información importante para usted'. (Read the entire leaflet carefully because it contains information important for you).

Each of the Danish, German and Spanish texts uses the imperative mood. In contrast, the translation into English is the polite 'Please read the entire patient information leaflet carefully as it contains important information on using the medicine', and the French is 'Veuillez lire attentivement cette notice avant de prendre ce medicament car elle contient des informations importantes pour vous' (Please read attentively this information before you take this medicine as it contains information that is important for you). Interestingly, the German insert encourages people to consult their doctor after three or four days if they do not feel better, the English opts for four days, whereas Danes must suffer for a full seven days. French and Spanish people are advised to consult their doctor after three days if their ailment is a fever, but after five days if they are taking the medication to control pain. Given the near-identical physical make-up, from a medical point of view, of the average member of each of the relevant nations, these differences are likely to be guided as much (or maybe more) by cultural conventions and customs relating to consulting a doctor as by medical science.

Section 1 of the inserts also explains what Aspirin is for and how it is to be used. The remainder of the insert is divided into five sections. These are phrased as questions (interrogative sentences) in German and in English, and as information (declarative sentences or noun phrases) in Danish. Section 2 explains what a person must be aware of before taking Aspirin, including circumstances in which Aspirin should not be taken. Section 3 explains how Aspirin is to be used, and section 4 focuses on possible side effects. Section 5 concerns appropriate storage of the tablets, and Section 6 provides further information about the contents of the packet and of the tablets, about what the tablets look like, and the addresses of the manufacturer and the holder of the rights to distribution.

Exercise 3.11 Texts that share structures across languages

This exercise is intended to illustrate that particular text types may share characteristic structures across languages.

EITHER

A. Compare what has been said above about the structure of medicine packet insets in Danish, English, German and Spanish with medical packet inserts in another language (or other languages).

OR

B. Select another text type with a clear, characteristic structure across languages and identify the purpose of the different sections of the texts.

Although terminology is important in monolingual text creation, it is also crucial in translation. In fact, according to the UN's website, 'the standardization of terms in the six official languages [of the union]' is a key responsibility of translators who work for the UN. The UN's multilingual database UNTERM and the European Union's terminology database Interactive Terminology for Europe (IATE) are both available to the public via the organizations' websites.

Summary

This chapter began with a discussion of the societal conditions that surround translations. We noted a lack of match between languages and countries and between societal bilingualism and bilingualism in the individuals living in those societies. Translation flourishes within officially bilingual countries because every sector of their populations is catered for in its own language. We noted that it is more common for economically secure cultures to translate between one another than it is for poor economies to translate into the languages of other poor economies or into the languages of rich economies. We discussed the networks and associations that translators form, which may adhere to codes of conduct. We examined one such code as well as the etiquette guiding members of a less formal translator community. In the second part of the chapter, we discussed whether translated language differs in identifiable ways from non-translated language, and in the third section, we looked at different types of translators and their working conditions. We discussed the gatekeeping roles that translators play in terms of what they decide to translate, in terms of who they admit to societies that they form, and in terms of providing access to other cultures.

Further Reading

Angelone, E., Ehrensberger-Dow, M. and Massey, G. (eds.) (2020). *The Bloomsbury Companion to Language Industry Studies*. London: Bloomsbury.

This volume contains sixteen articles by experts in their fields on the impact of new technologies on traditional translation work and on the new types of language work they enable.

Cordingly, A. (ed.) (2013). *Self-Translation: Brokering Originality in Hybrid Culture*. London: Bloomsbury.

The twelve articles in this volume concern self-translation in literary history, self-translation in interaction with disciplines like sociology, psychoanalysis and philosophy, and self-translation from the perspective of post-colonialism. The volume as a whole at once explains and challenges the concept of self-translation, and analyses the work of several practitioners.

Hinchliffe, I., Oliver, T. and Schwartz, R. (eds. and compilers) (2014). *101 Things a Translator Needs to Know*. WLF Think Tank. United Kingdom: WFL 101 Publishing.

This collection of 101 small pieces of wisdom and helpful advice for translators, provided and compiled by successful translators, cannot fail to make the life of novice as well as experienced translators easier, whether by providing novel ideas (for the former) or by confirming much of what the latter may have hoped they already knew.

CHAPTER 4

How Translation Happens

Preview

The process of translating begins with the acceptance of a text to be translated and ends with the delivery of the translation. Everything that happens during this process can be encompassed under the umbrella term 'translation workflow', and the translation workflow includes the important components, editing and revising. Industry standards for human translation services such as the American Society for Testing and Materials' ASTM 2575 and the International Organization for Standardization's ISO 17100 require these components to be part of the translation workflow (Mellinger 2018: 310). Therefore, in whatever manner a text has been translated (whether generated mainly by a translation machine aid or generated mainly by a human), prior to the delivery of the translation, the text will typically have undergone an editing process during which a person other than the translator will have tried to ensure that the translation is a fair representation of its first-written text and a suitable representation, given the translation brief. We will discuss the processes of editing and revising in Section 4.3. The chapter begins with a discussion of human translation and the conditions under which it takes place in Section 4.1, before moving on to focus on the state of the art in machine translation and in the use of translation memories, activities which are closely related to technological developments, and which form the topics of Section 4.2. Section 4.4 discusses quality assurance.

4.1 Human Translation

According to Liu (2020: 2), the translation and interpreting market is forecast to have the highest percentage growth in the period leading up to 2026 of any occupation in the *US Department of Labor Occupational Outlook Handbook*. Human translation, unaided by electronic tools, will not account for all or even most of this, but humans will be involved throughout, whether as translators, revisers of human or of machine-assisted translations, or as editors. In Section 4.2, we will chart the types of interaction between humans and machines that translating typically involves; however, we begin, in this section, with a consideration of human translation.

Human translation is, as Alves and Lykke Jakobsen (2022: 34) remark, 'physical, behavioural and mental. There is material text representation, there is body movement involved in reading and writing text, and there is thinking.' In Chapter 1, we examined ways of researching each of these aspects of human translation, including comparative text analysis, think-aloud protocol studies, keyboard logging, eye tracking, electroencephalography and brain imaging technology. The process of producing a translation, however, also involves receiving the text, tracking its progress through the translating institution, ensuring that it is treated appropriately in terms of who translates it and the suitability of the translation-to-be for the purpose it is intended to serve, checking it for linguistic and content accuracy, and delivering the translation to its intended receiver. In a translation agency, a project manager will usually ensure that all this happens successfully. Naturally, the translation workflow will differ depending on whether the translator is self-employed or working in a translation agency, although some systematizing of the workflow is helpful, and almost always necessary, irrespective of the size of the translation organization involved, and even if it is a one-person band.

Even when we speak of human translation as opposed to machine-aided translation or machine translation, the human in question will almost without exception use resources of various kinds to assist them in their activity. They may, for example, consult dictionaries as well as documents that exemplify the kind of text to be produced or which contain information about products related to products mentioned in the source text, and so on. Furthermore, given the physical aspects of the translating process, it is important for a translator to ensure that their working environment is one that will enable them to maintain and promote their physical well-being: a good chair at the right height relative to a desk or other type of work surface, providing suitable support and positioned in the right relationship to a work surface large enough to hold documentation of various kinds, writing paper and pens, along with a computer screen and keyboard. A well-lit workspace is also essential, although it must be protected against the glare of the sun through its windows; it is generally preferable for the light source to be at the left for right-handed people and at the right for left-handed people, though for typing this is less important than it is for handwriting. Physical aids such as dictionaries and documents need to be placed within easy reach of the translator so that they are readily available when the translator needs to consult them while typing. In a shared office space, privacy and protection from noise from colleagues is also important, and there must be access to fresh water as a minimum, and preferably also to tea, coffee, juices or similar light refreshments. These consumables are typically easily accessible for translators who work at home, but they are equally important for translators working within larger organizations.

In Chapter 1, Section 1.3, we addressed research methods employed to gain insight into the translating process, along with their advantages and disadvantages. As mentioned there, these research methods include think-aloud protocols, that is, recordings of translators verbalizing their thoughts while they are translating, something that may interfere with translators' normal way of working, and which tended to focus only on problematic and usually rather short passages of text. We also discussed Translog, which tracks translators' typing behaviour, and programs that track translators' gaze foci and gaze movement across the two texts prominently involved in a translating process, the first-written text and the developing translation. It is also possible to monitor translators' use of translating aids that are separate from the computer. These research methods offer evidence of translators' physical behaviour – evidence that is used by researchers to draw inferences about the mental processes underlying the physical behaviour. However, it is only the behaviour that is empirically available. Finally, we discussed methods for observing the translating brain, including positron emission tomography (PET), functional magnetic resonance imaging (fMRI) and functional near-infrared spectroscopy (fNIRS). Observations gained through the use of these various tools have strongly suggested that translating involves different parts of the brain than those involved when monolingual tasks are undertaken. This important insight testifies to the need for translators to be educated and practised in the translating task and in the subtasks that it involves; that is, having two (or more) languages and gaining practice in using them does not in and of itself suffice to enable a person to translate well.

Unfortunately, aside from the fourth research method that we discussed in Chapter 1, which focuses on the involvement of the emotions in translating, concerning which some extensive self-reporting is available, which we will outline below, relatively little is written by translators about their own understanding of the translating processes that they set in motion and undertake; and much of what is written tends to concentrate on literary translation. Examples include Selver (1966), Briggs (2017) and Hahn (2022). Selver (1966) concentrates on the translation of poetry. He lists the 'main ingredients' of a poem: its contents, its rhythmic structure and its verbal effects, claiming that 'the quality of a poetical translation will therefore be judged by the extent to which it reproduces these ingredients'. While it is easy to pour scorn on this ingredients metaphor for poetry, a sympathetic reading allows for a liberal understanding of the notion of reproduction, as exemplified, for example, in books like Briggs (2017) and Hahn (2022). Briggs (2017: 18) remarks that in a translation 'the question ... of what was *really* said or written gets suspended slightly', and that there is something 'novelistic about the translator's project, whatever the genre she is writing in'. Briggs writes, further, about the 'deep pleasures' there are in translating:

> There is often a strong writing desire, great conscious audacity and difficult identification, somehow together with the more familiar humility and willing apprenticeship.
>
> There is the making of a piece of writing: a new volume in a new context with very different materials. (2017: 91)

Similarly, Hahn (2022: 3) feels compelled to dwell on and stress his love of translating, because, as he puts it, 'I'm not sure the diary you are about to read conveys how much I love it. There's, um, a lot of complaining. But don't be fooled' (2022: 3, note 3). There is, in other words, creativity and often perhaps almost compulsion involved in the translating activity. I have charted a number of literary translators' testaments to this in Malmkjær (2020: Chapter 4). These after-the-fact self-reports have the advantage over measures that seem more objective in that they tend to report on the translating of full texts, or sizeable sections of texts, whereas more empirical measures tend to track the translation of words, expressions or, at most, sentences. Particularly, also, translators' self-reports, like these longer statements, testify to the responsibility translators tend to feel towards their source texts as texts, a responsibility that reaches beyond the search for smaller-scale equivalences.

Exercise 4.1 The demands of genres

This exercise is designed to encourage you to think about whether and to what extent texts of different genres make different types of demand of translators.

A. Do you think that poetry translation is more challenging than prose translation?

   OR

   Do you think that poetry translation is less challenging than prose translation?

   OR

   Do you think that poetry translation and prose translation are equally challenging?

   AND

   Do you think that literary translating of any kind is more or less challenging than other types of translating?

Explain your opinions.

Over the centuries, poetry translating has been classified as especially challenging. However, it is also possible to argue that translating difficulty depends less on the genre of a text than on the characteristics of the text itself, whatever its genre. The issue is unlikely to be resolved, and attempts to resolve it may be in vain because of the number of variables involved, including, among other factors, the complexity of a given text, an individual translator's familiarity with and appreciation of different genres, and a host of characteristic cultural attitudes and beliefs about these. It is particularly interesting to see that for some translators, the challenges posed by translating make the process more pleasurable than routine translation tasks might be.

In addition to self-reports such as those discussed above, attempts to gain understanding of translators' perceptions of their métier more broadly have been made by means of questionnaire studies. Drugan (2013) presents conclusions based on interviews with and questionnaires distributed to translators, both freelancers and in-house translators, as well as to others involved in the process of producing translations. The translators who took part in Drugan's study expressed concerns and discomfort about being asked to work on isolated text extracts without having access to the full text (in cases where only sections of a document need to be updated while the remaining text is held constant), and about instructions to produce low-quality text to maintain consistency. Further, they found that 'time spent extracting text or working on non-translation tasks such as formatting is effectively unpaid' (Drugan 2013: 29). The translators did, however, enjoy working with conceptually complex texts, and they enjoyed the teamwork that is often involved in large translation projects; translating that they considered routine gave them less job satisfaction (Drugan 2013: 30). Despite the frustrations that these translators of non-literary texts experienced, Drugan's study testifies to the pleasure that translators experience when engaged in challenging translation tasks.

One type of translating that is often claimed to pose particular challenges is legal translation (see e.g. Ainsworth 2016: 43; Vlachopoulos 2018: 433 and Sosoni, O'Shea and Stasimioti 2022: 94), also discussed in Chapter 2, Section 2.1.5. The challenges involved in translating legal texts arise in part because different countries have varying legal systems so that concepts relevant in one system may not be relevant in another. For example, the UK, the US and Australia employ so-called common law, a system of law in which precedent is set by previous cases of judgement. These precedents then inform and sometimes influence judgement in future cases. In civil law jurisdictions, in contrast, which include mainland Europe, core principles of the law are set down in documents to which reference can be made in individual cases. Other legal systems may combine civil or common law with aspects of religious law; for example, India combines common law with aspects of Hindu law, the latter covering family and inheritance matters; and Arab countries may use Islamic law for family and inheritance issues, and common law for commerce. In addition, legal systems have of course developed over time under varied influences, so it is not surprising that what Prieto Ramos (2021: 175) refers to as Legal Translation Studies has, as he puts it, 'become one of the most prominent and prolific within Translation Studies'. Translation between texts relating to different legal systems may be done via a lingua franca, often English or French, and as Mattila (2016: xxi) points out, this poses some danger of meaning distortion. But however legal translation is carried out, Engberg (2020: section 1, Introduction) is clearly right to emphasize that 'a prerequisite to create good translations of legal texts is to have sufficient knowledge about the legal systems behind the source and target texts and also specific comparative knowledge about significant differences'.

Differences between legal systems, however, is not the only reason that legal translation is challenging. Linguistic conventions pertaining to legal texts also differ between countries; for example, Biel (2022: 382) mentions that 'legal English is tolerant of repetitions and redundancy' as in the case of 'terms and conditions' and 'the contract made by and between', for example. This tolerance, or predilection even, for repetitions in English legal parlance can be confusing for lawyers (and others) if they are replicated in translation into a language where such duplication is not the norm in legal (or possibly any other) texts. Further, as Sosoni et al. (2022: 95) point out, the register of legal texts differs in most languages from the standard register, in being

> rich in terminology, passive and impersonal forms, hypotactic structures, and complexity of modifiers. This specialised language lacks emotivity and seeks precision, yet is simultaneously characterised by vagueness, generality, ambiguity, and declarative and pompous style.

This makes legal translation challenging not only for human translators but also for machine-aided translation, a mode of translation to be discussed in Section 4.2.

In order to ameliorate the difficulties that beset legal translation, a translation team consisting of translators and lawyers, or others with knowledge of law, from both relevant language and legal backgrounds can be engaged. If it is not possible to assemble such a team, however, it can help significantly if the translator understands '*Who does What locally*', because this will enable them to name 'the status and powers of investigating authorities', which 'facilitates the appreciation of another country's legal system at the international justice level, and as far as translation is concerned, supports decision-making' (Halimi 2017: 24, italics in the original). In other words, translators can familiarize themselves with the operation of legal systems by identifying the roles that are fulfilled within them and the processes engaged in by the people who act in these roles. This will help them to establish parallels between systems. Of course, such parallels may not be precise, and systems may contain processes and procedures with no parallels in another system. In such cases, paraphrase can be used, or explanatory notes can be added, provided these are not precluded by constraints on the permissible features of the document to be created. In addition, the approach advocated by Vienne (1994) and discussed in Section 3.3, which involves careful analysis of the translational situation as well as of the text to be translated, of parallel texts, and perhaps of translations that already exist of texts of the relevant type, will be immensely helpful. Such an approach is also advocated by Prieto Ramos (2016), who adds a focus on terminology. He argues that terminology problems can be tackled by way of a three-step process consisting of (i) analysis of the term in the text to be translated, (ii) comparative analysis of the relevant legal systems and of the terms employed within them, searching for functionally equivalent terms – that is, terms as closely equivalent to each other as possible, and (iii) a search for acceptable reformulations (Prieto Ramos 2016: 125).

Within the European Union (EU) and the United Nations (UN), a special category of legal translator is employed known as a lawyer-linguist. Lawyer-linguists in the EU are required to have a legal education qualification, perfect command of one relevant language of the Union and knowledge of at least two other official Community languages; legal translators working for the UN require a law degree, knowledge of local and international law, translation training and language skills. The UN employs a special category of translator known as lawyer-linguists for translation tasks related to human rights issues (Arturo 2015). Human rights issues are extensive and varied. The Universal Declaration of Human Rights includes thirty Articles, each article covering one particular right, and each of these rights falling under one of either civil and political rights, which include freedom of speech and religious liberty, or human rights classified as economic, social, and cultural rights, which include the right to health and housing (Chen and Renteln 2022: 5). Chen and Renteln (2022) discuss international human rights in chapters focusing on socio-economic rights, cultural rights, Indigenous rights, the rights of persons with disabilities, labour rights, children's rights, women's rights, and LGBTQ+ rights. The Declaration was adopted on 10 December 1948, at the Palais de Chaillot in Paris, France, largely as a reaction to the atrocities that had been committed during the second world war, which had then recently ended. Chen and Renteln explain:

> At the Nuremberg tribunals ... which began in 1945, prosecutors sought to hold the perpetrators accountable for war crimes and crimes against humanity. At that juncture, the world community decided to define international human rights standards that would apply to every country to protect every human being. Although some argued that the criminal standards used were being applied retroactively, the international community was determined to prevent future crimes such as these; formal recognition of the norms would preclude others from subsequently raising that type of argument. This led to the successful drafting of an 'international bill of rights'. (2022: 3)

Interestingly, given that the Declaration is 'universal', Chen and Renteln (2022) do not include 'translation' as an indexed term, although they do discuss a case where Spanish-speaking parents of a child who had been injured by a medicine took the producer of the medicine to court for not providing patient information in Spanish; but the parents of the injured child lost the case (see Chen and Renteln 2022: 248).

At the time of writing (2024), the Declaration is available in 562 different translations, which can be accessed at www.ohchr.org/en/human-rights/universal-declaration/universal-declaration-human-rights/about-universal-declaration-human-rights-translation-project, where you can also listen to the Declaration being read aloud. The website encourages submission of the Declaration in languages in which it is not yet available on the website.

Exercise 4.2 The Universal Declaration of Human Rights

Since, as its name indicates, the Universal Declaration of Human Rights is considered to hold universally, it is especially important that each of its existing manifestations describes and identifies the rights that the Declaration covers using expressions that will both denote and connote the same concepts. The difference between denotation (picking out a phenomenon) and connotation (the varied ethereal associations people have with phenomena) is difficult to maintain for long, but it serves as a useful, if ultimately vain, way of seeking to dissociate 'hard reality' from diverse ways of describing it and different attitudes to aspects of it. Given the variations between languages and the differences between their respective legal genres and registers, it is particularly challenging to achieve the desired identities between concepts relevant to human rights across the diverse ways of expressing them in different languages. This exercise is intended to allow you to explore the complex relationship between expression and connotation by studying text versions in which it is especially important to keep the relationship between expression and connotation stable across different language manifestation.

A. At www.ohchr.org/en/universal-declaration-of-human-rights, read and analyse the Declaration in English. Then either go to 'Other Languages' and look for one or more languages of your choice (other than English) and compare the language versions; or provide a translation of your own into any language or languages other than English. Note any variations you find between the existing translation or translations and your own preferred translation.
B. In language groups, if possible, discuss your findings, and report to other language groups. Compare the groups' findings.
C. The website mentioned in A above offers the opportunity to listen to the Universal Declaration of Human Rights being read aloud in a number of languages. Select one or more spoken versions and note and comment on how well suited to speech the declaration is in the relevant languages.

Comment

One feature that stands out especially in a comparison between the Declaration in English and the Declaration in Danish is the following: the English version begins each of the seven paragraphs which introduce the Declaration's 'Preamble' with the term 'whereas', as is common in English legal register; but the Danish version uses the term 'da', which means 'as' or 'since', and which is used in the same context in non-legal registers in Danish. The Danish version is, in this respect, closer to 'normal' language than the English version is, but this is not to say that the Danish version is without formality. An expression like 'den mennesket iboende værdighed' (as opposed to the less formal 'menneskets medfødte værdighed', for example), which corresponds to 'the inherent dignity ... of all members of the human family' in the English version, is fairly formal. In addition, the repeated use of 'da' to introduce seven successive paragraphs is as unusual in 'normal' written Danish as the repetition of the paragraph opening is in the English version, even though the term selected for the Danish version, 'da', seems more 'normal' in its position here than 'whereas' does in the English version.

The type of sensitivity to features of texts as wholes which the preceding paragraphs illustrate is characteristic of human translation; a translator of texts of any length typically makes decisions about individual text items with the whole text and any patterns found in it in mind. This is one reason many translators read through the texts they are to translate before they begin translating (see e.g. Jääskeläinen 2020: 224). It is true that in Chapter 1 Section 1.2 we came across the opposite trend – the preference of one translator identified there was to begin to translate as soon as she was faced with the text and before reading through it; obviously, there is no reason to suppose that there are no other translators like her. Nevertheless, the tendency among translation teachers and among many self-reporting translators remains to consider the text to be translated in its entirety, as a whole which both surrounds and is composed of the individual sites of translation choices that it presents. Furthermore, human translators are typically highly conscious of contextually relevant features of their work, as highlighted by Vienne (see above), and, as obvious as it may seem, of the meaning of the texts they are working with – the first-written text and the translation they are producing. Arguably, none of this is true of the machines that assist humans in their translation efforts, in our era of 'augmented translation' (Angelone, Ehrensberger-Dow and Massey (2020: 3). A translation memory or a piece of machine translation software does not understand the meaning of the first-written text, nor, for that matter, of the text it is helping to produce. Translation machines do not enjoy what Dennett (1991: 452) refers to as a 'belief environment'; they are machines. Belief environments are functions of brains, and 'Brains are alive; computers are not' (Dennett 2017: 156). There are, of course, limits to brains, but by their very power, 'brains have become equipped with additions, thinking tools by the thousands, that multiply our brains' cognitive powers by many orders of magnitude' (373). However, as Dennett points out (2017: 398), these additions 'are tools, not colleagues'. Claims hinting at the contrary can have severe consequences. For example, Blake Lemoine, a software engineer at Google, was swiftly dismissed after claiming that an AI system he had been working on was sentient and publicizing this belief in *The Washington Post* (Tiku 2022; see also *The Guardian*, 23 July 2022). In Section 4.2, we explore translation technology. Before we leave human translation, though, I want to introduce an account of 'A translator at work', written by the translator himself, which is printed in Quah (2006: 14–17).

4.1.1 An Account of a Translator at Work

The translator's name is Stephen Moore, and he translates between English and Japanese. He specializes in texts related to the chemicals industry and he also writes journalism in this field. He uses hard-copy and online dictionaries related to the chemicals industry and to relevant organizations, as well as Google and relevant company websites to help with terminology, and he consults colleagues on a translators mailing list, commenting that 'At the end of the day, the less I trouble my clients with requests for assistance, the more likely I am to receive more work' (Quah 2006: 16). Moore complements these strategies with the use of translation software; however, he concludes his account by stressing that he feels 'that in order to remain a creative translator, I have to continue to exercise my brain'. In other words, he resists over-reliance on translation aids, because he thinks that overuse of these might adversely affect his ability to translate without them and perhaps, by implication, dull his feeling for the finer details of human translation.

Exercise 4.3 Using translation aids

This exercise is intended to allow you to test out Moore's suspicion that using translation aids reduces the demands that translating imposes on translators' brains. It will also serve as preparation for work in Section 4.3 on editing and revising.

A. Select two texts, each around 600 words long. Divide each text in two. Translate the first half of one text yourself using any dictionaries you normally use, but no translation software. Next, use translation software to translate the other half of the first text. For the second text, use the software to translate the first half of the text and translate the second half of the text using any dictionaries you normally use but no translation software.
B. Examine the text parts produced by the translation software and make any changes you think are required.
C. Compare your experience of adjusting the electronically produced text halves with your experience of translating the text parts without the help of electronic translation aids.
D. Do you agree with Moore's suspicion that using translation aids reduces the demands that translating imposes on translators' brains (in cases where the translator post-edits the electronically produced text)?
   Explain your answer.

Comment
Assessing and adjusting someone else's translation can be very demanding. It imposes a need not only to check an existing translation but also to justify to yourself any alternative choices you propose to make. Perhaps when 'the other translator' is a piece of translation software, the discomfort you may experience when disagreeing with it will be less than when the other is a live translator.

We can assume that translation aids have improved since Quah published Moore's account of his translating experience. However, a further criticism levelled at machine translation programs and at translation memories is that they encourage sentence-by-sentence translation; it is worth bearing this in mind when working with electronic translation aids and using your knowledge of the longer text to help you when editing and revising your machine-aided translations.

4.2 Machine Translation and Translation Memories

Human translation aided only by traditional tools such as hard-copy dictionaries and relevant types of documentation has become increasingly rare, and while precise calculation is difficult (though see Google's calculations below), it is probable that since the turn of the century, most translating has been aided by some form of automation. Automation has been considered a threat to what Desjardins, Larsonneur and Lacour (2021: 3) refer to, within quotation marks, as 'human translation'; but, as they explain, 'a more nuanced take' understands that although 'technology, digitization, and automation affect ... human translators ... they do not eradicate human involvement in translation' (2021: 3). In fact, according to Schaeffer (2022: 576), who had been encouraged to speculate about how translation might develop in the third millennium, 'It is highly likely that ... technology will become much more integrated with humans', and that, as a consequence, the roles of translators will change dramatically. He believes that the roles of translators will be enhanced rather than diminished through this change, envisaging that human brains will connect with each other directly, although translation between them will be needed whether or not the individuals whose brains they are speak the same or different languages.

In the meantime, the general consensus is that translation technologies 'are getting better and better at helping people lower language barriers' (Van der Meer 2020: 285), and as Drugan (2013: 31) points out, translation tools also

> have clear positive effects for some aspects of quality. They enhance consistency, accuracy and increasingly allow for some elements to be checked automatically. Automated QC [quality control] processes outstrip some traditional checks due to human fallibility. A computer never mistakes a comma for a full stop; a human's tired eyes can easily do so. Such errors in translated engineering or pharmaceutical texts can be critical.

Desjardins et al. (2021: 4, 5) elaborate: 'Automation ... simply shifts where and how human involvement is needed'; and 'digital and online tools have allowed translators to rethink their roles and to advocate more recognition and visibility'. On the other hand, according to Kenny (2022: v), although

> machine translation ... can help professional human translators to work more productively ... the technology ... could be used in ways that gloss over potential problems with the output it produces, so that consumers don't realize when texts they are reading contain machine-translation induced inaccuracies or biases [such as an overuse of masculine as opposed to feminine pronouns, for example].

Clearly, then, there are both advantages and potential disadvantages associated with the increasing use of technology-aided translation. Kenny advocates, referring to Bowker and Ciro (2019), that the use of machine translation be underpinned by machine translation literacy, by which she means that (2022: vi) 'all users of machine translation should have some basic understanding of why the technology is important ... [and] of how the technology works, so that they can use it intelligently and avoid common pitfalls'; indeed translation courses in universities tend to include modules designed to ensure that at least this basic understanding is imparted to students.

Not all translation companies require new recruits to come armed with knowledge of how to use computer-assisted translation (CAT) tools. However, a survey undertaken by the five major European language industry associations and the European Masters' in Translation, published in 2018, found that fewer than one per cent of the companies surveyed did not use these tools (Rodríguez de Céspedes 2020: 116), and Liu (2020: viii) estimates that 99 per cent of translation is machine mediated. These 99 per cent constitute a very large amount of text indeed: at a 'Made by Google' event on 9 October 2018, Google announced 'that around 143 billion words are translated every single day across 100 languages' by Google Translate alone (Davenport 2018). Some translation companies provide their own in-house training, and it is becoming increasingly unusual for any translator, save possibly for translators of literature, not to avail themselves of the technological facilitators of their métier. There are, as Sakamoto (2022: 55) points out, 'a wide range of electronic tools and systems ... available to support the production of translation', and a number of these offer free trials on their websites, which can of course be especially helpful for freelancers.

A major distinction in the area of machine-aided or machine-mediated translation, which we must dwell on, is that between machine translation (MT) and translation memory (TM).

4.2.1 Machine Translation

Melby (2020: 419) defines machine translation as 'a fully automatic process that starts with a text in one language and produces a corresponding text in another language, using a machine of some kind', and according to van der Meer (2020: 285), 'MT may with good reason be considered the grandfather of all translation automation technologies'. Machine translation can be of one of three kinds: rule-based (RBMT, rule-based machine translation), statistical (SMT, statistical machine translation), and neural (NMT, neural machine translation). RBMT applies rules devised for it by human designers, and the rules typically involve dividing sentences into words, looking up words in a dictionary, undertaking syntactic analysis, and finally generating text in the language being translated into. In contrast, SMT and NMT search through data available to the machine in the form of large numbers of first-written texts and (human or at least post-edited by humans) translations of them. They then apply the results of the search to new cases the machines are presented with. These translation modes are, in that sense, 'data-driven'. Rule-based systems were dominant from the 1950s until the 1980s, and Melby (2020: 420) sees a transition period between the 1980s and 2000, when SMT began to replace RBMT. He adds that for a viable NMT system, sufficient training data only exists for around twenty languages, and 'for the rest (over 99 % [of languages]), either RBMT or SMT or, in most cases, human translation are the only option'.

4.2.1.1 Data-Driven Machine Translation Systems

Most machine translation systems are data-driven rather than based on translation rules; that is, the system produces translations by calculating the most probable translation of a stretch of text on the basis of translations that it searches through in corpora of first-written texts and translations of them made, or at least classed as adequate for their purpose, by humans. Raw MT is rarely publishable, but it can be edited and revised by human translators, in which case it is defined as 'human-assisted machine translation' (Sakamoto 2022: 56). The more specific in terms of genre the corpus the computer searches through is, and the more closely the genre of a text to be translated matches the corpus text type, the more acceptable and appropriate the translation is likely to be. Guerberof Arenas (2020: 338) provides an MT output error typology which includes errors related to Accuracy, Language, Terminology, Style, Country Standards (e.g. the ways in which given countries refer to dates, numbers, currency and addresses), and Formats (e.g. layouts).

Exercise 4.4 Machine translation and text genres

Select a text in a standard format (e.g. a set of instructions for use) and a text in a less standardized format (e.g. the opening paragraph of a literary text) and translate both texts using a machine translation system of your choice.

A. Compare each source text with its translation, noting any changes you think should be made to the translations.
B. Were there notable differences between the two sets of changes (the changes to the translations of the text that followed a standard format and the changes to the translation of the text that did not follow a standard format)? If so, what were these differences?

The European Union has its own machine translation service, eTranslation, which, at the time of writing, is freely available for use by 'EU institutions, public administrations, universities, EU freelance translators, SMEs [small and medium enterprises], European NGOs and projects funded by the Digital Europe Programme, located in an EU country, Iceland, Norway, Lichtenstein or Ukraine' (https://commission.europa.eu/resources-partners/etranslation_en; accessed 9 January 2024).

Machine translation systems can be interactive (with a human) in ways that can take the use of MT beyond the sentence level, as Carl and Planas explain:

> The online, real-time learning capacities of MT systems now open the possibility for completely new approaches to translation production in which a human and an MT system collaborate in an interactive process on an unprecedented scale. The MT system produces an initial segment of a translation which is validated or corrected by a human translator. Every correction is sent back to the MT server in real time and thereby immediately considered for the enhanced suggestions of successive translations of the same segment and the rest of the text. It is hoped that with the human corrections in a feedback loop, the MT system may produce better translation proposals for the remaining part of the text or sentence that has not been validated yet. In this way, the human and machine iterate through the translation in a fashion where the system listens and learns from the corrections with the aim of increasing the acceptability of the next translation proposal. (2020: 369–370)

4.2.2 Translation Memories (TM)

Whereas a machine translation system translates a document it is presented with without any human assistance (until at a later editing stage), a translation memory system assists the translator by storing text and translation segments as the translator works, so that these can be used later in the text or in future translation jobs. This will ensure consistency of terminology and expression, and will record individual clients' 'styles' or different companies' house styles. This is immensely helpful for translators who undertake repeat translations of texts that are updated regularly to match new versions of a given product; the memory will reuse text that has not been altered in the new first-written text, saving the translator the effort of having to check for this themselves, and only presenting for translating text that has been altered in the new first-written text. It will also help ensure consistency when several translators are engaged in one large translation project. Translation produced with the use of such a system is called machine-assisted human translation (Sakamoto 2022: 56).

A potential problem with a translation memory system is that because many terms are polysemous (have several meanings), the same sentence form can have different meanings in different non-linguistic contexts; but the non-linguistic context for any given sentence is not known to the translation system. Or, as Sakamoto (2022: 61) more aptly puts it, 'When a sentence is stored in a TM, the context is stripped away'. To take a basic and often-quoted example, the sentence 'I went to the bank' may be used in an utterance about visiting the side of a river, or in an utterance about visiting an institution concerned with money. 'Bank' is an ambiguous term and its presence in a sentence can make the sentence lexically ambiguous ('lexically' because the ambiguity arises from a lexical item (a word)). A related difficulty, which is exacerbated by the TM's inability to use contextual information to aid its translation suggestions, can be caused by structural ambiguity ('structural' because the ambiguity stems from the way the linguistic item, usually a sentence, is structured). For example the sentence 'We decided on the boat' has a different grammatical structure depending on whether it is used to indicate that a decision has been made aboard a boat [Subject 'We', Verb 'decided', Adverb of place 'on the boat'], or whether it is used to indicate that a decision has been made to travel by (or buy, or paint . . . etc.) a boat [Subject 'We', Phrasal verb 'decided on', Object 'the boat'].

For humans, instances like this are generally, if not always, non-problematic because the context for the utterance is shared by the people involved in the interaction and will disambiguate the utterance (indicate which meaning is intended) for them. If misunderstanding occurs, humans can generally resolve it through discussion. Consider the following genuine interaction about a room heater:

A: Is it going down there, then?
B: It is already down there; you saw me carry it down!
A: No, I mean, is it lit and working?

In contrast, for a translation system, polysemy may be viciously problematic. For some languages, A's utterance will have to be translated either into a question about moving an item, or as a question about whether the item is working.

Human post-editing of both translation memory-aided translation and of machine translation is therefore almost always called for, and will certainly be required if the translation being made is meant for publication for use by the general public. It is one of three basic forms of interaction between humans and machines identified by O'Brien (2017: 313), who also refers to it as revision. Editing and revision are the subjects of Section 4.3 next.

4.3 Editing and Revising Translations

The criterion that strictly speaking distinguishes editing from revision is the reliance, during revision, on comparison with the first-written text. Translation editing, in contrast, involves only the target language text, the translation. Editing is described by Do Carmo (2001: 3) as 'a technical dimension of the writing task performed by translators when they apply four actions to previous text: deleting, inserting, replacing, and moving words and groups of words'. Revision, in contrast, involves checking the developing translation against the source text, so it can, as Shih (2006: 296) points out, be considered part of the translating process. In fact, according to Jakobsen (2019a: 65), 'Revision is so integral to writing and translation that we cannot truly say where text production begins, and where text revision ends.'

Editing may be carried out in order to make a translation adhere to an organization's style guide, or to ensure that the translation conforms to target language writing conventions for referring to dates (e.g. the order in which the month and the date are presented), numbers (e.g. the conventions for the use of commas and full stops to separate series of digits), currency (e.g. whether and when it is acceptable to use an abbreviation like GBP to refer to British pounds, and whether to use a capital initial letter for the currency when it is written out in full) and addresses (e.g. the placing of house number, street, city and country relative to each other), or to the many and varied conventions governing the relevant text type or genre in the target culture.

Revision, on the other hand, is undertaken to ensure that the translation is a fair representation of the first-written text, in light of the translation brief (the set of guidelines or instructions concerning what the translation is to be used for, where it is to be published, whether there will be illustrations that the text needs to be relevant to in terms of, say, placing, and so on). The translation brief may be to produce a translation of a quality that is good enough for a certain purpose, for example to provide the gist of the first-written text, or for a translation that matches the quality of a human translation. Clearly, the exact details of 'good enough' may vary depending on the brief, and the quality of human translation may vary depending on the capabilities and habits of individual human translators. Guerberof Arenas (2020: 336) provides the following guidelines for what she refers to as good enough translation quality and human translation quality respectively, but the first category, especially, is problematic in several respects, as indicated.

Good enough quality translation is:

- semantically correct (that is, it gives the correct meaning; but meaning is a complex phenomenon)

- includes all and only the information from the first-written text (this is problematic because it may be necessary to add information in the case of some genres, to ensure that the text conforms to the conventions that govern the genre in the language and culture being translated into)
- includes no offensive, inappropriate or culturally unacceptable content (this is a problematic criterion because what is offensive, inappropriate or unacceptable to some members of a society may not be judged to be so by other members of the same society; besides, the original may include such content)
- includes as much of the MT output as possible (in cases of machine translation)
- is spelled correctly
- is stylistically acceptable
- flows naturally (exact criteria for natural flow are difficult to provide, and may vary in different circumstances and across different text types).

Human quality translation:

- is grammatically and semantically correct
- uses correct terminology
- keeps terms that are on the client's 'Do not translate' list as they appear in the first-written text
- contains no accidentally added information (some information may be added on purpose, for example for clarification)
- does not leave out any information accidentally (some information in the first-written text may purposefully be excluded from the translation, for example because it is likely to be so obvious for the projected target text readers that including it would seem to be verging on the offensive, or because it would be immensely offensive for the projected audience for the translation)
- includes as much of the MT output as possible
- is spelled, punctuated and hyphenated correctly
- is correctly formatted.

Mossop (2014: 1) distinguishes between two types of translation revision: revision of one's own work (self-revision) and revision of another person's work (other-revision). Obviously, one person may engage in both types of revision, but translation standard ISO 17100 requires translations provided by translation services providers to be revised by a person other than the translator. According to Jakobsen (2019a: 69), this is also the custom among company in-house translation departments and language service providers. Revision by someone other than the translator typically takes place late in the translation process, and it may take place at a late stage too when undertaken by the translator themselves. Jakobsen (2019a: 66) distinguishes, within self-revision, between revision as part of the translation process and revision after the first full draft of a text has been completed. Mellinger (2018: 314) considers self-revision a hybrid of editing and revision.

Some texts for machine translation are pre-edited, that is, edited in preparation for being translated, as well as edited after the translating has been carried out. Pre-editing 'controls' the language in a text for translation so that it is void of ambiguities and grammatical complexity (Guerberof Arenas 2020: 334). In addition:

> Pre-editors follow certain rules, not only to remove typographical errors and correct possible mistakes in the content but also to write shorter sentences, to use certain grammatical structures (simplified word order and less passive voice, for example) or semantic choices (the use of consistent terminology), or to mark certain terms (product names, for example) that might not require translation.

Pre-editing can be either prescriptive or proscriptive. A proscriptive rule set specifies which linguistic structures are not allowed, while a prescriptive set specifies which structures are allowed (Mitamura and Nyberg 2001, referred to by Carl and Planas 2020: 365). Post-editing can be used to identify and resolve translation errors (2020: 376). It can be light or full (Guerberof Arenas 2020: 335). Full editing is done to ensure that a text is as close as possible to the standard of human translation; the purpose of light editing is to provide a text that reflects the gist of the first-written text. Any translation may lie anywhere between these two ends of a scale, as agreed with the translation commissioner.

The aim of pre-editing is to change the first-written text in such a way that the quality of the machine translation output will be as high as possible (Carl and Planas 2020: 365). It is typically reserved for texts which are intended for wide international distribution, and since this is probably a minority of texts, pre-editing is less common than post-editing.

It is customary, and helpful, for translators and other revisers of translations to rely on a revision checklist, and Shih (2006) remarks that although a variety of such checklists are recommended in the literature on translation revision, they generally share an emphasis on accuracy of the translation as being among the most important characteristics to check for. She presents as an example Graham's (1983) checklist which includes accuracy, typing errors, spelling, misleading statements, ambiguities, omissions, style, consistency of style and register (Shih 2006: 297), but as this and other lists that Shih refers to show, the distinction drawn above between editing and revising is exceedingly blurred in the field, since typing and spelling errors are certainly matters of editing as there defined. Indeed, it stands to reason that a reviser who comes across a spelling or typing error is likely to feel inclined to correct it. It is less likely that an editor will revise, if their only brief is to ensure that a translation conforms to the linguistic, cultural and genre conventions of the target culture and language. It is unlikely that they will spot inaccuracies in the translation; in fact, they may not even have access to the first-written text or understand its language. Clearly, there are a number of issues that an editor thus understood is unlikely to identify and would perhaps also be unable to correct because of their lack of access to the first-written text.

Consider the text below, which is a rendering by Microsoft's Bing Translator of Danske Bank's information (in Danish) about their FlexLife loan (https://danskebank.dk/privat/db/laan/bolig/flexlife50plus?section=mereomflexlife#tip1 (accessed 28 February 2023); Danske Bank is a Danish bank); obviously no professional translations would or should be made in reliance solely on Bing Translator, but the example illustrates the point I am making about an editor's potential difficulties when faced with a text that appears odd without being linguistically flawed. At least one of the infelicitous translation choices made in the translation below by Bing Translator cannot be identified without access to the first-written text:

> *With FlexLife® you can – within the agreed framework – shape your loan to suit your life and plans, and you can change your mind along the way. We put together a plan for how large your monthly payments on the loan should be. The benefits may be the same throughout the term of the loan, or may vary depending on your finances and plans.*
>
> *For example, at some point you might want to work less for a period of time and want to reduce your monthly allowance to suit your income. When you go up in time again, you can turn up the performance. This can be done if the plan we have put in place gives you the necessary financial leeway.*
>
> *How often you can change your performance depends on whether you have chosen fixed or variable interest rates. If you have fixed interest, you can change your repayments every quarter. If you have variable interest rates, you can change when your loan needs to be refinanced.*
>
> *It costs a fee to change the loan.*

As a minimum, this text needs editing (as opposed to revision; we will discuss the need for revision of the text shortly) so that it reads as below (altered stretches of text underlined; questionable stretches double underlined; I have numbered the sentences for ease of reference).

> *(1) With FlexLife® you can – within the agreed framework – shape your loan to suit your life and plans, and you can change your mind along the way. (2) We put together a plan for how large your monthly payments on the loan should be. (3) The benefits may be the same throughout the term of the loan, or may vary depending on your finances and plans.*
>
> *(4) For example, at some point you might want to work less for a period of time and want to reduce your monthly allowance to suit your income. (5) When you start to work more again, you can turn up the performance. (6) This can be done if the plan we have put in place gives you the necessary financial leeway.*
>
> *(7) How often you can change your performance depends on whether you have chosen fixed or variable interest rates. (8) If you have fixed interest, you can change your repayments every quarter. (9) If you have variable interest rates, you can change when your loan needs to be refinanced.*
>
> *(10) There is a fee to change the loan.*

The first two sentences clearly indicate that the topic of the text is a flexible loan, which allows the borrower to change the amount of their monthly loan repayment. It is unclear, against this background, what the benefits mentioned in sentence 3 are, or the allowance in sentence 4 or the performance sentences 5 and 7. Sentence 8 again mentions repayments, and we might suspect that this should in fact replace the terms, 'benefits', 'allowance' and 'performance'.

Comparing the translation with the first-written text confirms this suspicion, and shows that the Danish term 'ydelse' is used consistently in the relevant sentences of the first-written text. In this context, 'ydelse' means 'contribution', that is, in the context of a bank loan, a repayment. In other contexts, though, for example, in the context of paid employment, it refers to the service which the person being paid delivers for payment or, confusingly, to the payment the person is given for a service.

The comparison, however, also reveals inaccuracies that could not be identified as such without comparison with the first-written text.

In sentence (2), the first-written text says 'Vi lægger sammen en plan for, hvor store dine månedlige ydelser på lånet skal være.' A near-to-gloss translation of this sentence would be 'we lay together a plan for how large your monthly repayments of the loan shall be', but the intended meaning is certain to be 'Together (sammen) we make a plan for . . .' (To arrive at the translation provided by Bing Translator the first-written text stretch would have had to be 'Vi planlægger hvor store dine månedlige ydelser på lånet skal være'). In sentence (4), the 'allowance' should be 'housing costs'. These inaccuracies could not have been identified by looking at the translation alone, that is, they could not have been identified by 'pure' editing.

Exercise 4.5 Revision and editing

This exercise is intended to heighten your awareness of the differences between the process of editing and the process of revising.

A. Select a short (300–400 words) text in a language that you know, and use one of the translation providers freely available on the internet to translate it.
B. Identify stretches of the translation that need to be edited (to suit your target language conventions) and those that need to be revised (to reflect the first-written text accurately).

Revision is not necessarily undertaken only once; in fact, it is probably rarely undertaken once only, even when it is done after the completion of a translation. Shih (2006) reports on an interview study involving twenty-six professional translators who were asked about their revision behaviour. There were seventeen reports of revising twice and thirteen reports of revising once, but this varied depending on the kind of text being translated, on its length, and on the deadline for submitting the translation. Most translators did not avail themselves of 'drawer-time' – setting aside the translation for a while before returning to it to revise it – but this was to an extent dependent on the length of the translation: clearly, very long texts simply cannot be completed in one setting. Where drawer-time was used, it was mostly for one day or overnight.

The foci of the translators' revision fell into three major categories, which Shih (2006: 304–305) labels and defines as follows:

(i) Source Text Meaning Transfer: ensuring that the information focus of the first-written text is reproduced in the translation and that the translation is accurate and complete (no omissions; correct format used for numbers and dates)
(ii) Target Text Linguistic Features: spelling, punctuation, grammar, naturalness (no translationese), register, cohesion, conciseness and consistency of style
(iii) Other Target Text Issues.

While the foci mentioned under (i) and (ii) are to be expected, those reported under (iii) go beyond the obvious issues of correctness, completeness and accuracy. Here, the translators mentioned checking the formatting and formulation of the text, for example whether illustrations were placed appropriately, whether the concepts mentioned in the translation made sense and whether arguments were valid (e.g. not self-contradictory, not unsubstantiated), whether terminology was used correctly and consistently, whether the most suitable expressions were selected and whether the meaning could be expressed more explicitly and simply. Finally, Shih indicates that although seven of the translators in her study reported that they compared the translation sentence by sentence with the first-written text and that a further two translators also compared the two texts, albeit not on a sentence-by-sentence basis, 'seven other translators reported that they did not refer back to the ST unless they sensed some problems in the TT. Another two claimed that they did not check their TT against the ST at all' (Shih 2006: 308–309); these two, then, were effectively editing only rather than revising.

Overall, Shih's study indicates that there is no fixed way, perhaps perceived as the only correct way, to deal with a translation, at least as far as this body of practising translators are concerned, something that should remind us of the translator in Jakobsen's study (2019b) mentioned in Chapter 1, Section 1.3, whose preferred reading strategy for the source text, contrary to most trainers' recommendation about careful reading, was 'as little as possible' or 'only as much as necessary' (Jakobsen 2019b: 105). For textbook writers and for teachers of translation and trainers of would-be translators, possibly even for many readers of books such as this one who might like firm direction, this kind of insight can engender some discomfort; however, perhaps it should not. Most processes can take multiple forms, and not all doers and thinkers behave comfortably in the same way. Therefore, it is generally helpful if guidance allows room for variation according to individual preferences. Nevertheless, it is important to note that, as mentioned above, the International Standard for Translation Services (ISO 17100:2015 (E), reviewed and confirmed in 2020) requires that translation service providers ensure that the content of translations is revised and that the reviser 'shall be a person other than the translator' (ISO 2015); clearly, anyone wishing to claim to be translating to this standard will need to comply with its requirements.

Arthern (1983) identifies a tendency among revisers in the European Commission's translation department to hyper-revise, and some studies of trainee revisers identify the same tendency (see Künzli 2007). Therefore, it is important, when revising, to ask oneself (or to explain to the translator) what the justification is for a given revision suggestion. Personal preferences for certain stylistic options or for certain expressions over others are not sufficient justification in this context.

Exercise 4.6 Justifying revisions

Return to Exercise 4.5 and justify the revisions that you made to the translations.

As Künzli (2007: 124) remarks, the right question to ask in any given instance is not whether something *can* be changed, but whether something *has to be* changed.

Bisiada (2018: 291) reports a magazine editor's account of the revision process undertaken for the *Harvard Business Manager* (although Bisiada translates the editor's German term, 'Redigatur' as editing, what is being described at the beginning of the quotation is clearly revision; original in German; translated by Bisiada):

> When we start editing the translated text, we usually place next to us the original text from the HBR [*Harvard Business Manager*] and compare both texts sentence by sentence, with regard to both language and content. We also edit the language of the translations, at times significantly, depending on the quality and effort of each translator. Thus, we split convoluted sentences into more comprehensible pieces, reformulate nominalisations and passive constructions and remove superfluous auxiliary verbs.

Whether one is revising or editing, it is important to bear in mind that, in Jakobsen's words,

> In a superficial sense, revision is all about words, but our use of words is motivated by our will to best represent and convey the flux of our thoughts, emotions, and ideas, and so we keep on formulating, reformulating, paraphrasing, and revising them to make our meaning shareable. (2019a: 77)

4.4 Quality Assurance

One way of helping to ensure that a translation will be of good quality is to make the process of its production as efficient, meticulous and highly functional as possible. In other words, quality assurance (QA) can be an important part of establishing translation quality. Quality assurance includes 'systems put in place to pre-empt and avoid errors or quality problems at any stage of a translation job' (Drugan 2013: 76). Drugan (2013: 77–80) provides details of each of the stages of a translation job, which, in common with other scholars we have discussed, she considers to be (i) a pre-translation stage, (ii) a translation stage and (iii) a post-translation stage. However, in addition to the text editing processes mentioned in Section 4.3, Drugan mentions a number of equally important activities that need to be undertaken in preparation for translating, namely pricing, planning, identifying the human resources required, source-file preparation and quality assessment, identifying terminology and translation resources, project management resources such as databases, software and perhaps division of large projects, and training for all involved, including translators and terminologists. Drugan's translation stage includes research, resource preparation, translating, cost monitoring and, if necessary, cost allocation, self-checking by the translator and participation in the feedback cycle during which the client may provide feedback. Her post-translation stage allows language service providers to identify problems that have arisen during a given translation project with a view to preventing similar problems from arising in the future (project review). It also includes invoicing and the archiving of resources and their secure storage.

While Drugan's focus is on the translation provider, Swisher (2020) focuses on stages that a client needs to go through when ordering a translation from a translation service provider. These include (i) a stage before the text is delivered to the translation provider, (ii) a delivery stage when the content to be translated is delivered to the translation provider, (iii) a stage during which the translation is undertaken, (iv) a stage of returning the translation, and (v) a stage after translation.

During stage (i), the client and the translation provider need to agree how their relationship is going to work, including apportioning the responsibilities each will have. During the delivery stage, stage (ii), the content to be translated needs to be delivered to the translation provider according to the agreement reached during stage (i), the pre-translation stage. For example, the text to be translated may be delivered by email, or via a cloud-based platform, or even by hand or surface mail if the text to be translated only exists in hard copy. During the translation stage, stage (iii), client and translator may discuss relevant practical issues concerning the text to be produced, and during stage (iv), the resultant translation is returned to the client, again according to an agreement reached at stage (ii). Finally, after the translation is completed and received by the client, during stage (v) the client decides what to do with the translation. Obviously, a client will have had a reason for having a text translated and that will influence what they do with the translation, but beyond the translation hopefully having fulfilled the client's need, the client might decide to keep the translation for future reference, perhaps simply out of interest, or in case it might turn out to be useful in other respects. For example, if the text is one of a series of texts of a particular genre or related to a specific product, process or concept, it may be valuable to retain the translation for future reference.

Before we leave the subject of revising and editing, it is worth pointing out that post-editing can also be used 'to track and understand issues in the performance of

MT engines and to make the necessary adjustments to improve them' (Van der Meer 2020: 293). No doubt some clients and translation service providers will also adopt this practice even when their translator is human.

Summary

We began this chapter with an account of human translation and of the working conditions that human translators should be able to enjoy, whether within a translation agency or in their own workspace. Mention was made of accounts of their métier by translators, who tend to stress their enjoyment of the translating activity and the responsibility that they often feel towards their source texts as texts. The findings of Drugan's (2013) interview study which targeted freelancers, in-house translators and others involved in the process of producing translations showed the participants' concerns and discomfort at having to work on isolated text extracts and about occasional instructions to produce low-quality text to maintain consistency.

In Section 4.2, we turned to a discussion of machine translation and translation memories. These phenomena can be seen as threatening to human translation, but the section focused on arguments by scholars to the effect that the main consequence of the success of translation automation is likely to be an enhancement of the roles of translators. Raw MT output is rarely publishable without revision by human translators, in which case it is defined as 'human-assisted machine translation' (Sakamoto 2022: 56).

In Section 4.3, we drew a distinction between editing and revision. Revision is undertaken to ensure that the translation is a fair representation of the first-written text, in light of the translation brief, whereas during editing only the target language text, the translation, is consulted and checked for compliance with the rules for writing in the culture where it is to operate, for example the rules for referring to dates, numbers, currency and addresses. We noted the difference between post-editing and pre-editing: pre-editing is undertaken to ensure that a first-written text can be rendered into another language as unproblematically as possible, using so-called controlled language. Controlled language contains rules for what must and what must not occur.

In Section 4.4, we discussed the important issue of quality control of translators' output. A set of stages of translation was identified, along with the practical measures that can be taken at each stage to ensure that the translation reaches the quality agreed between client and translation provider.

Further Reading

Chen, C. W. and Renteln, A. D. (2022). *International Human Rights: A Survey*. Cambridge: Cambridge University Press.

This book provides an overview of international human rights issues. It defines key concepts and suggests activities and discussion questions which are available on the accompanying website.

Drugan, J. (2013). *Quality in Professional Translation: Assessment and Improvement.* London: Bloomsbury.

Joanna Drugan's book reports on approaches to quality assurance in the translation industry globally, addressing both individual freelancers and large translation suppliers. The book highlights the needs and expectations of employers of translators and how these relate to levels of quality that translators can provide. Drugan also discusses issues of quality assessment and quality guarantee in professional translation contexts.

Kenny, D. (2022). *Machine Translation for Everyone: Empowering Users in the Age of Artificial Intelligence.* Berlin: Language Science Press.

This book addresses the advantages and disadvantages of machine translation, gradually building up readers' understanding of each issue addressed in its nine chapters. The book is accompanied by a set of internet-based interactive activities.

Krings, H. P. (2001). *Repairing Texts: Empirical Investigations of Machine Translation Post-Editing Processes.* Kent, OH: The Kent State University Press.

Hans Krings' *Habilitation* (a thesis which enables its author to apply for full professorships in German universities) is one of the most approachable and thorough accounts of the mental processes involved in machine translation post-editing as hypothesized on the basis of translators' verbalizations during translating. It also contains a chapter (Chapter 3) which outlines the state of empirical research into translation processes at the time when Krings wrote the book. It remains an extremely valuable historical account of one of the most fruitful approaches in translation process-oriented research to date, even though modern research methods such as eye tracking and keyboard recording have overtaken the research method Krings charts as more objective procedures.

O'Hagan, M. (ed.) (2019). *Routledge Handbook of Translation and Technology,* London: Routledge.

O'Hagan's handbook is a comprehensive guide to the relationships between translation and technology. Translating technology has evolved rapidly and is likely to keep evolving, so interested readers would do well to keep a keen eye on relevant publisher and journal outputs.

Schwartz, L. (2018). The history and promise of machine translation. In I. Lacruz (ed.) *Innovation and Expansion in Translation Process Research.* Amsterdam: John Benjamins: 161–190.

This chapter provides a thorough account of its subject matter for readers with a particular interest in the history of machine translation program development.

CHAPTER 5

How to Do Translating

Preview

In this chapter, we explore methods of undertaking a variety of modes of translating and the type of editing that might be required in each case. We begin by exploring ways of working with machine-generated texts. Such texts typically require post-editing, which is time consuming. However, machine translation is likely to boost productivity, albeit potentially at the cost of text quality. Next, we consider the processes and practices involved in working with internet-based material and colleagues. Finally, the chapter introduces a method of translating, adaptation and revision known as translational stylistics.

5.1 Working with Machine-Generated Text

As mentioned in Chapter 4, the production of machine-generated translation has become increasingly common because of its potential to enable a translation organization or an individual translator to increase their output significantly (Farrell 2018: 50). In addition, demand for translation often outstrips the capacity of human translation alone to meet it (Daems et al. 2017: 246), and even though raw machine translation (MT) output almost always needs to be post-edited by a human translator if it is to reach the quality level that a human translator is able to reach when translating using only standard dictionaries and supporting documentation, the increase in output volume generally justifies the editing effort. The amount of post-editing required by a piece of MT output, and the amount of effort it will take to post-edit it, will clearly affect the level of advantage it will provide. At the time of writing (2024), the translation service provider Sandberg Translation Partners, for example, advises on its website that if, after a quick look at a given segment of machine-translated text (Sandberg advocates two seconds), a translator does not think they can turn it into a good translation easily by editing it, it is better to discard the segment and translate the relevant source segment themselves.

In fact, any form of text editing may be more time consuming than original writing because it tends to raise questions in the editor's mind about the justification for the changes they might be proposing. Nevertheless, according to Daems et al. (2017: 246), 'Companies and researchers report an increase in productivity when using post-editing compared to regular human translation . . . while at the same time still delivering products of comparable quality'. However, opinions about the quality of machine translation output vary. For example, Toral (2019: 279–280) finds (i) that even post-edited machine translations tend to display lower lexical density and less lexical variety than human translations do (lexical density is the proportion of content words to grammatical words in a text); (ii) that the sentence length of machine translations tends to be closer to that of the first-written text than is the case in human translations; and (iii) that post-edited machine translation outputs resemble the first-written texts more in terms of parts of speech than human translations made without help from any computer technology, including translation memories, do.

According to Sandberg's website, the most common errors found in machine-translated text are incorrect sentence structures, wrong tenses, misuse of definite and indefinite articles, inconsistent terminology use and incorrect or missing tags. It is likely that broad generalizations in favour of either stance (MT versus human translation) are futile, though, because, just like human translations, individual machine translation outputs are likely to vary widely. Of course, the reasons for the variation in the quality of machine translation output are likely to be different from the reasons that influence variation in the quality of human translations. In the case of machine translation output, quality is likely to be influenced by, for example, the size of the database available to the machine translation program and variation in the size of the database depending on the languages involved. In contrast, human translations depend for their quality on the translator's talent, experience and ability to consult both linguistic and extra-linguistic context, as well as their access to and good use of supporting documentation and their understanding of the first-written text. Another factor is the 'courage' of the translator to diverge from the first translational response (the translation that immediately springs to mind), which tends to be close to the first-written text and therefore perhaps more literal than a translation choice that would suit the language habits of the translation's prospective audience and culture better.

Nevertheless, both translation output types (human produced and machine produced) can almost invariably benefit from both post-editing and revision. Post-editing involves checking a translation without access to the first-written text to ensure that it conforms to linguistic, genre-related and cultural conventions; revision involves checking to see that the translation is related to the first-written text in the way that is specified in the translation brief. Exercise 5.1 is designed to address the issue of editing machine-generated translation.

Exercise 5.1 Post-editing

This exercise asks you to post-edit two texts translated from Danish into English by Microsoft Bing Translator. Both texts are newspaper articles and they focus on aspects of an event that took place in Denmark but which is of interest internationally, since it concerns the security of items on display in museums. The first text is from the Danish newspaper *Berlingske Online* (www.berlingske.dk/), published on 13 March 2023, and the second is from the Danish newspaper *Jyllandsposten Online* (https://jyllands-posten.dk) published on the same day, 13 March 2023.

A. Post-edit both articles, noting any changes you want to make, and justifying each change.

Article 1, translated from *Berlingske Online*, 13 March 2023

Heading: Vandalism has made Jorn painting fragile and perhaps better known

Sub-heading: The work 'The Disturbing Duckling' was among Museum Jorn's spearheads, but after vandalism it cannot be lent.

Main text: Although it is not apparent to the naked eye that the Asger Jorn painting 'The Disturbing Duckling' has been pasted in glue and written on with permanent marker, there are still relics of glue in cracks and crevices.

The remains can be seen with a microscope, and the vandalism has made the known work more fragile and thus almost impossible to lend.

So says Jacob Thage, director of Museum Jorn.

'It's become more vulnerable.'

'When exposed to fluctuations in temperature and humidity, there is a risk that the glue that still remains in the very, very fine cracks will expand in a different way than the paint and thus spoil the image,' he says.

Therefore, according to Jacob Thage, the painting needs to be supervised at Museum Jorn.

The painting 'The Disturbing Duckling' dates from 1959 and hangs daily at Museum Jorn in Silkeborg.

It was created by the Danish painter and visual artist Asger Jorn, who died in 1973. He bought a work at a flea market, painted it over and thereby made the picture his own.

According to the museum director, the work is among the museum's spearheads and then a coveted work for other museums to borrow. But this has been blocked with the vandalism.

The serious vandalism took place in the museum in April last year. Here, a provo artist walked in and used glue to stick a picture of himself on Asger Jorn's duckling.

Next to the duckling, but still at the work, she wrote her signature with a black permanent marker.

It penetrated paint, cracks and crevices, and art conservators have been able to remove so much that it is impossible to see the glue with the naked eye.

The case of vandalism has put the spotlight on the painting and the museum. But still, Jacob Thage sees nothing positive about the case.

'We don't support the kind of disaster tourism where you suddenly want to see a picture that has either become very, very expensive or has been destroyed.'

'We have always wanted the picture to be displayed exactly as the artist wanted it. But the question is whether you can do it in the future or put up special protection,' says Thage.

The painting was gone from the walls of the museum for almost half a year, during which it was restored, but it is exhibited again at Museum Jorn. Now behind glass to prevent vandalism.

On Monday, the provo artist was sentenced by the Court in Viborg to one and a half years in prison for the vandalism. In addition, she will have to pay almost DKK 1.9 million in compensation for damage and loss of value for the plant.

/ritzau/

Article 2, translated from *Jyllandsposten Online*, 13 March 2023

Heading: Ibi-Pippi sentenced to one and a half years in prison for vandalism

Sub-heading: Ibi-Pippi Orup Hedegaard has been sentenced to prison and must pay DKK 1.9 million. She is appalled by the verdict and appeal.

Photo caption: Conservators have succeeded in restoring Asger Jorn's painting 'The Disturbing Duckling', but it was an expensive game. Photo: Anders Holst Pedersen

Main text: Provo artist Ibi-Pippi Orup Hedegaard, who last week confessed to vandalism committed against an Asger Jorn painting, is sentenced to a year and a half in prison.

In addition, she must pay almost DKK 1.9 million in compensation for the vandalism she carried out on the painting 'The Disturbing Duckling'.

This was decided by the Court in Viborg on Monday.

The prison sentence has been made unconditional. That is, it must be served.

Thus, the court has followed special prosecutor Søren Kløvborg Laustsen's sentencing claim. He also takes note of the reasons for the verdict.

'As I understand it, the court has emphasized that it has been planned for a few days. Of course, this has a strongly aggravating significance'.

'And when you vandalize a recognized art object, of which there is only one, it has such an aggravating significance that we have to face a significant custodial sentence, and that it is also made unconditional,' he told Ritzau Bureau.

Søren Kløvborg Laustsen hopes that the punishment can act as a deterrent to others who may consider doing something similar.

In its decision, the court referred to the vandalism as 'exceptionally serious' and emphasized that there has been damage and loss of a significant amount.

Ibi-Pippi Orup Hedegaard admitted in a court hearing last week that she used glue and permanent marker to vandalize an Asger Jorn painting at Museum Jorn in Silkeborg in April last year.

In addition, she said that she was prepared to pay the claim for damages brought against her. The case has been treated as a confession case.

She used the glue to stick a picture of herself on top of the duckling in the foreground of the painting. To the right of the attached picture, she signed the painting.

Later, Ibi-Pippi said she had now taken artistic ownership of the photo, which she called 'The Disturbing Bitch'.

According to her, the deed took place because she wanted to create debate about artistic ownership of pictures, as Asger Jorn himself has painted his nationally known painting on top of a landscape painting he found at a flea market.

The landscape painting forms the background of the painting.

The marker Ibi-Pippi Orup Hedegaard wrote with during the vandalism penetrated the paint, and the glue settled into the cracks and cracks in the painting. The sticky picture slipped off.

Therefore, it had to be restored, and the painting 'The Disturbing Duckling' was not to be seen on any of Museum Jorn's walls for almost half a year.

During the absence, art conservators worked to review the work with a microscope and restore it piece by piece. We managed to remove so much of the damage that 'it's not a made-up corpse or a heavily restored image we've got back'.

Museum director Jacob Thage told Midtjyllands Avis in October 2022. When the work came up to hang again, it was behind glass to protect against new vandalism.

The amount of almost DKK 1.9 million covers the work behind the restoration, as well as an estimated impairment of the work as a result of the vandalism. The exact amount is DKK 1,889,350.

Although Ibi-Pippi Orup Hedegaard told TV Midtvest last week that she was still 100 percent on target for her actions and 'I will not regret a single year', she has decided to appeal.

'I am appalled by the verdict. It couldn't have gone worse, and that's why I'm appealing the verdict,' she told Jyllands-Posten.

Thus, the Western High Court must assess the case.

Exercise 5.2 Comparing post-editing suggestions

Below are my own editing suggestions for comparison with your own. I recommend that you do not look at my suggestions until you have made your own edits. In the edited texts, I have put brackets around the text parts produced by Microsoft Bing Translator and underlined my own substitute suggestions.

A. Compare my editing suggestions with your own. Discuss any differences between the two sets of editing suggestions.

Article 1, translated from *Berlingske Online (with my editing suggestions)*

Heading: Vandalism (has made) weakens Jorn painting (fragile) but may have raised its profile (and perhaps better known)

Sub-heading: 'The (Disturbing) Disquieting Duckling' was among Museum Jorn's (spearheads) main exhibits, but having been vandalized (after vandalism) it (can) will (not be) no longer be available to borrow (lent).

Main text: Although it is not apparent to the naked eye that the Asger Jorn painting 'The (Disturbing) Disquieting Duckling' has been (pasted) plastered with (in) glue and written on with a (permanent) felt tip pen (marker), remnants of (here are still relics of) glue remain in folds (cracks) and (crevices) creases.

The (remains) remnants are visible with a (can be seen with a) microscope, and the vandalism has made the well-known (known) work more fragile and thus made it almost impossible for the museum to lend it out according to Jacob Thage, director of Museum Jorn.

(So says Jacob Thage, director of Museum Jorn).

'(It's) It has become more vulnerable.'

('When) There is a risk that exposure (exposed) to fluctuations in temperature and humidity might make (there is a risk that) the glue that (still) remains in the very, very fine (cracks) creases (will) expand in a different way than the paint and thus spoil the image,' he says.

Therefore, according to Jacob Thage, the painting needs to (be) remain in the care of (supervised at) Museum Jorn.

The painting 'The Disquieting(turbing) Duckling' dates from 1959 and is normally (hangs daily) on display at Museum Jorn in Silkeborg.

It was created by the Danish painter and visual artist Asger Jorn, who died in 1973. He bought a work at a flea market and painted (it) over it (and) thereby (made) making the picture his own.

According to the director of the museum (director), the work is among the most important exhibits in the museum (museum's spearheads) and a popular (then a coveted) work for other museums to borrow; (.) (But) but the vandalism (this) has (been blocked with the vandalism) put a stop to this.

The serious vandalism attack (took place) happened in the museum in April last year, when (. Here) a provo artist walked in and (used glue to stick) glued a picture of (himself) herself (on) onto Asger Jorn's duckling.

Next to the duckling (but still at the work) she (wrote her signature) signed her name on the painting with a black (permanent marker) felt tip pen.

(It) The glue penetrated paint, (cracks) folds and (crevices) creases, but (and) art conservators have been able to remove (so much) enough to make (that) it (is) impossible to see the glue with the naked eye.

The (ease of) vandalism attack has put the spotlight on the painting and the museum. (But still) Yet Jacob Thage sees nothing positive about the case.

'We don't support the kind of disaster tourism where you suddenly want to see a picture that has either become very, very expensive or has been destroyed.'

'We have always wanted the picture to be displayed exactly as the artist wanted it. But the question is whether (you) we will be able to (can) do so (it) in the future or whether we need to put up special protection,' says Thage.

The painting was (gone) missing from the walls of the museum for the nearly six months it took to restore it, but (it) is now back on display (exhibited) again at Museum Jorn, albeit (. Now) behind glass to (prevent) protect it against vandalism.

On Monday, the provo artist was sentenced by the Court in Viborg to one and a half years in prison for the vandalism attack. In addition, she will have to pay almost DKK 1.9 million in compensation for damage and loss of value to (for) the (plant) museum.

/ritzau/

Article 2, translated from *Jyllandsposten Online (with my editing suggestions)*

Heading: Ibi-Pippi to serve an 18 months (sentenced to one and a half years in) custodial prison sentence for vandalism

Sub-heading: Ibi-Pippi Orup Hedegaard has (been sentenced) received a prison sentence and a fine of (must pay) DKK 1.9 million. She is appalled by the verdict and is going to appeal.

Photo caption: Conservators have succeeded in restoring Asger Jorn's painting 'The (Disturbing) Disquieting Duckling', but (it was an expensive game) at a cost. Photo: Anders Holst Pedersen

Main text: Provo artist Ibi-Pippi Orup Hedegaard, who (last week confessed to) admitted vandalizing (vandalism committed against) an Asger Jorn painting last week has been sentenced to a year and a half in prison.

In addition, she must pay almost DKK 1.9 million in compensation for the vandalism she (carried out on) exposed the painting 'The (Disturbing) Disquieting Duckling' to.

This was the decision reached (decided) by (the Court in) Viborg Court on Monday.

The prison sentence (has been made unconditional) is custodial. (That is, it must be served.)

Thus, the court has followed special prosecutor Søren Kløvborg Laustsen's sentencing (claim) recommendation. He comments on (also takes note of) the reasons for the verdict: 'As I understand it, the court has (emphasized) taken into consideration the fact that the attack (that it has been) was pre-planned over (planned for) a (few) number of days, which of course has (Of course this has) a strongly aggravating significance'.

'And when you vandalize a recognized piece of art (object), a unique work, (of which there is only one. It has such an) the aggravating significance is such that (we have to face) a significant sentence is inevitable, and (that it is also made unconditional) must be custodial' he told Ritzau News (Bureau).

Søren Kløvborg Laustsen hopes that the punishment (can) will act as a deterrent to others who may consider doing something similar.

In (its decision) passing sentence, the court referred to the vandalism as 'exceptionally serious' and emphasized that there has been a significant level of damage and loss (of a significant amount) of value.

Ibi-Pippi Orup Hedegaard admitted during (in) last week's (a) court hearing (last week) that she used glue and a felt tip pen (a permanent marker) to vandalize an Asger Jorn painting at Museum Jorn in Silkeborg in April last year.

In addition, she said that she was prepared to pay the claim for damages brought against her. The case has been treated as (a confession case) uncontested.

She used the glue to stick a picture of herself on top of the duckling in the foreground of the painting. To the right of the attached picture, she signed the painting.

Later, Ibi-Pippi said she had now taken artistic ownership of the (photo) work, which she called 'The (Disturbing) Disquieting Bitch'.

According to her, (the deed) she acted as she did (took place) because she wanted to (create) encourage debate about artistic ownership of pictures, as Asger Jorn himself (has) painted his (nationally known) famous painting on top of a landscape painting he had found at a flea market.

The landscape painting forms the background of the painting.

The (marker) felt tip pen Ibi-Pippi Orup Hedegaard (wrote with) used (during the vandalism) penetrated the paint, and the glue (settled) seeped into the (cracks) folds and creases (cracks) in the painting. The (sticky) attached picture slipped off.

(Therefore) Consequently, the painting had to be restored, and (the painting) 'The (Disturbing) Disquieting Duckling' was not (to be seen) displayed on any of Museum Jorn's walls for almost half a year.

During (the) its absence, art conservators (worked to review) examined the work with a microscope and (restore) restored it piece by piece. We managed to remove (so much) enough of the damage that 'it's (not) neither a made-up corpse (or) nor a heavily restored image we've got back' museum director Jacob Thage told Midtjyllands Avis [newspaper] in October 2022. When the work (came up to hang again) was put on display again, it was placed behind glass to protect it against (new) further vandalism.

The amount of almost DKK 1.9 million covers the (work behind) cost of the restoration, as well as an estimated (impairment) loss of (the work) value (as a result of) due to the vandalism. The exact amount is DKK 1,889,350.

Although Ibi-Pippi Orup Hedegaard told TV Midtvest last week that she (was still) stood by her actions 100 percent (on target for her actions and) adding 'I will not regret a single year', she has decided to appeal.

'I am appalled by the verdict. It is the worst possible outcome (couldn't have gone worse), and that's why I'm appealing against the verdict,' she told Jyllands-Posten.

(Thus, the) The Western High Court must therefore review (assess) the case.

Exercise 5.3 Revision

I have made the revisions below to the two texts in the light of my access to the source texts. The texts display revision only; that is, I have not included the stylistic adjustments made in the edited texts above but concentrated on inaccuracies that a comparison between the first-written texts and the translations show. Occasionally, the two categories overlap. For example, 'relic' is both stylistically inappropriate and factually inaccurate. In the title of the painting, I have changed 'disturbing' to 'disquieting' in both sections, because 'The Disquieting Duckling' is the title under which the painting 'Den foruroligende ælling' by the Danish artist Asger Jorn is usually known in English.

A. Compare my revisions with the texts as translated by the translating software. Do you think that my revisions correct distortions of the source text's sense that the machine translation software had caused?

Article 1, translated from *Berlingske Online (revised)*

Heading: Vandalism has made Jorn painting fragile and perhaps better known

Sub-heading: The work 'The Disquieting Duckling' was among Museum Jorn's spearheads, but after vandalism it cannot be lent.

Main text: Although it is not apparent to the naked eye that the Asger Jorn painting 'The (Disturbing) Disquieting Duckling' has been pasted in glue and written on with permanent marker, there are still (relics) remnants of glue in cracks and crevices.

The (remains) remnants can be seen with a microscope, and the vandalism has had the effect that (made) the well-known work has become more fragile and (thus) therefore almost impossible to lend.

So says Jacob Thage, who is the director of Museum Jorn.

'It's become more vulnerable.'

'When exposed to fluctuations in temperature and humidity, there is a risk that the glue that still remains in the very, very fine cracks will expand in a different way than the paint and (thus spoil) thereby ruin the (image) painting,' he says.

Therefore, according to Jacob Thage, the painting needs to be under observation in (supervised at) Museum Jorn.

The painting 'The (Disturbing) Disquieting Duckling' dates from 1959 and normally hangs (daily at) in Museum Jorn in Silkeborg.

It was created by the Danish painter and visual artist Asger Jorn, who died in 1973. He bought (a work) an artwork at a flea market, painted (it) over it and thereby made the picture his own.

According to the museum director, the work is among the museum's spearheads and (then) therefore a coveted work for other museums to borrow. But the vandalism has created a stumbling block to this (has been blocked with the vandalism).

The serious vandalism took place in the museum in April last year. Here, a provo artist walked in and used glue to stick a picture of (himself) herself on Asger Jorn's duckling.

Next to the duckling, but still (at) on the work, she wrote her signature with a black permanent marker.

It penetrated paint, cracks and crevices, and art conservators have been able to remove so much that it is not possible (impossible) to see the glue with the naked eye.

The vandalism case (of vandalism) has put (the spotlight) a focus on the painting and the museum. But still, Jacob Thage sees nothing positive about the case.

'We don't support the kind of disaster tourism where (you) people suddenly want to see a picture that has either become very, very expensive or has been subject to an attempt to destroy it (destroyed).'

'We have always wanted the picture to be displayed exactly as the artist wanted it. But the question is of course whether (you) that can (do it) be done in the future or whether we must put up special protection,' says Thage.

The painting was gone from the museum walls (of the museum) for (almost) just under half a year, during which it was restored, but it is (exhibited) on display again at Museum Jorn. Now behind glass to prevent vandalism.

On Monday, the provo artist was sentenced by the Court in Viborg to one and a half (years) year in prison for the vandalism. In addition, she (will have) has to pay almost DKK 1.9 million in compensation for damage and loss of value for the work (plant).

/ritzau/

Comment

Non-Danish speakers may be intrigued by the erroneous last word in the translation, 'plant', which I have changed to the correct 'work'. The word 'work' here is a translation of the Danish word 'værk' which can be used to refer to an industrial business in Danish (a 'plant' (or 'works') in English) as well as to a work of art; here, it is obviously a work of art that is at issue.

Article 2, translated from *Jyllandsposten Online* (revised)

Heading: Ibi-Pippi (sentenced to) given a one and a half years (in prison) custodial prison sentence for vandalism

Sub-heading: Ibi-Pippi Orup Hedegaard has (been sentenced to) received a prison sentence and must pay (DKK) 1.9 million. She is (appalled) shaken by the verdict and will appeal.

Photo caption: Conservators have succeeded in restoring Asger Jorn's painting 'The (Disturbing) Disquieting Duckling', but it was an expensive game. Photo: Anders Holst Pedersen

Main text: Provo artist Ibi-Pippi Orup Hedegaard, who last week confessed to vandalism committed against an Asger Jorn painting, is sentenced to a year and a half in prison.

In addition, she must pay (almost) just short of DKK 1.9 million in compensation for the vandalism she carried out on the painting 'The (Disturbing) Disquieting Duckling'.

This (was decided) has been determined by the Court in Viborg on Monday.

The prison sentence has been made unconditional. That (is) means that it must be served.

(Thus) Thereby, the court has followed special prosecutor Søren Kløvborg Laustsen's sentencing claim to the letter. He also takes note of the reasons for the verdict.

'As I understand it, the court has emphasized that it has been planned for (a few) several days. This of course (Of course, this) has a strongly aggravating significance.

'And when you vandalize a recognized art object, (of) which there is only this one of, it has such an aggravating significance that we must go up to (have to face) a significant custodial sentence, and that it is also made unconditional,' he told Ritzau Bureau.

Søren Kløvborg Laustsen hopes that the punishment can act as a deterrent to others who (may) might consider doing something similar.

The court has in (In) its decision referred to the vandalism as 'exceptionally harsh (serious)' and emphasized that (there has been) damage and loss (of) to the cost of a significant amount have occurred.

Ibi-Pippi Orup Hedegaard admitted in a court hearing last week that (she used) with the use of glue and permanent marker she carried out significant vandalism to (to vandalize) an Asger Jorn painting at Museum Jorn in Silkeborg in April last year.

In addition, she said that she was prepared to pay the claim for damages brought against her. The case has been treated as a confession case.

She used the glue to stick a picture of herself on top of the duckling in the foreground of the painting. To the right of the attached picture, she signed the painting.

Later, Ibi-Pippi said she had now taken artistic ownership of the (photo) painting, which she called 'The (Disturbing) Disquieting Bitch'.

(According to her the) The deed took place according to her because she wanted to create debate about artistic ownership of pictures, as Asger Jorn himself has painted his nationally known painting on top of a landscape painting he found at a flea market.

(The) That landscape painting forms the background of the painting.

The marker Ibi-Pippi Orup Hedegaard wrote with during the vandalism penetrated the paint, and the glue seeped into the (cracks) creases and cracks in the painting. The (sticky) glued-on picture slipped off.

Therefore, it had to be restored, and the painting 'The (Disturbing) Disquieting Duckling' was not to be seen on any of Museum Jorn's walls for almost half a year.

During (the) this period of absence, art conservators worked to review the work with a microscope and restore it piece by piece. (We) It was possible (managed) to remove enough (so much) of the damage that 'it's not a made-up corpse or a heavily restored image we've got back'.

So said museum (Museum) director Jacob Thage (told) in Midtjyllands Avis [newspaper] in October 2022. When the work (came up to hang again) was re-hung, it was behind glass to protect it against (new) further vandalism.

The amount of almost DKK 1.9 million covers the work (behind) involved in the restoration, as well as an estimated (impairment) devaluation of the work (as a result of) resulting from the vandalism. The exact amount is DKK 1,889,350.

Although Ibi-Pippi Orup Hedegaard told TV Midtvest last week that she (was) still stood 100 per cent (on target for) behind her actions and 'I will not regret a single year', she has decided to appeal.

'I am (appalled) shaken by the verdict. It couldn't have gone worse, and therefore I (that's why I'm) am naturally appealing against the verdict,' she (told) tells Jyllands-Posten.

(Thus) Therefore, (the Western High Court) Vestre Landsret [High Court West] (must) has to assess the case.

5.2 Navigating Net-Translation

As McDonough Dolmaya and Sánchez Ramos (2019: 129) note, translators have made use of online translation technologies since the early days of the internet.

Translators use the internet in two main ways: to search for information and to translate texts online. While the online dimension of searching for information and translating does not alter the basic nature of the activities, it can radically affect the translator's experience of undertaking them; and there are clear potential time-scale implications. Online information resources proliferate. They include dictionaries, encyclopaedias, term banks, specialist databases, text collections of numerous types for multiple specializations, including corpora of 'naturally occurring' spoken and written discourse, that is discourse drawn from situations and sources that have not been manipulated by researchers, such as everyday newspapers and conversations.

While the advantages of having easy access to vast amounts of information are clear, the quantities involved and the sources they may derive from raise questions of selection and of trust. For example, which is the most pertinent information relative to a given query? And what guarantees are there that what seems most pertinent is also accurate? In addition, the sheer scale of resource availability and translators' potential feeling that all these resources need to be assessed can be overwhelming. One way that translators may deal with these dilemmas was illustrated in a study by Shih (2023) involving eleven student translators from University College, London and ten professional translators. Tracking these translators' use of online resources, Shih finds that many translators settle for 'good enough' information; that is, they use information directly available on search engines without clicking on hyperlinks to read the more detailed information available (2023: 31). The participants in Shih's study all had English as one of their languages, but their other languages included Arabic, Chinese, German, Japanese, Russian and Spanish. The specializations of the professional translators included legal, medical, audiovisual, and literary translation, as well as localization (2023: 27), so this population, albeit small, can be considered representative of a fair proportion of translators. Google was the most popular search engine among the participants in the study; in fact, for many, it was the only search engine they used, although Chinese translators also used the Chinese search engine Baidu (2023: 29). In addition to search engines, online dictionaries were popular among this group of translators.

The interactive web also offers opportunities to bid for translation jobs online and to translate directly online. Online translation is often collaborative and collaborative translation has been greatly facilitated by the interactive web. A translation can be divided into parts and each part can be translated by one member of a group of translators assigned to the translation task. These different contributions can then be revised and formed into a final end product by a reviser (Zwischenberger 2022: 4); the reviser may have been chosen by the job provider. Crucially, in comparison with more traditional forms of collaborative translation, online collaboration can take place in real time; that is, translators can work on the same text at the same time and take the kinds of action agreed on immediately (Zielinska-Elliott and Kaminka 2017: 178), even if the translators are not co-located. Zielinska-Elliott and Kaminka describe their own experience of the advantages of online translation collaboration:

> Translators brainstorm and learn from one another; collaboration is based on a non-hierarchical relationship of equality and is driven by the desire to help each other and get help when needed. ... While talking about the difficulties of translating particular phrases or speech patterns, each [translator] considers

> whether a certain solution would work in their particular linguistic, cultural and sociolinguistic context. Sometimes [they] manage to find common ground, but arriving at a consensus is not the point of the discussion; no one is made to follow a given suggestion or strategy. The point is to find a solution that works within one's own language; and with that in mind, it is extremely useful to learn how colleagues working in other languages have addressed an identical problem. (2017: 183)

In contrast to Zielinska-Elliott and Kaminka's (2017) generally positive assessment of online translation collaboration, Jones (2019: 77) focuses on 'the difficult processes of fierce conflict and debate which often characterise interactions within [online communities of volunteer translators]'. These conflicts and debates between translators, he argues, 'also have a major shaping influence on their output' (2019: 79) and include 'clashes that arise between expert and lay understandings' (2019: 92–93).

The kind of collaborative translation under discussion here is referred to as 'concurrent translation (CT)' by Gough et al. (2023), who focus on 'cloud-based collaborative translation platforms that can . . . scale up the translation process' (2023: 45). A translation platform is a set of technologies that enables the recruitment of translators, the management of translation workflows, and communication between the agents involved in the translation process, including project managers, editors, clients and support staff. Gough et al. (2023: 47) present a survey of 804 translators' views of the efficacy of these platforms. Between them, the translators surveyed worked with 84 languages, 233 language pairs, 365 language directions, and used 49 translation platforms. Forty-eight per cent of the translators taking part in the survey worked on more than one platform, 67 per cent of the translators had had formal training in translation and 55 per cent were male (Gough et al. 2023: 53). Most of the translators surveyed devoted a relatively small percentage of their time to collaborative translation. The survey identified a number of 'unfavourable consequences' (Gough et al. 2023: 66) of collaborative translation, namely 'compromised quality and consistency, lack of satisfaction and ownership of the translation task as a whole and devaluation of translation' (2023: 66). However, underlying the first of these disadvantages, compromised quality and consistency, was 'extreme time pressure leading to less revision, less research and less thought devoted to the translation' (66). In other words, it was not the collaboration as such that compromised quality and translator satisfaction. As Zielinska-Elliott and Kaminka (2017: 183) testify (see above) there is no reason in principle why collaboration between translators should not be satisfactory and successful. Indeed, what has been termed 'the most important book in the English language' (Campbell 2010: 2), The King James Version of the Bible, published in 1611, was made by six 'Companies' whose members numbered altogether fifty-four translators. There were also a number of revisers of both the first and subsequent editions (Campbell 2010: Appendix I).

Clearly, technological breakdowns, whether affecting equipment, servers or platforms, if they occur, can have a major negative impact on online translation.

Exercise 5.4 Exploring translation platforms

This exercise encourages you to explore several translation platforms, as a lone translator and if possible, in the company of colleagues.

A. Identify three translation platforms and assess whether each
   a. requires registration for access to all or some jobs
   b. offers assignments for the languages you can offer
   c. offers jobs for editors and proofreaders.
B. List any other services that the platform offers.
C. Which platform would suit your needs and abilities best, and for what reasons?

Comments

Smartcat (www.smartcat.com/blog/top-15-websites-to-get-freelance-translation-jobs/, accessed 29 January 2024) compares what it considers the five most popular online translation agencies in terms of numbers of site visits, LinkedIn followers and fees. It also lists several pros and cons for each. If Smartcat lists the three translation platforms you have selected, do you agree with its ratings?

If Smartcat does not list the three platforms you have chosen, how would you rate them using Smartcat's criteria?

5.3 'Equivalence' in Translation Studies

In Section 4.1, we discussed what most translators, probably, and most translator trainers almost certainly see as a need to read first-written texts for translation carefully before beginning the translating process, but what does it mean to 'read a source text carefully'? It might mean reading it slowly, taking in and savouring every word; but a text is more than a number of individual words – more, even, than a number of individual sentences. A text has to cohere, hold together, in a certain way if it is to tell its story, and it is the sequencing of, and connections between the sentences and words in a text, with their senses in their contexts, that enable it to do so.

Assuming that a translator wants to convey in a translation the story told by the first-written text, they will try, as far as possible, to re-create that story (as they understand it) in the target language, and this aim may, or it may not, be best achieved by attempting to replicate in the translation the sequencing and relationships between the textual items in the first-written text. However, we must bear in mind that the very notion of 'the same story' is problematized by the fact that an audience for a story always receives it in the context of their personal, and, more broadly, their cultural background, and this affects their understanding.

The relationship between the first-written text and a translation of it is traditionally referred to in translation studies as 'equivalence', a concept that we touched on in Chapter 1, Section 1.1. The term 'equivalence' has created a good deal of controversy in the translation studies community over the years. The problem with the term when used in the context of translation is that it echoes a notion of equivalence that is not well suited to language issues. The term derives from the first of Euclid's (c. 300 bce) so-called common notions. According to Euclid, 'Things that are equal to the same thing are equal to one another.' This implies that there must exist a means of assessment, Euclid's 'same thing', which can be used to decide whether other things are equal to each other. This Euclidean notion of equivalence is an excellent account of how equivalence is established between (physical) phenomena: if you go to buy ten metres of ribbon, for example, the seller will measure a stretch of ribbon against a measuring stick which indicates what the length that we class as one metre is. You measure your ribbon by holding successive stretches of it against this stick ten times. Normally, the seller will not measure one metre of ribbon and then another metre against the first piece and so on. They will measure the ribbon against the metre measure – the 'same thing' that each metre of ribbon is equal to.

The metre having been defined as one ten-millionth of the distance from the equator to the North Pole, in 1789 'authorities in Paris constructed a platinum bar with a length of exactly one metre to serve as an official reference point'. The measure has been redefined three times, most recently in 1983, as 'the length of the path travelled by light in a vacuum during a time interval of 1/299 792 458 of a second' (Lucy 2018). So, if we wanted or needed to assess a length that someone claims is one metre, we could ultimately test the claim by comparing the asserted metre with this official reference point. In theory, all our means of measuring one metre replicate the platinum bar in Paris.

Similarly, if I want to tune three guitars, I will tune each to a tuning fork rather than to another guitar, usually a tuning fork that sounds the musical note A above middle C, which has the musical pitch or audio frequency of 440 hertz (Hz) – at least I will do so ideally, to prevent any gradual distortion that might be introduced if I were to tune one guitar to another, and then the third guitar to the recently tuned one. If a constant is used to measure all new instances, minor inaccuracies in individual instances will not be replicated or increased for other individual instances.

So a metre is a metre whatever material is used and whatever the context; and A above middle C is A above middle C whatever instrument is used and whatever the relevant tune and context.

But this concept of equivalence cannot be used to refer to the relationship between languages, because there is no constant (like 'the length of the path travelled by light in a vacuum during a time interval of 1/299 792 458 of a second' or the audio frequency of 440 Hz) that individual expressions can be measured against and which can be kept constant across and independent of situations. 'Meaning' will not do as such a measure, because meaning arises for language users in situations, and these will differ along with the different configurations of sets of language users and the situations they find themselves in. In addition, languages differ in what can or must be expressed on certain occasions: they offer their speakers different resources, and speakers create varying rules and habits of use for their languages. In other words, no two languages correspond to each other in a one-to-one manner, and nor do most terms within those languages.

Nevertheless, translations proliferate, as the Israeli translation scholar Gideon Toury pointed out (Toury 1978, 1995), and there must certainly exist a relationship between first-written texts and their translations if one text is to be considered a translation of the other. But what relationship is that, then? According to Toury, it is the observable relationship between the two texts, and he names this relationship 'translational equivalence'; and each realization of this relationship can be studied.

Many analyses of translation are carried out with the first-written text as the starting point. That is, the analyst begins by identifying segments of the first-written text and proceeds to check the translation to see whether equivalent segments exist there. Clearly, this requires the analyst to have an idea of what kinds of relationships between the two texts (or text segments) will count as equivalence prior to the analysis; otherwise, how would the analyst know what to check for?

Toury, in contrast, advocates an analysis that proceeds from the segments in the translation rather than from segments in the first-written text. The analyst will check which features in the first-written text these segments within the translation represent. This means that relationships between the two texts are not preconceived but, rather, identified as the analysis progresses. If a large number of pairs of translation segments and their first-written text segments are examined in a language, or in an author's opus, or in a specific text type, it may be possible to identify similarities between the relationships between these pairs, and this may be taken as evidence that certain norms guide translation in the culture that the translated texts belong to. These norms of the target culture generally guide translation into its language, either insofar as translators seek to follow them, or, indeed, insofar as translators may deliberately break them. Identifying the norms can, in turn, be sociologically informative, because the analyst may be able to perceive certain taboos, habitual mentions and various language- and culture-specific phenomena in the culture whose language is being translated into which do not exist, or which play different roles, in the culture whose language is being translated from.

In my own research, I have named this type of analysis of translations and their first-written texts 'translational stylistics', and I have used translational stylistics to identify and explain relationships between the original versions of Hans Christian Andersen's stories and their translations into English (Malmkjær 2003, 2004, 2014). In the sections that follow, I describe and illustrate the translational stylistic analysis method.

5.4 Stylistics and Translational Stylistics

As mentioned in the preceding paragraph, I use the term 'translational stylistics' to stand for a particular type of analysis of the style of translated texts. The term echoes the term 'stylistics' which is often used to refer to the study of style, and in the following sections I will discuss the notions of style, stylistics and translational stylistics in more detail.

5.4.1 Style

The style of a text is realized by features of language that recur in it with a certain regularity and in certain patterns. Some styles are 'institutionalized' or specialized in the sense that they are characteristic of certain genres or text types, as discussed in Chapter 2, Section 2.1. Indeed, some genres, including, prominently, literary genres, are defined in large part in terms of the ways in which language is used in them. For example, a thirteenth-century sonnet has fourteen lines and a particular rhyme scheme. For another example, according to Aristotle's *Poetics*, the action in a play must be set at one time and in one place; it must focus on one action, and it must have a beginning, a middle and an end.

5.4.2 Stylistic Analysis

An analysis of the style of a text or set of texts may focus mainly on the text itself, or it may focus on how a reader or a set of readers interact with the text, or on the writer's potential reasons for shaping the text in a certain way (among other possible primary foci – for example, manuscript authentication, authorship ascription and forensic linguistics – see Coulthard 2002: 139).

5.4.3 Translational Stylistics

Translated texts can be analysed in the same way as non-translated texts if the focus is on the text itself, or on the reader's interaction with the text. But it is clearly not possible to use a translated text to study the original writer's textual choices, because in the translation, these are swathed in the translator's selections of expressions. Therefore, a stylistic analysis of a translation, or a set of translations, that is focused on the reasons for the choice of particular textual items in the translation cannot be carried out in the same manner as such a stylistic analysis of non-translated texts. In translational stylistics, it is always necessary to take into consideration the relationship between the translated text and the first-written text that it translates when translational choices are under discussion. In the case of some texts, this issue is particularly acute. For example, Davies (2018: 27) suggests that what might be seen as disloyalty to a witness voice, namely Curt Meyer-Clason's choice of the term 'Gaskammer' (gas chamber) for 'crématoir' (crematorium) in his translation into German of Elie Wiesel's Holocaust memoir *La Nuit* (1958 (The Night); 2008 *Die Nacht: Erinnerung und Zeugnis*) is made because

> The voice of the witness is of less importance than the effect of the text in the new context: where those who experienced Auschwitz knew exactly what was meant by the term 'crematorium' and what happened there, the translation is being made in a context in which doubt can be cast on the existence of gas chambers.

(The term used in *Night* (2006), Marion Wiesel's translation into English of her husband's memoir, is 'crematorium'.)

Literary texts, especially those aimed primarily or in part at children, very often display adjustments to their new audience, and these adjustments may be signalled clearly by their translators. For example, Ker Wilson carefully explains the reasons for the choices made in Nancy Sheppard's adaptation and translation of Lewis

Carroll's *Alice in Wonderland* (1865) into Pitjantjatjara, a Western Desert language spoken in the west of South Australia, part of Western Australia and the Northern Territories. The projected readership and listeners are Aboriginal children, and,

> Like all languages, Pitjantjatjara is the cultural expression of its people, descriptive of the terrain, the fauna and flora and the way of life known to them; it follows that the characters and settings of *Alice* have been adapted accordingly. The White Rabbit, with his gloves and fan, becomes the Kangaroo, with dilly-bag and digging-stick – not, it should be emphasized, because there is no Pitjantjatjara word for 'rabbit', but simply because an Aboriginal Alice would naturally have seen a kangaroo in her dream. The Caterpillar becomes a Witchety Grub … (Sheppard 1975, Ker Wilson's Introduction; 1992: Notes)

The types of adjustment we have just seen may be met with protest and arguments to the effect that they leave their readers with a skewed impression of the originals. There are at least two ways of countering this argument. One is that it is unlikely that any two people ever form the same impression as one another of anything, and that the further apart people are in terms of background knowledge and culture, the less likely they are to coincide on understanding. This is a sound argument in defence of translational adjustment, although a counter argument might be that a translator might at least try to enable their audience to share the experiences that the readers of the first-written text are likely to enjoy. But this takes us to a second argument which, as we saw in Section 1.3., is elegantly expressed by Boase-Beier and de Vooght (2019: 17), who suggest that

> Translation … is never about getting it right, about approximating the form or content of the original, about making a copy for those who do not speak Yiddish, or Latvian or French. It is about recognising someone else's story, understanding the way the teller has chosen to tell it, and passing it on to others.

Translation, in other words, is not chiefly about language (counterintuitive as this may seem); it is about replicating for a readership something akin to what a prior text offered its projected audience. And although this may seem more relevant in the case of literature translation, it is quite possible to argue that any text tells a story, even if the stories in non-literary texts tend to concern actuality whereas the stories in literature need not do so.

In any case, recognizing and re-telling someone's story often requires considerable knowledge, sensitivity and creativity on the part of the translator – much more than a mere linguistic matching would require. The 'mere linguistic matching' as I have just expressed it, is of course often very challenging, and is certainly the first step in any translating process; indeed, it is crucial to the success of any translation. It requires of the translator excellent language skills and excellent understanding of the cultures involved; but these skills are not enough. Cultural understanding must be applied carefully, with considerable thought if 'someone else's story' is to be made acceptable and appropriately available to others. We may hope that humans are endowed with what Bucciarelli and Johnson-Laird (2019: 89) call 'an innate system of basic emotions' which enable them to empathize with one another

(Oatley and Johnson-Laird 2014: 135), that is, to share the emotions of others, or, at least, to understand them. Readers' experience of much literature and of much other writing depends on this. A translator is a reader for whom empathy has to reach both back to the first-written text's author and readership and forward to the readership for the translation. A translator will understand the first-written text and often their first translational response will be the closest, most literal translation. So when this is not what is found in a translation, we may, as analysts, think about why this should be. Of course, such speculation depends crucially on acquaintance with the first-written text which, in the nature of things, most readers of a translation do not enjoy.

An argument for deliberate choice in stylistic analysis is often supported by identification of patterns of expression which contribute significantly to the development of the characterization of people or story themes. In translational stylistic analysis, significant patterns may additionally be identified in the relationships between the translation and the first-written text. For example, in Malmkjær (2003) I describe the translator Henry William Dulcken's determination to maintain a respectful distance in his translations between the heavenly and the earthly spheres in Hans Christian Andersen's stories (Dulcken 1864), in which in fact there is no such distance, or, at least, a much less pronounced one. For example, in a story entitled 'De vilde svaner' (1838) (The wild swans) a character, Elisa, has a vision in which

> Trægrenene oven over hende gik til side og *vor Herre* med milde øine saae ned paa hende, og smaa Engle tittede frem over hans Hoved og under hans Arme.
>
> (The tree branches over above her parted and *our Lord*'s gentle eyes looked down on her, and little angels peeped out above his head and under his arms.)

In this example, a greater physical distance between heaven and earth is suggested in Dulcken's translation, which even elevates the position of the angels to 'on high':

> It seemed to her as if the branches parted above her head, and mild eyes of angels looked down upon her from on high.

In addition, by removing God altogether from the scene, Dulcken avoids any suggestion of intimacy between the divine and the human, along with the description of a positively avuncular God who lets the angels crawl around on his body. Finally, since the name of God is deleted from the translation, a linguistic distance is also maintained. Similar variations in distancing occur throughout Dulcken's translations vis-à-vis Andersen's first-written texts, which suggests that Dulcken seeks to maintain a more formal relationship between the divine and the earthly spheres than the more romantically minded Andersen seeks to portray.

In a related example of translational stylistic analysis, Choi (2021) discusses the missionary translator James Scarth Gale's translations into English of Korean folk tales (1913 and 1915). She shows that Gale, who was a Canadian Presbyterian missionary as well as a scholar of Korean studies, deliberately adapted Christian concepts and Christian ideology when representing Korean folk beliefs and Buddhism in order to Christianize these texts (2021: 2–4), perhaps to ease English-speaking readers' access to them (8–9), but also because he considered the two systems of faith and belief closely related and of equal value (23).

Summary

We began this chapter by exploring ways of working with machine-generated or machine-stored texts. Texts produced with the aid of machine translation (MT) or with the aid of translation memories (TM) can enhance productivity, but almost without exception require significant editing – MT at the end of the process, TM typically during the process itself. We distinguished editing from revision, and practised each activity with reference to machine-generated translations into English of two newspaper articles in Danish on the same topic. Next, we explored translators' potential uses of the internet for individual or group collaborative translation, and their varying attitudes to this type of collaboration. Finally, we introduced an approach to translation analysis known as translational stylistics.

Further Reading

Boase-Beier, J. (2006). *Stylistic Approaches to Translation*. Manchester: St. Jerome.

This book introduces several approaches to stylistic analysis of translation and a number of theories underlying this activity.

Boase-Beier, J. (2020). *Translation and Style*. London: Routledge.

Expands and updates Boase-Beier (2006).

Daems, J., Vandepitte, S., Hartsuiker, R. J. and Macken, L. (2017). Translation methods and experience: A comparative analysis of human translation and post-editing with students and professional translators. *Meta: Journal des traducteurs/ Meta: Translators' Journal* 62(2), 245–270.

This journal article addresses the differences between human translation and post-editing with reference to eye tracking and keystroke logging. It examines the final quality of the product as well as translators' attitudes towards both methods of translation.

Gough, J., Temizöz, Ö., Hieke, G. and Zilio, L. (2023). Concurrent translation on collaborative platforms. *Translation Spaces* 12(1), 45–73.

This journal article draws on a study of 804 translators' experiences to examine commercial translation performed on collaborative platforms by multiple agents (translators, editors, subject-matter experts, etc.) with concurrent access. It indicates that despite advantages like peer learning, positive competition, speed, flexibility of the volume of work and working time, and reduced pressure of responsibility and reduced stress, collaborative translation brings with it challenges of time pressure, negative competition, reduced opportunity for self-revision and research.

Malmkjær, K. (2003). What happened to God and the angels: An exercise in translational stylistics. *Target* 15(1), 39–62.

Malmkjær, K. (2004). Translational Stylistics. *Language and Literature* 13(1): 13–24

These two journal articles discuss and illustrate the method of translational stylistics.

CHAPTER 6

Returning to the Theory of Translation and Looking Ahead

Preview

This book began with a chapter that considered attitudes to translation and common conceptions about what translation involves. Next, the chapter introduced methods of investigating translation processes and products, and Chapters 2, 3, 4 and 5 presented and drew on the findings of these investigations. In this final chapter, we look back at the issues that have been introduced in the book, in Sections 6.1 and 6.2, and we look forwards to potential future scenarios for our discipline in Section 6.3.

6.1 Where We Have Been

In Chapter 1, we explored beliefs about translation and attitudes to it. We surveyed a number of theories of translation which have held sway from the 1960s onward. The earliest of these were largely language-focused, although some held the translation's purpose and the needs of its projected audience to be the overall determinant of the content and structure of a translation, rather than equivalence with the language (content and structure) of the source text. We saw, also, how later theories turned the focus more towards actual, existing translations than towards an ideal concept of translation equivalence. We considered empirical methods that have been employed to investigate these products of the process of translating as well as the processes themselves.

In Chapter 2, we examined a number of genres of translation. Genres, the chapter illustrates, are manifestations of agreements and understandings that obtain between producers and consumers of texts regarding how typical texts of certain types are structured and about what they tend to concern, so the chapter also examined the relationships between translators and the people and organizations who employ them, and between translators and those who may be reading translations. These relationships are varied and complex. We focused especially on texts types (genres) for which these relationships are well understood, such as recipes, brochures, tourism texts, community information materials, instructions for use, legal texts, and medical texts, as well as official documents, such as contracts, refugee statements, driving licences, statutory declarations, and certificates of birth, baptism, education, employment, marriage and death. We also examined scientific writing, news texts and subtitles. We introduced the important concepts of lexical sophistication and textual complexity, as well as the possibly more familiar notion of formality. The notions of corpora and collocation were also explained, and a section is devoted to the relationship between speech and writing, and its consequences for subtitling and other forms of representation of speech in written text. Section 2.2 discussed translators' clients, in the sense of the people and agencies who want a given text to be made available to people whose language differs from the language the text is written in. We noted that readers of translations may live within the country where the language of the first-written text is used, and that such readers will have different requirements of translations than readers foreign to that country. We covered translators' working practices and working conditions, which vary between self-employment and employment by agencies or within national or international institutions. The section following discussed readers of translations and their varied needs and interests, and the requirement for translators to have extensive understanding of these needs and interests to ensure that the translations they create are fit for purpose. In this, translators are aided by the translation brief, which is discussed in Chapter 3.

Chapter 3 concerns the location of translating in societies and international organizations, and translators' roles within and relationships with these varied sites. Translators work in a world in which more than 7,000 languages are spoken, although just twenty-three of these languages serve more than half of the world's population. Equity in this numerical setting is clearly difficult to establish, although organizations like the United Nations and the European Union strive for that goal through their language and translation policies. Online translating by enthusiasts has also enhanced availability of content originally expressed in minority languages, although the quality of such translating is not monitored in the same manner as translations that are formally commissioned. Volunteer translation is often questioned on moral grounds and in consideration of the potential damage that the activity may cause to translators' pay bargaining power. The chapter outlines the nature of translators' networks and more formal associations and the codes of conduct that such networks and associations often expect their members to follow. These associations can form a type of barrier to practice by way of barring from membership translators who do not have certain qualifications and experience; but they can also offer early-career translators support, for example through pairings with more experienced colleagues.

The issues of translation copyright and the relationship between a first-written text and successive different translations of it, along with the issue of using translations as sources for further translations into other languages were also broached. Translations are of course made of language, and in Chapter 3, we also looked at the question of whether the language in a text that is made against the direct background of a previously existing text in a different language differs in nature from the language that makes up first-written texts. For example, it has been argued that translated texts tend to be more explicit than first-written texts. Finally in Chapter 3, we considered the many kinds of human agents that are involved in the process of making translations, and, prominently among these, of course, translators (who may also undertake several or all of the relevant roles themselves). Many translators work on a freelance basis, which gives them considerable freedom to organize their working time and practices, but which also imposes on them the need to obtain and update their working equipment, to advertise their services, and to keep abreast of developments in fields relevant to their specialisms and within the countries whose languages they use in their work. In contrast, company translators typically benefit from resources provided by their employers, including a workspace, relevant documentation, and colleagues to discuss their work with.

Most translators translate texts written by other people, but a group, known as self-translators, translate text that they have authored themselves. Self-translation is more common in literary translation than in translation of other text types, and self-translators typically allow themselves more freedom to make translations that deviate from the first-written texts than other translators tend to. The chapter illustrates this by way of an example of a self-translated poem. Significant deviations from a first-written text often result in texts that are labelled 'adaptations' rather than translations, a phenomenon illustrated in the chapter by way of a piece of translated literature and a set of translated songs. When making deviations of this type, as well as less radical changes, translators effectively localize their texts, that is, they make their translations relevant to a current time and to norms that may deviate from those operating in the locale of the first-written text. The chapter offers several illustrations of the need for localization.

Translators' work benefits from the scrutiny of a reviser. A reviser is typically a translator; indeed, it may be the same translator who made the translation, but given the tendency of authors of text to be blind to their own errors, having one's text revised by another person is preferable. Given the number of tasks that have to be completed for a translation to be made ready for publication, the services of a project manager are extremely helpful. Several translation memory tools can be used to undertake project management tasks, which is clearly helpful for freelance translators working on their own. Translation memory tools will also help with terminology management, ensuring that terminology is consistent across documentation relevant to the same or closely similar projects across a range managed by one translation service provider, and across an area of interest more broadly. Terminology standardization is one of the key responsibilities of translators working for the United Nations.

A final type of 'translator' discussed in Chapter 3 is the so-called pseudotranslator: a person who publishes a text which they have in fact authored but which they claim is a translation, and which they endow with features which they believe are characteristic of translated text in the relevant language and culture. Pseudotranslators protect themselves and their authored publications against potential censure in this way, and they may benefit from the exoticism that often attaches to a work of foreign origin, or from the kudos that may be provided by a work's alleged historical heritage, for example.

Exercise 6.1 Pseudotranslations

A. Write a pseudotranslation of approximately 300 words in a language of your choice.
B. Next, list the features of the text that you think are characteristic of translations. If possible, form groups of up to four people, preferably sharing the same languages, and compare your lists of what you consider characteristics of translations into the relevant language or languages and culture(s).

All translators have a degree of power deriving from their ability to choose to introduce or refuse to introduce certain content into a culture. For example, *The Times of Israel*, 9 March 2023, reports on a translator's refusal to translate for the Israeli Prime Minister Benjamin Netanyahu during his visit to Italy. Opinions vary about the degree to which translators are free to, or indeed ought to, exercise that power. Translators may argue that they need to make a living, and that their individual likes or dislikes are not grounds for censorship; besides, what one translator turns down, another may take on. Nevertheless, I would strongly argue for a negative answer to House's question (2016: 133) 'if a translator refuses to translate a text that offends her own and others' religious feelings, is she acting unethical [sic] because she steps outside the ethical consensus of "freedom of the pen", "freedom from censure", "freedom of speech"?' I would delete 'religious' here, or add many more types of feeling; there are other sensibilities than religious convictions that can offend and be offended. But no translator is *obliged* on ethical grounds, and even less on the grounds that someone else will undertake the job anyway, to translate what they find offensive or believe to be damaging.

Exercise 6.2 Declining translation assignments

In groups, if possible, discuss scenarios in which you might decline a translation assignment. You can find a debate on the subject at www.youtube.com/watch?v=DIlVWkLdQc0 (accessed 12 June 2024; the introduction is in Hebrew but the debate following is in English).

Chapter 4 focuses on how translations come into being via the agency of humans, increasingly aided by machines. They are typically subjected to a process of editing and revision before they are released for use. We looked at the need for translators to work in a comfortable, functional environment, and explored translators' general enjoyment of their métier and their keen sense of responsibility towards their texts and their clients. We noted some of the results of the kinds of research methods outlined in Chapter 1, as well as the challenges posed by the translation of a number of the genres discussed in Section 2.1, and translators' responses to these challenges. We explained that translators who work within organizations like the European Union and the United Nations may be required to have specific qualifications in addition to their translating abilities to qualify for the translation of certain text types. For example, lawyer-linguists, who translate mainly legal texts, typically require a degree in law.

In Chapter 4, we also emphasized that an important difference between human and machine translation is that human translators are conscious of features of context that may be relevant for the choices that they make in translating, whereas machine translation programs are dependent on features internal to their programming. That is, human translators typically respond more successfully than machine translation programs do to novel or unusual circumstances. Machines, however, far outstrip humans in terms of memory and speed of recall, and they do not typically need to rest to remain alert; the chapter explained the distinction between machine translation (MT, which translates by itself) and translation memory (TM, which a translator can draw on while translating), emphasizing the need to post-edit text generated by way of either method (as well as by purely human translation).

Post-editing may take the form of either editing, which is essentially proofreading a text for linguistic accuracy, sense and adherence to cultural or client-related conventions, or revision, which involves comparing the first-written text with the translation. Of course, a combination of both may also be used. Post-editing is distinguished from pre-editing, which is undertaken to ensure that a text is free of ambiguities, unnecessary complexities, errors, and other matters that might interfere with the flow of the translating process or militate against adherence to the translation brief.

Chapter 5 opens with a discussion of the advantages of machine translation. The raw versions of such texts commonly contain a number of error types, although the use of machine translation has been shown to allow translation service providers to increase productivity despite the human post-editing that they require. Next, the chapter addresses the processes and practices involved in working with internet-based material and colleagues. The advantages of online translation collaboration include its facilitation of co-temporal work even when translators and other agents involved in the translating process are not co-located; some disadvantages that have been claimed include lower translation quality and less consistency of, for example, terminology. A further perceived risk is that the technology that enables online collaboration may fail. Finally, Chapter 5 discusses two examples of translational analysis using a translation framework known as translational stylistics. This framework stresses the importance of considering translational choices in the light of their relationship to choices made in the first-written text. The argument is not that translations should only ever be analysed in the light of the first-written texts that they represent, only that certain questions about the translation vis-à-vis the first-written text are best answered in the light of the social and other norms at play in the societies in which the translations are to function.

6.2 Where We Are Now

We are more than fifty years forward in the era which knows our discipline as Translation Studies, the name recommended for it by James Stratton Holmes during a conference on Applied Linguistics in Copenhagen, Denmark, in 1972 (see Holmes 1988: 66). Developments over these years, especially in the use of translation technology to translate and in methods used for exploring the translation process, have enabled increasing amounts of translating to be undertaken and have allowed for a significantly enhanced understanding of the processes involved in translation, both physical and mental. With the growth in the market for translating and translation-related activities has come increasing need and demand for translator training. And with advances in our understanding of translation-relevant processes have come enhancement and growth in the provision of training. The translation profession and the subject of translation studies lag some way behind other professions and subjects in which humanities meet science in terms of the public respect and understanding they enjoy. However, in our increasingly internationalized and interconnected world, we may hope for improvements in the general awareness of and respect for translation as an important player in the communication industry.

6.3 Where We Are Going

As mentioned in Section 4.1, the 2020s have been referred to by Angelone, Ehrensberger-Dow and Massey (2020: 3) as the era of 'augmented translation'. It is indeed likely, as Schaeffer (2022: 576) suggests, that 'technology will become much more integrated with humans' in the future. This, we may hope, will alter translators' working lives for the better, and although it is most unlikely to obviate the need for translators, it is highly likely that their activities will diversify. It lies, we may argue, in the nature of machine translation programs, which learn from their past activity, that the quality of the augmentation they provide will be enhanced. It is not, however, likely that translation machines will make humans redundant. They are, as Dennett (2017: 398) remarks with reference to computers, 'tools, not colleagues', and they can neither look forward nor deal with the unexpected in the way that humans can and do. But it is overwhelmingly likely that we will be able to rely increasingly on machine-aided translation, that machine translation will improve steadily for some time to come, and that the better the programs become, the more help they will have to offer. As Carl and Planas (2020: 370) put it, together with human correction in a feedback loop, a machine translation system

> may produce better translation proposals for the remaining part of the text or sentence that has not been validated yet. In this way, the human and machine iterate through the translation in a fashion where the system listens and learns from the corrections with the aim of increasing the acceptability of the next translation proposal.

This is a good job. For as we noted in Section 4.1, the translation and interpreting market is forecast in the *US Department of Labor Occupational Outlook Handbook* to have the highest percentage growth in the period leading up to 2026 of any occupation. Assuming that this prospect is confined neither to the United States nor to the period leading up to 2026 only, we may hope that the expansion of translator training mentioned in Section 6.2 will continue apace, that some understanding of the nature of translation will become more widespread, and that the esteem in which our discipline is held will be enhanced, something that will in turn enhance translators' working lives.

References

Abercrombie, D. (1965). *Studies in Phonetics and Linguistics*. London: Oxford University Press.

Adami, E. and Ramos Pinto, S. (2020). Meaning-(re)making in a world of untranslated signs: Towards a research agenda on multimodality, culture, and translation. In Boria, M., Carreres, Á., Noriega-Sánchez, M. and Tomalin, M. (eds.), *Translation and Multimodality: Beyond Words*. London: Routledge, 71–93.

Ainsworth, J. (2016). Lost in translation? Linguistic diversity and the elusive quest for plain meaning in the law. In Cheng, L., Sin, K. K. and Wagner, A. (eds.), *The Ashgate Handbook of Legal Translation*. London: Routledge, 43–55.

Alves, F. and Lykke Jakobsen, A. (2022). The translation process. In Malmkjær (ed.), 34–54.

Alves, F., Pagano, A. and da Silva, I. (2010). A new window on translators' cognitive activity: Methodological issues in the combined use of eye tracking, key logging and retrospective protocols. In Mees, I. M., Alves, F. and Göpferich, S. (eds.), *Methodology, Technology and Innovation in Translation Process Research: A Tribute to Arnt Lykke Jakobsen*. Copenhagen: Samfundslitteratur, 267–291.

Alves, F., Szpak, K. S. and Buchweitz, A. (2019). Translation in the brain: Preliminary thoughts about brain-imaging study to investigate psychological processes involved in translation. In Li, D., Lei, V. L. C. and He, Y. (eds.), *Researching Cognitive Processes of Translation*. Singapore: Springer.

Anderman, G. and Rogers, M. (2008). *Incorporating Corpora: The Linguist and the Translator*. Clevedon: Multilingual Matters.

Angelone, E., Ehrensberger-Dow, M. and Massey, G. (eds.) (2020). *The Bloomsbury Companion to Language Industry Studies*. London: Bloomsbury.

Anselmi, S. (2018). Self-translators' rewriting in freedom: New insights from product-based translation studies. *Testo e Senso* 19, 1–16.

Arthern, P. (1983). Judging the quality of revision. *Lebende Sprachen* 2, 53–57.

Arturo, P. (2015). Legal-linguistics for the United Nations, states and other non-state actors. ProZ.com Translation Article Knowledgebase. www.proz.com/doc/4090 (accessed 11 November 2024).

Austin, J. L. (1962). *How to Do Things with Words*. Oxford: Oxford University Press.

Baker, C. (2010). Bilingualism and multilingualism. In Malmkjær, K. (ed.), *The Routledge Linguistics Encyclopedia*, 3rd ed. London: Routledge, 51–60.

Baker, M. (1993). Corpus linguistics and translation studies: Implications and applications. In Baker, M., Francis, G. and Tognini-Bonelli, E. (eds), *Text and Technology: In Honour of John Sinclair*. Amsterdam: John Benjamins, 233–250.

Baker, M. (1997). Corpus-based translation studies: The challenges that lie ahead. In Somers, H. (ed.), *Terminology, LSP and Translation: Studies in Language Engineering in Honour of Juan C. Sager*. Amsterdam: John Benjamins, 175–186.

Balmer, J. (2013). *Piecing Together the Fragments: Translating Classical Verse,*

Creating Contemporary Poetry. Oxford: Oxford University Press.
Barley, N. (1983). *The Innocent Anthropologist: Notes from a Mud Hut*. London: Penguin.
Baumgarten, S. and Cornellà-Detrell, J. (eds.). (2019). *Translation and Global Spaces of Power*. Bristol: Multilingual Matters.
BBC Good Food (nd). Recipe for pancakes. www.bbcgoodfood.com/recipes/easy-pancakes (accessed 24 January 2024).
Beeching, K. (2011). The translation equivalence of *bon, enfin, well* and *I mean*. *Revue française de linguistique appliquée* 2(xvi), 91–105.
Behrens, B. (2022). Translated text. In Malmkjær (ed.), 96–115.
Bell, R. T. (1991). *Translation and Translating: Theory and Practice*. London: Longman.
Berger, P. L. and Luckman, T. (1976). *The Social Construction of Reality*. London: Penguin.
Bernardini, S. (2000). *Competence, Capacity, Corpora: A Study in Corpus-Aided Language Learning*. Bologna: Libraria Universitaria Editrice Bologna.
Bernardini, S. (2001). Think-aloud protocols in translation research: Achievements, limits, future prospects. *Target* 13(2), 241–263.
Bever, T. G. (1970). The cognitive basis for linguistic structures. In Hayes, R. (ed.), *Cognition and Language Development*. New York: Wiley & Sons, 279–362. Reprinted in Sanz, Laka and Tannenhaus (eds.) (2013), 1–80.
Biel, Ł. (2014/2016). Phraseology in legal translation: A corpus-based analysis of textual mapping in EU law. In Cheng, L., Sin, K. K. and Wagner A. (eds.), *The Ashgate Handbook of Legal Translation*. London: Routledge. First published in 2014 by Ashgate Publishing, 177–192.
Biel, Ł. (2022). Translating legal texts. In Malmkjær, K. (ed.), 379–399.
Birch, D. (1988). Expanding semantic options for reading Early Modern English, in Birch, D. and O'Toole, M. (eds.), *Functions of Style*. London: Pinter Publishers, 157–168.
Bisiada, M. (2018). The editor's invisibility: Analysing editorial intervention in translation. *Target* 30(2), 288–309.
Blixen, K. (1935). *Syv Fantastiske Fortællinger*. Copenhagen: Gyldendal.
Blum-Kulka, S. (1986). Shifts of cohesion and coherence in translation. In House, J. and Blum-Kulka, S. (eds.), *Interlingual and Intercultural Communication: Discourse and Cognition in Translation and Second Language Acquisition Studies*. Tübingen: Gunter Narr, 17–35.
Blum-Kulka, S. and Levenston, E. A. (1978/1983). Universals of lexical simplification. In Færch, C. and Kasper, G. (eds.), *Strategies in Interlanguage Communication*. London: Longman, 119–139. Revised version of an article originally published in *Language Learning* 28: 399–425, 1978.
Boase-Beier, J. (2006). *Stylistic Approaches to Translation*. Manchester: St. Jerome.
Boase-Beier, J. (2020). *Translation and Style*, 2nd ed. London: Routledge (1st ed. 2006).
Boase-Beier, J. and de Vooght, M. (eds.) (2019). *Poetry of the Holocaust: An Anthology*. Todmorden: Arc Publications.
Bowker, L. (2020). Terminology management. In Angelone, Ehrensberger-Dow and Massey (eds.), 261–283.
Bowker, L. and Ciro, J. B. (2019). *Machine Translation and Global Research*. Bingley: Emerald Publishing.
Briggs, K. (2017). *This Little Art*. London: Fitzcarraldo Editions.
Brodie, G. (2022). Translating for the theatre. In Malmkjær (ed.), 423–439.
Bucciarelli, M. and Johnson-Laird, P. N. (2019). Deontics, meaning, reasoning, and emotion. *Materiali per una storia della cultura giuridica* XLIX(1), 89–112.

Byrne, J. (2010). *Technical Translation: Usability Strategies for Translating Technical Documentation*. Dordrecht: Springer.

Cao, D. (2007). *Translating Law*. Clevedon: Multilingual Matters.

Campbell, G. (2010). *Bible: The Story of the King James Version 1611–2011*. Oxford: Oxford University Press.

Carl, M. (2012). Translog-II: A program for recording user activity data for empirical translation process research, *International Journal of Computational Linguistics and Applications* 3(1), 153–162.

Carl, M. and Planas, E. (2020). Advances in interactive translation technology. In Angelone, Ehrensberger-Dow and Massey (eds.), 361–386.

Carl, M., Bangalore, S. and Schaeffer, M. (eds.) (2016). *New Directions in Empirical Translation Process Research: Exploring the CRITT TPR-DB*. Cham: Springer.

Carl, M., Schaeffer, M. and Bangalore, S. (2016). The CRITT Translation Process Research Database. In Carl, Bangalore and Schaeffer (eds.), 13–54.

Carroll, M. and Ivarsson, J. (1998). *Code of Good Subtitling Practice*. Berlin: European Association for Studies in Screen Translation. www.esist.org/wp-content/uploads/2016/06/Code-of-Good-Subtitling-Practice.PDF.pdf (accessed 24 November 2024).

Catford, J. C. (1965). *A Linguistic Theory of Translation: An Essay in Applied Linguistics*. Oxford: Oxford University Press.

Chalmers, A. F. (1978/1999). *What Is This Thing Called Science?* Maidenhead: Open University Press.

Chan, S.-W. (2013). Approaching localization. In Millan, C. and Bartrina, F. (eds.), *The Routledge Handbook of Translation Studies*. London: Routledge.

Chartered Institute of Linguists (CIOL) (nd). *Professional Code of Conduct*. www.ciol.org.uk/code (accessed 20 November 2024).

Chen, C. W.and Renteln, A. D. (2022). *International Human Rights: A Survey*. Cambridge: Cambridge University Press.

Choi, J. (2021). What happened to heaven and Buddha? James Scarth Gale's translation stylistics. *Acta Koreana* 24(2), 1–30.

Choi, J. (2022). *Government Translation in South Korea: A Corpus-Based Study*. London: Routledge.

Chomsky, N. (1957). *Syntactic Structures*. 's-Gravenhage: Mouton.

Cicero, M. (46 BCE). *Libellus de optimo genere oratorum 'On the Best Kind of Orators'*.

Cirillo, L. and Niemants, N. (2017). *Teaching Dialogue Interpreting*. Amsterdam: John Benjamins.

Conboy, M. (2007). *The Language of the News*. London: Routledge.

Constantine, D. (2011). Service abroad: Hölderlin, poet-translator: A lecture. *Translation and Literature* 20(1), 79–97.

Cook, V. (2004). *The English Writing System*. London: Arnold.

Cordingly, A. (ed.). (2013). *Self-Translation: Brokering Originality in Hybrid Culture*. London: Bloomsbury.

Cornbleet, S. and Carter, R. (2001). *The Language of Speech and Writing*. London: Routledge.

Coulthard, R. M. (2002). Forensic linguistics. In Malmkjær, K. (ed.), *The Linguistics Encyclopedia*, 2nd ed. London: Routledge, 139–143 (1st ed. 1991).

Crossley, S. A., Skalicky, S. and Dascalu, M. (2019). Moving beyond classic readability formulas: New methods and new models. *Journal of Research in Reading* 42(3–4), 541–561.

Csikszentmihalyi, M. (1990). *Flow: The Psychology of Optimal Experience*. New York: Harper & Row.

Dagut, M. B. (1971). *A Linguistic Analysis of Some Semantic Problems of Hebrew–English Translation*. Unpublished doctoral thesis, Jerusalem.

Daems, J., Vandepitte, S., Hartsuiker, R. J. and Macken, L. (2017). Translation methods and experience: A comparative analysis of human translation and post-editing with students and professional translators. *Meta* 62(2): 245–270.

Davenport, C. (2018). Google Translate processes 143 billion words every day. Android Police, 9 October 2018. www.androidpolice.com/2018/10/09/google-translate-processes-143-billion-words-every-day/ (accessed 24 February 2023).

Davies, P. (2018). *Witness between Languages: The Translation of Holocaust Testimonies in Context*. Rochester, NY: Camden House Publishing.

Dennett, D. C. (1991). *Consciousness Explained*. London: Penguin Books.

Dennett, D. C. (2017). *From Bacterias to Bach and Back: The Evolution of Minds*. London: Allen Lane.

Desjardins, R. (2017). *Translation and Social Media: In Theory, in Training and in Professional Practice*. London: Palgrave Macmillan.

Desjardins, R., Larsonneur, C. and Lacour, P. (2021). Introduction. In Desjardins, R., Larsonneur, C. and Lacour, P. (eds.), *When Translation Goes Digital: Case Studies and Critical Reflections*. Cham: Palgrave Macmillan, 1–16.

Díaz Cintas, J. and Remael, A. (2007). *Audiovisual Translation: Subtitling*. Manchester: St. Jerome.

Dinesen, I. (Karen Blixen). (1934). *Seven Gothic Tales*. London: Random House.

DK-Kogebogen (nd). Recipe for pancakes. www.dk-kogebogen.dk/opskrifter/31044/pandekager-gammeldags (accessed 24 January 2024).

Do Carmo, F. (2021). Editing actions: A missing link between translation process research and machine translation research. In Carl, M. (ed.), *Explorations in Empirical Translation Process Research*. Cham: Springer, 3–38.

Dollerup, C. (2000). 'Relay' and 'support' translations. In Chesterman, A., Gallardo San Salvador, N. and Gambier, Y. (eds.), *Translation in Context: Selected Contributions from the EST Congress, Granada 1998*. Amsterdam: John Benjamins, 17–26.

Drugan, J. (2013). *Quality in Professional Translation: Assessment and Improvement*. London: Bloomsbury.

Dudley-Evans, T. (1987). Introduction. *ELR Journal* 1(1), 1–9.

Dulcken, H. W. (1864). *Hans Christian Andersen's Stories for the Household. Stories and Tales*. London: Routledge. Reissued as *The Complete Illustrated Works of Hans Christian Andersen* (London: Chancellor Press) in 1983, reprinted 1994.

d'Ydewalle, G. and De Bruycker, W. (2007). Eye movements of children and adults while reading television subtitles. *European Psychologist* 12(3), 196–205.

Engberg, J. (2020). Comparative law for legal translation: Through multiple perspectives to multidimensional knowledge. *International Journal for the Semiotics of Law – Review international de Sémiotique juridique*. Online first version at https://pierre-legrand.com/ewExternalFiles/Engberg.pdf (accessed 11 January 2023).

Erdmann, B. and Dodge, R. (1898). *Psychologische Untersuchung über das Lesen auf experimenteller Grundlage*. Niemeyer: Halle.

Erkazanci-Durmuş, H. (2011). A critical sociolinguistic approach to translating marginal voices. In Federici, F. M. (ed.), *Translating Dialects and Languages of Minorities: Challenges and Solutions*. Oxford: Peter Lang, 21–30.

Euclid (c. 300 bce). *The Elements* (Greek: Στοιχεῖα *Stoikheîa*).

European Commission Directorate-General (nd).Translation. https://ec.europa.eu/info/departments/translation_en) (accessed 07 June 2024).

European Union Publications Office (2023). *Translation in Figures 2023*. Publications

Office of the European Union. https://op.europa.eu/en/publication-detail/-/publication/86b29f2e-bc97-11ed-8912-01aa75ed71a1; accessed 20 November 2024.

Farrell, M. (2018). Machine translation markers in post-edited machine translation output. In *Proceedings of the 40th Conference Translating and the Computer*. London: AsLing, 50–59.

Fillmore, C. (1977). Scenes-and-frames semantics. In Zampolli, A. (ed.), *Linguistic Structure Processing*. Amsterdam: North Holland, 55–81.

Firth, J. R. (1957). Modes of meaning. In *Papers in Linguistics, 1934–1951*. Oxford: Oxford University Press.

Fischbach, H. (ed.) (1998). *Translation and Medicine*. Amsterdam: John Benjamins.

Fowler, R. (1991). *Language in the News: Discourse and Ideology in the Press*. London: Routledge.

Fowler, R., Hodge, R., Kress, G. and Trew, T. (1979). *Language and Control*. London: Routledge.

Fraser, J. (1996). The translator investigated. *The Translator* 2(1), 65–79.

Fujii, A. (1988). News translation in Japan. *Meta* 33(1), 32–37.

Gagnon, D. (2015). Self-translation. Literary creativity, and trans-lingual aesthetics: A Québec writer's perspective. *Linguaculture* 1, 45–55.

Gale, J. G. (trans.) (1913). *Korean Folk Tales: Imps, Ghosts and Fairies*. London: J. M. Dent and Sons.

Gale, J. G. (1915). *The Life of the Buddha*. Unpublished manuscript held at the University of Toronto.

García, A. M. (2019). *The Neurocognition of Translation and Interpreting*. Amsterdam: John Benjamins.

Ghassempur, S. (2011). Fuckin' Hell! Dublin soul goes German: A functional approach to the translation of 'fuck' in Roddy Doyle's *The Commitments*. In Federici, F. M. (ed.), *Translating Dialects and Languages of Minorities: Challenges and Solutions*. Oxford: Peter Lang, 49–64.

Giroud, V. (2010). Translation. In Suarez, M. F. and Woudhuysen, H. R. (eds.), *The Oxford Companion to the Book*, Vol. 2. Oxford: Oxford University Press, 1215–1217.

Giusti, G. (1873). *Proverbi toscani*. Rome: Spese dell' editore.

Gottlieb, H. (2004). *Screen Translation: Seven Studies in Subtitling, Dubbing and Voice-Over*. Copenhagen: Centre for Translation Studies, Department of English, University of Copenhagen.

Gough, J., Temizöz, Ö., Hieke, G. and Zilio, L. (2023). Concurrent translation on collaborative platforms. *Translation Spaces* 12(1), 45–73.

Graham, J. D. (1983). Checking, revision and editing. In Picken, C. (ed.), *The Translator's Handbook*. London: Aslib, 99–105.

Grainger, S., Lerot, J. and Petch-Tyson, S. (2003). *Corpus-Based Approaches to Contrastive Linguistics and Translation Studies*. Amsterdam: Rodopi

Grimes, J. E. (1975). *The Thread of Discourse*. The Hague: Mouton.

The Guardian (2022). Google fires software engineer who claims AI chatbot is sentient. *The Guardian*, 23 July 2023. www.theguardian.com/technology/2022/jul/23/google-fires-software-engineer-who-claims-ai-chatbot-is-sentient (accessed 26 January 2024).

Guerberof Arenas, A. G. (2020). Pre-editing and post-editing. In Angelone, Ehrensberger-Dow and Massey (eds.), 333–360.

Gutt, E.-A. (1991). *Translation and Relevance: Cognition and Context*. Oxford: Basil Blackwell.

Hahn, D. (2022). *Catching Fire: A Translation Diary*. Edinburgh: Charco Press.

Halliday, M. (1961). Categories of the theory of grammar. *Word* 17(3), 241–292.

Halliday, M. (1989). Spoken and Written Language, *2nd ed.* Oxford: Oxford University Press (1st ed. 1985).

Halliday, M., McIntosh, A. and Strevens, P. (1964). *The Linguistic Sciences and Language Teaching*. London: Longmans.

Halimi, S. A. (2017). Contextualizing translation decisions in legal system-bound and international multilingual contexts: French–Arabic criminal justice terminology. *Translation and Translanguaging in Multilingual Contexts* 3(1), 20–46.

Hansen, G. (1999). Das kritische Bewustsein beim Übersetzen: Eine Analyse der Übersetzungsprozesses mit Hilfe von *Translog* und Retrospektion. In Hansen, G. (ed.), *Probing the Process in Translation: Methods and Results*. Copenhagen: Samfundslitteratur, 43–67.

Hansen, M.-B. M. (2005). A comparative study of the semantics and pragmatics of *enfin* and *finalement*, in synchrony and diachrony. *Journal of French Studies* 15, 153–171.

Hansen-Schirra, S., Neumann, S. and Steiner, E. (2012). *Cross-Linguistic Corpora for the Study of Translations*. Berlin: de Gruyter.

Harris, B. (2011). *¡Cuéntame cómo pasó!* – a memoir of machine translation in Montreal circa 1970. In Blasco Mayor, M. and Jimenez Ivars, M. (eds.), *Interpreting Naturally: A Tribute to Brian Harris*. Bern: Peter Lang, 11–32.

Hasselgård, H. and Oksefjell, S. (1999). *Out of Corpora: Studies in Honour of Stig Johansson*. Amsterdam: Rodopi.

Henkel, D. and Lacour, P. (2021). Collaboration strategies in multilingual online literary translation. In Desjardins, R., Larsonneur, C. and Lacour, P. (eds.), *When Translation Goes Digital: Case Studies and Critical Reflections*. Cham: Palgrave Macmillan, 153–171.

Hennecke, I. (2017). The impact of pragmatic markers and hedging on sentence comprehension: A case study of *comme* and *genre*. *Journal of French Studies* 27, 355–380.

Hinchliffe, I., Oliver, T. and Schwartz, R. (eds. and compilers) (2014). 101 Things a Translator Needs to Know. *WLF Think Tank*. United Kingdom: WFL 101 Publishing.

Hölderlin, J. C. F. (1804). *Die Trauerspiele des Sophokles*. Frankfurt am Main: F. Wilmans.

Holmes, J. (1972/1988). The name and nature of translation studies. In *Translated! Papers on Literary Translation and Translation Studies*. Amsterdam: Rodopi: 67–80. This is an expanded version of a paper presented in the Translation Section of the Third International Congress on Applied Linguistics held in Copenhagen, 21–26 August 1972.

Horace (c. 19 BCE). *Ars Poetica* (The Art of Poetry).

House, J. (2016). *Translation and Communication Across Cultures*. London: Routledge.

Howes, D. H. and Solomon, R. L. (1951). Visual duration threshold as a function of word-probability. *Journal of Experimental Psychology* 41(6), 401–410.

Hubscher-Davidson, S. (2018). *Translation and Emotion: A Psychological Perspective*. London: Routledge.

Hunston, S. (2002). *Corpora in Applied Linguistics*. Cambridge: Cambridge University Press.

Hyland, K. (1994). Hedging in academic writing and EAP textbooks. *English for Specific Purposes* 13(3), 239–256.

Institute of Translation and Interpreting (ITI) (nd). www.iti.org.uk (accessed 7 June 2024).

International Organization for Standardization (ISO) (2015). *ISO 17100:2015 (E) Translation Services – Requirements for Translation Services*. www.iso.org/standard/59149.html (accessed 26 January 2024).

Iser, W. (1978). *The Act of Reading: A Theory of Aesthetic Response*. Baltimore, MD: Johns Hopkins University Press.

Jääskeläinen, R. (2002). Think-aloud protocol studies into translation: An annotated bibliography. *Target* 14(1), 107–136.

Jääskeläinen, R. (2020). Verbal reports. In Schwieter, J. W. and Ferreira, A. (eds.), *The Handbook of Translation and Cognition*. Hoboken, NJ: Wiley-Blackwell, 213–231.

Jacquemond, R. (1992). Translation and cultural hegemony: The case of French-Arabic translation. In Venuti, L. (ed.), *Rethinking Translation: Discourse, Subjectivity, Ideology*. London: Routledge, 139–158.

Jakobsen, A. L. (1998). Logging time delay in translation. In Hansen, G. (ed.), *LSP Texts and the Process in Translation*. Copenhagen: Copenhagen Business School, 73–101.

Jakobsen, A. L. (1999). Logging target text production with *Translog*. In Hansen, G. (ed.), *Probing the Process in Translation: Methods and Results*. Copenhagen: Samfundslitteratur, 9–20.

Jakobsen, A. L. (2016). Foreword. In Carl, Bangalore and Schaeffer (eds.), 13–54.

Jakobsen, A. L. (2017). Translation process research. In Schwieter, J. W and Ferreira, A. (eds.), *The Handbook of Translation and Cognition*. New York: John Wiley and Sons, 21–49.

Jakobsen, A. L. (2019a). Moving translation, revision, and post-editing boundaries. In Dam, H. V., Nesbett Brøgger, M. and Zethsen, K. K. (eds.), *Moving Boundaries in Translation Studies*. London: Routledge, 64–80.

Jakobsen, A. L. (2019b). Segmentation in translation: A look at expert behaviour. In Li, D. V., Lei, D. V. L. and He, Y. (eds.) *Researching Cognitive Processes of Translation*. Singapore: Springer, 71–108.

Jakobsen, A. L. and Jensen, K. T. H. (2008). Eye movement behaviour across four different types of reading task. In Göpferich, S., Jakobsen, A.L. and Mees, I.M. (eds.), *Looking at Eyes: Eye Tracking Studies of Reading and Translation Processing*. Copenhagen: Samfundslitteratur, 103–124.

Jakobsen, A. L. and Schou, L. (1999). Translog documentation. In Hansen, G. (ed.), *Probing the Process in Translation: Methods and Results*. Copenhagen: Copenhagen Business School, Appendix.

Javal, E. (1878). Essai sur la physiologie de la lecture. *Annales d'ocullistique* 80, 61–73.

Jones, F. R. (1989). On aboriginal sufferance: A process model of poetic translating. *Target* 1(2), 183–199.

Jones, F. R. (2001). Bringing Mak Dizdar into the mainstream: Textual and cultural issues in translating Dizdar's *Kameni spavač*. *Forum Bosnae* 11, 261–285.

Jones, H. (2019). Wikipedia as a translation zone: A heterotopic analysis of the online encyclopedia and its collaborative volunteer translator community. *Target* 31(1), 77–97.

Juel, C. and Solso, R. L. (1981). The role of orthographic redundancy, versatility and spelling-sound correspondences in word identification. In Kamil, M. L. (ed.), *Directions in Reading: Research and Instruction*. Rochester, NY: National Reading Conference, 74–82.

Jung, V. (2002). *English–German Self-Translation of Academic Texts and Its Relevance for Translation Theory and Practice*. Frankfurt am Main: Peter Lang.

Just, M. A. and Carpenter, P. A. (1980). A theory of reading: from eye fixations to comprehension. *Psychological Review* 87(4), 329–354.

Kenny, D. (2001). *Lexis and Creativity in Translation: A Corpus-Based Study*. Manchester: St. Jerome.

Kenny, D. (2022). *Machine Translation for Everyone: Empowering Users in the Age of*

Artificial Intelligence. Berlin: Language Science Press.
Kingscott, G. (2002). Technical translation and related disciplines. *Perspectives: Studies in Translatology*. 10(4), 247–255.
Koskinen, K. (2008). *Translating Institutions: An Ethnographic Study of EU Translation*. Manchester: St. Jerome.
Krings, H. P. (1986). *Was in den Köpfen von Übersetzern vorgeht: Eine empirische Untersuchung zur Struktur des Übersetzungsprozesses an fortgeschrittenen Französisschlernern*. Tübingen: Gunter Narr Verlag.
Krings, H. P. (2001). *Repairing Texts: Empirical Investigations of Machine Translation Post-Editing Processes*. Kent, OH: Kent State University Press.
Krouwer, M. (1981). Verfangen (Involvement). *Orbis: The International Literary Magazine* 41, 15.
Künzli, A. (2007). Translation revision: A study of the performance of ten professional translators revising a legal text. In Gambier, Y., Shlesinger, M. and Stolze, R. (eds.), *Doubts and Directions in Translation Studies*. Amsterdam: John Benjamins, 115–126.
Labinaz, P. and Sbisà, M. (2014). Certainty and uncertainty in assertive speech acts. In Zuczkowski, A., Bongelli, R., Riccioni, I. and Canestrari, C. (eds.), *Communicating Certainty and Uncertainty in Medical, Supportive and Scientific Contexts*. Amsterdam: John Benjamins, 31–58.
Laviosa, S. (2002). *Corpus-Based Translation Studies: Theory, Findings, Application*. Amsterdam: Rodopi.
Lewin, K. (1947). Frontiers in group dynamics: Concept, method and reality on social science; social equilibria and social change. *Human Relations* 1(1), 5–41.
Li, C. and Thompson, S. (1981). *Mandarin Chinese: A Functional Reference Grammar*. Berkeley, CA: University of California Press.
Li, Wei. (2006). Bilingualism. In Brown, K. (ed.), *Encyclopedia of Language and Linguistics*, 2nd ed., Vol. 2. Amsterdam: Elsevier, 1–12.
Li, Wenjie. (2017). *The Chinese Versions of Hans Christian Andersen's Tales: A History of Translation and Interpretation*. Odense: University Press of Southern Denmark.
Liu, H. (2020). Foreword. In Angelone, Ehrensberger-Dow and Massey (eds.), viii–xi.
Liu, Y., Zheng, B. and Zhou, H. (2019). Measuring the difficulty of text translation: The combination of text-focused and translator-oriented approaches. *Target* 31(1), 125–149.
Lörscher, W. (1986). Linguistic aspects of the translation process: Towards an analysis of translation performance. In House, J. and Bloom-Kulka, S. (eds.), *Interlingual and Intercultural Communication: Discourse and Cognition in Translation and Second Language Acquisition*. Tübingen: Gunter Narr Verlag, 277–292.
Lu, F. and Yuan, Z. (2019). Explore the brain activity during translation and interpreting using functional near-infrared spectroscopy'. In Li, D., Lei, V. C. L. and He, Y. (eds.), *Researching Cognitive Processes of Translation*. Singapore: Springer, 109–120.
Lucy, M. (2018). The measure of a metre. *Cosmos*, April 6 2018. https://cosmosmagazine.com/people/society/the-measure-of-a-metre/ (accessed 11 November 2024).
Luther, M. (1530). *Sendbrief vom Dolmetschen*. Nürnberg: Georg Rottmaier.
McDonough, J. (2007). How do language professionals organize themselves? An overview of translation networks. *Meta* 52(4), 793–815.
McDonough Dolmaya, J. (2011). The ethics of crowdsourcing. *Linguistica Antverpiensia* 10, 97–110.

McDonough Dolmaya, J. (2022). Translator associations and networks. In Malmkjær (ed.), 198–213.
McDonough Dolmaya, J. and Sánchez Ramos, M. del M. (2019). Characterizing online social translation. *Translation Studies* 12(2), 129–138.
McEnery, T. and Wilson, A. (1996). *Corpus Linguistics*. Edinburgh: Edinburgh University Press (2nd ed. 2001).
McEnery, T., Xiao, R. and Tono, Y. (2006). *Corpus-Based Language Studies: An Advanced Research Book*. London: Routledge.
McKay, C. (2006). *How to Succeed as a Freelance Translator*. Colorado: Two Rats Press.
Macpherson, J. (1765). *The Works of Ossian, the son of Fingal, in two volumes. Translated from the Galic language by James Macpherson. The Third Edition. To which is subjoined a critical dissertation on the poems of Ossian. By Hugh Blair, D.D.* London: T. Becket and P. A. De Hondt.
Maginot, C. (2018). Is there a future in freelance translation? Let's talk about it. *The ATA Chronicle* 31(May/June). www.atanet.org/business-strategies/is-there-a-future-in-freelance-translation/ (accessed 11 November 2024).
Maher, B. (2011). *Recreation and Style: Translating Humorous Literature in Italian and English*. Amsterdam: John Benjamins.
Malmkjær, K. (1998). Love thy neighbor: Will parallel corpora endear linguists to translators? *Meta* 43(4), 534–541.
Malmkjær, K. (2003). What happened to God and the angels: An exercise in translational stylistics. *Target* 15(1), 39–62.
Malmkjær, K. (2004). Translational stylistics. *Language and Literature* 13(1), 13–24.
Malmkjær, K. (2011). Translation universals. In Malmkjær, K. and Windle, K. (eds.), *The Oxford Handbook of Translation Studies*. Oxford: Oxford University Press, 83–93.
Malmkjær, K. (2014). What happened to God and the angels: An exercise in translational stylistics. Special Issue of *Journal of the Association of North-East Asian Cultures* 40(9), 63–86.
Malmkjær, K. (2020). *Translation and Creativity*. London: Routledge.
Malmkjær, K. (ed.) (2022). *The Cambridge Handbook of Translation*. Cambridge: Cambridge University Press.
Marling, W. (2020). What does the gatekeeper do? In Guerrero, G., Loy, B. and Müller, G. (eds.), *World Editors: Dynamics of Global Publishing and the Latin American Case between the Archive and the Digital Age*. Berlin: De Gruyter, 229–244.
Matsushita, K. (2019). *When News Travels East: Translation Practices by Japanese Newspapers*. Leuven: Leuven University Press.
Mattila, H. E. S. (2016). Foreword: New challenges for legal translation. In Cheng, L., Sin, K. K. and Wagner, A. (eds.), *The Ashgate Handbook of Legal Translation*. London: Routledge, xix–xxi.
Melby, A. K. (2020). Future of machine translation: Musings on Weaver's memo. In O'Hagan, M. (ed.), *Routledge Handbook of Translation and Technology*, London: Routledge, 419–436.
Mellinger, C. D. (2018). Re-thinking translation quality: Revision in the digital age. *Target* 30(2), 310–331.
Mellinger, C. D. and Hanson, T. (2017). *Quantitative Research Methods in Translation and Interpreting Studies*. London: Routledge.
Merkle, D. (2022). Translation in the second millennium. In Malmkjær (ed.), 556–575.
Mesmer, H. A. (2005). Decodable text and the first grade reader. *Reading and Writing Quarterly* 21(1), 61–86.
Mesmer, H. A., Cunningham, J. W. and Hiebert, E. H. (2012). Toward a

theoretical model of text complexity for the early grades: Learning form the past, anticipating the future. *Reading Research Quarterly* 74(3), 235–258.

Meylaerts, R. and Marais, K. (eds.) (2023). *The Routledge Handbook of Translation Theory and Concepts*. Oxford: Routledge.

Miller, C. R. (1984). Genre as social action. *Quarterly Journal of Speech* 70, 151–167.

Mitamura, T. and Nyberg, E. (2001). Automatic rewriting for controlled language translation. In *Proceedings of the NLPRS2001 Workshop on Automatic Paraphrasing: Theories and Applications*. ACM Digital Library.

Montalt Resurrecció, V. (2010). Medical translation and interpreting. In Gambier, Y. and van Doorslaer, L. (eds.), *Handbook of Translation Studies*, Vol. 2. Amsterdam: John Benjamins, 79–82.

Montalt Resurrecció, V. and González-Davies, M. (2007/2014). *Medical Translation Step by Step: Learning by Drafting*. London: Routledge. First published in 2007 by St Jerome, Manchester.

Moore, F., Lowe, S. and Hwang, K.-S. (2007). *Language, Power and Integration: The Translator as Gatekeeper in the Korean Business Community in London (UK)*. www.researchgate.net/publication/242080689_Language_Power_and_Integration_The_Translator_as_Gatekeeper_in_the_Korean_Business_Community_in_London_UK (accessed 6 January 2021).

Mossop, B. (2009). Positioning readers. In Dimitriu, R. and Shlesinger, M. (eds.), *Translators and Their Readers. In Homage to Eugene A. Nida*. Brussels: Les Éditions du Hasards, 235–251.

Mossop, B. (2014). *Revising and Editing for Translators*, 3rd ed. London: Routledge.

Mounin, G. (1955). *Les Belles Infidèles*. Lille: Presses Universitaires de Lille.

Mousten, B. (2008).*Globalisation and Localisation Influences on Web Site Text Distribution: A Case Study of Text Travel between Two VELUX Web Sites*. PhD, Copenhagen University.

Muñoz-Miquel, A. (2018). Differences between linguists and subject-matter experts in the medical translation practice. *Target* 30(1), 24–52.

Nida, E. (1964). *Toward a Science of Translating: With Special Reference to Principles and Procedures Involved in Bible Translating*. Leiden: Brill.

Nord, C. (1988/2005). *Text Analysis in Translation: Theory, Methodology and Didactic Application of a Model for Translation-Oriented Text Analysis*. Amsterdam: Rodopi (2005). Translated into English by C. Nord and P. Sparrow from *Textanalyse und Übersetzen: Theoretische Grundlagen, Methode und didaktische Anwendung einer übersetzungsrelevanten Textanalyse*. Heidelberg: Gross (1988).

Nord, C. (2008). Defining translation functions: The translation brief as a guideline for the trainee translation. Ilha do Desterro. A Journal of English Language Literatures in English and Cultural Studies, 41–55.

Nunberg, G. (1990). *The Linguistics of Punctuation*. Stanford, CA: Center for the Study of Language and Information.

Oatley, K. and Johnson-Laird, P. N. 2014. Cognitive approaches to emotions. *Trends in Cognitive Science* 18(3): 134–140.

O'Brien, S. (2011). Introduction. In *Cognitive Explorations of Translation*. New York: Continuum, 1–15.

O'Brien, S. (2017). Machine translation and cognition. In Schwieter, J. W. and Ferreira, A. (eds.), *The Handbook of Translation and Cognition*. Hoboken, NJ: Wiley-Blackwell, 313–331.

Olohan, M. (2016). *Scientific and Technical Translation*. London: Routledge.

Olohan, M. and Baker, M. (2000). Reporting that in translated English: Evidence for subconscious processes of

explicitation? *Across Languages and Cultures* 1(2): 141–158.
Opdag Jylland. (2018). *25 jyske attraktioner / 25 Jütland Attraktionen/ 25 Attractions in Jutland.* Copenhagen: Visit Denmark.
Øverås, L. (1996). *In Search of the Third Code: An Investigation of Norms in Literary Translation.* Unpublished Cand. Philol. Thesis, University of Oslo.
Øverås, L. (1998). In search of the third code: An investigation of norms in literary translation. *Meta* 43(4), 571–588.
Park, R. (1922). *The Immigrant Press and Its Control.* New York: Harper.
Perego, E., Del Missier, F. and Stragà, M. (2018). Dubbing vs. subtitling: Complexity matters. *Target* 30(1), 137–157.
Pérez-González, L. (2020). From the 'Cinema of Attractions' to *Danmu*: A multimodal-theory analysis of changing subtitling aesthetics across media cultures. In Boria, M., Carreres, Á.,Noriega-Sánchez, M. and Tomalin, M. (eds.), Translation and Multimodality: Beyond Words. London: Routledge, 94–116.
Phillips, J. (1953). Some personal reflections on New Testament translation. *The Bible Translator* 4, 53–59.
Pierini, P. (2009). Adjectives in tourism English on the web: A corpus-based study. *Círculo de Linguística Aplicada a la Comunicación (CLAC)* 40, 93–116.
Prieto Ramos, F. (2016). Parameters for problem-solving in legal translation: Implications for legal lexicography and institutional terminology management. In Cheng, L., Sin, K. K and Wagner, A. (eds.), *The Ashgate Handbook of Legal Translation.* London: Routledge, 121–134.
Prieto Ramos, F. (2021). Legal and institutional translation: Functions, processes, competences. *Target* 33(2), 175–182.
Pym, A. (2004). *The Moving Text.* Amsterdam: John Benjamins.
Pym, A. (2014). Translator associations: From gatekeepers to communities. *Target* 26(3), 466–491.
Pym, A. (2015). Translating as risk management. *Journal of Pragmatics* 85, 67–80.
Pym, A. (2016). Risk analysis as a heuristic tool in the historiography of interpreters: For an understanding of worst practices. In Takeda, K. and Baigorri-Jalón, J. (eds.), *New Insights in the History of Interpreting.* Amsterdam: John Benjamins, 247–268.
Pym, A. and Matsushita, K. (2018). Risk mitigation in translator decisions. *Across Languages and Cultures* 19(1), 1–18.
Quah, C. K. (2006). *Translation and Technology.* Basingstoke: Palgrave Macmillan.
Reiss, K. (1971/2000). *Möglichkeiten und Grenzen der Übersetzungskritik.* Munich: Max Hueber. Translation by Erroll F. Rhodes (2000) as *Translation Criticism: The Potentials and Limitations.* Manchester: St. Jerome.
Richards, D. B. (1979). *Goethe's Search for the Muse: Translation and Creativity.* Amsterdam: John Benjamins.
Richardson, J. T. E. (1975). The effect of word imageability in acquired dyslexia. *Neuropsychologia* 13(3), 281–288.
Risku, H. and Dickinson, A. (2009). Translators as networkers: The role of virtual communities. *Hermes – Journal of Language and Communication Studies* 42(20), 49–70.
Robinson, D. (1997). *Western Translation Theory: From Herodotus to Nietzsche.* Manchester: St. Jerome.
Rodríguez de Céspedes, B. (2020). Beyond the margins of academic education: Identifying translation industry training practices through action research. *The International Journal for Translation & Interpreting Research* 12(1), 115–126.
Sager, J. (1990). *A Practical Course in Terminology Processing.* Amsterdam: John Benjamins.

Sakamoto, A. (2022). Translation and technology. In Malmkjær (ed.), 55–74.
Salaga-Meyer, F. (1997). I think that perhaps you should: A study of hedges in written scientific discourse. In Miller, T. (ed.), *Functional Approaches to Written Text: Classroom Applications*. Washington: United States Information Agency.
Saldanha, G. and O'Brien, S. (2013). *Research Methodologies in Translation Studies*. Manchester: St. Jerome.
Sanz, M., Laka, I. and Tannenhaus, M. K. (eds.) (2013). *Language Down the Garden Path: The Cognitive and Biological Basis for Linguistic Structures*. Oxford: Oxford University Press.
Šarčević, S. (2006). Legal translation. In Brown, K. (ed.), *Encyclopedia of Language and Linguistics*, 2nd ed., Vol. 7. Amsterdam: Elsevier: 26–29.
Schaeffer, M. (2022). Translation in the third millennium. In Malmkjær (ed.), 576–587.
Schaeffer, M., Paterson, K. B., McGowan, V. A., White, S. J. and Malmkjær, K. (2017). Reading for translation. In Jakobsen, A. L. and Mesa-Lao, B. (eds.), *Translation in Transition: Between Cognition, Computing and Technology*. Amsterdam: John Benjamins, 17–53.
Schäffner, C. (2020). Translators' roles and responsibilities. In Angelone, Ehrensberger-Dow and Massey (eds.), 63–89.
Schwartz, L. (2018). The history and promise of machine translation. In Lacruz, I. (ed.), *Innovation and Expansion in Translation Process Research*. Amsterdam: John Benjamins, 161–190.
Scruton, R. (1974/1988). *The Aesthetic Attitude: A Study in the Philosophy of Mind*. London: Methuen. Reprinted in 1988 St. Augustine's Press, Indiana.
Selver, P. (1966). *The Art of Translating Poetry*. London: John Baker.
Setton, R. and Dawrant, A. (2016). *Conference Interpreting: A Complete Course*. Amsterdam: John Benjamins.
Sheppard, N. (1975). *Alitjinya Ngura Tjukurtjarangka / Alitji in the Dreamtime* (edited by B. Ker Wilson). Adelaide: The Department of Adult Education, The University of Adelaide
Sheppard, N. (1992). *Alitji in Dreamland*. East Roseville: Simon & Schuster.
Shih, C. Y. (2006). Revision from translators' point of view: An interview study. *Target* 18(2), 295–312.
Shih, C. Y. (2015). Problem-solving and decision-making in translation revision: Two case studies. *Across Languages and Cultures* 16(1), 69–92.
Shih, C. Y. (2023). *Navigating the Web: A Qualitative Eye Tracking-Based Study of Translators' Web Search Behaviour*. Cambridge: Cambridge University Press [Elements in Translation and Interpreting].
Shreve, G. M. (2020). Professional translator development from an expertise perspective. In Angelone, Ehrensberger-Dow and Massey (eds.), 153–177.
Smith, J. Jr. (1830). *The Book of Mormon: An Account Written by the Hand of Mormon, Upon Plates Taken from the Plates of Nephi, Palmyra*. New York: E. B. Grandin.
Snell-Hornby, M. (1988; revised ed. 1995). *Translation Studies: An Integrated Approach*. Amsterdam: John Benjamins.
Sosoni, V., O'Shea, J. and Stasimioti, M. (2022). Translating law: A comparison of human and post-edited translations from Greek to English. *Revista de Llengua i Dret / Journal of Language and Law* 78, 92–120.
Sperber, D. and Wilson, D. (1986). *Relevance: Communication and Cognition*. Oxford: Blackwell (2nd ed. 1995).
Steiner, G. (1975/1992). *After Babel: Aspects of Language and Translation*. Oxford: Oxford University Press.
Suojanen, T., Koskinen, K. and Tuominen, T. (2015). *User-Centered Translation*. London: Routledge.

Swales, J. M. (1981/2011). *Aspects of Article Introductions.* Aston ESP Research Report No. 1. Birmingham: Language Studies Unit, University of Aston in Birmingham. Reissued 2011, Michigan University Press.

Swisher, V. (2020). The Five Phases of the Translation Workflow. Content Rules ebook. https://contentrules.com/creating-translation-workflow/.

Taibi, M. and Ozolins, U. (2016). *Community Translation.* London: Bloomsbury.

Teich, E. (1999). System-oriented and text-oriented comparative linguistic research: Crosslinguistic variation in translation. *Languages in Contrast* 2(2), 187–210.

Tiku, N. (2022). The Google engineer who thinks the company's AI has come to life. *The Washington Post,* 11 June 2022.

Tirkkonen-Condit, S. (2002). Translationese – a myth or an empirical fact? A study into the linguistic identifiability of translated language. *Target* 14(2), 207–220.

Toral, A. (2019). Post-editese: An exacerbated translationese. In *Proceedings of Machine Translation Summit XVII: Research Track.* Dublin: European Association for Machine Translation, 273–281.

Toury, G. (1976/1980). The nature and role of norms in literary translation. Extended version of a paper read at the *International Leuven Colloquium on 'Literature and Translation: New Perspectives in Literary Studies',* The Catholic University of Leuven, 27–30 April 1976, and published in *In Search of a Theory of Translation* (1980). Tel Aviv: The Porter Institute for Poetics and Semiotics, 51–62.

Toury, G. (1977). *Normot sel tirgumve-ha-tirgum ha-sifruti le-ivrit ba-sanim 1930–1945 (Translational Norms and Literary Translation into Hebrew, 1930–1945).* Tel Aviv: The Porter Institute for Poetics and Semiotics, Tel Aviv University.

Toury, G. (1978/1980). Translated literature: System, norm, performance: Toward a TT-oriented approach to literary translation. Paper read at the *International Symposium on 'Translation Theory and Intercultural Relations',* Tel Aviv University, March 1978 and published in *In Search of a Theory of Translation* (1980). Tel Aviv: The Porter Institute for Poetics and Semiotics, 35–50.

Toury, G. (1991). What are descriptive studies into translation likely to yield apart from isolated descriptions. In van Leuven-Zwart, K. and Naaijkens, T. (eds.), *Translation Studies: The State of the Art. Proceedings from the First James, S. Holmes Symposium on Translation Studies.* Amsterdam: John Benjamins, 179–192.

Toury, G. (1995). *Descriptive Translation Studies – and Beyond.* Amsterdam: John Benjamins.

Toury, G. (2012). *Descriptive Translation Studies – and Beyond,* revised ed. Amsterdam: John Benjamins.

Truss, L. (2003). *Eats, Shoots and Leaves: The Zero Tolerance Approach to Punctuation.* London: Fourth Estate.

Tytler, A. (1792). *Essay on the Principles of Translation.* London: J. M. Dent and Sons.

United Nations General Assembly (2022). *Report A/77/91 Pattern of Conferences.* UN Secretary-General. https://documents.un.org/doc/undoc/gen/n22/389/25/pdf/n2238925.pdf (accessed 20 November 2024).

Van der Meer, J. (2020). Translation technology: Past, present and future. In Angelone, Ehrensberger-Dow and Massey (eds.), 285–309.

Van Dijk, T. A. (1972). *Some Aspects of Text Grammars: A Study in Theoretical Linguistics and Poetics.* Berlin: De Gruyter Mouton.

Van Doorslaer, L. (2009). How language and (non-)translation impacts on media

news-rooms: The case of newspapers in Belgium. *Perspectives* 17(2), 83–92.
Van Doorslaer, L. (2012). Translating, narrating and constructing images in journalism with a test case on representation in Flemish TV news. *Meta* 57(4), 1046–1059.
Vermeer, H. (1978). Ein Rahmen für eine allgemeine Translationstheorie (A framework for a general theory of translation). *Lebende Sprachen* 23(3), 99–102.
Vermeer, H. (1989/2000). *Skopos* and commission in translational action. In Chesterman, A. (ed. and trans.), *Readings in Translation Theory*. Helsinki: Oy Finn Lectura Ob, 173–187. Reprinted in Venuti, L. (ed.) (2000), *The Translation Studies Reader*. London: Routledge, 221–232.
Vienne, J. (1994). Toward a pedagogy of 'translation in situation'. *Perspectives: Studies in Translatology* 1, 51–59. Also published in French: 'Pour une pédagogie de la traduction en situation', in Snell-Hornby, M., Pöchhacker, F. and Kaindl, K. (eds.), *Translation Studies: An Interdiscipline*. Amsterdam: John Benjamins, 421–429.
Vlachopoulos, S. (2018). Language for specific purposes and translation. In Malmkjær, K. (ed.), *The Routledge Handbook of Translation Studies and Linguistics*. London: Routledge, 425–440.
Vuorinen, E. (1995). News translation as gatekeeping. In Snell-Hornby, M., Jettmarová, Z. and Kaindl, K. (eds). *Translation as Intercultural Communication*. Amsterdam: John Benjamins, 161–172. Also at www.arts .kuleuven.be/cetra/papers/files/ vuorinen-1999.pdf (accessed 27 July 2020).
Wagner, E., Bech, S. and Martínez, J. M. (2002). *Translating for the European Union Institutions*. Manchester: St. Jerome.
Wiesel, E. (1958). *La Nuit*. Paris: Les Éditions de Minuit. German translation by Curt Meyer-Clason (2008). *Die Nacht: Erinnerung und Zeugnis*. Freiburg: Verlag Herder. English translation by Marion Wiesel (2006). *Night*. London: Penguin Books. The book is based on the Yiddish און די וועלט האט געשוויגן (*Un di velt hot geshvign* 1955 And the world kept silent). Buenos Aires: Union Central Israelita Polaca.
Williams, J. and Chesterman, A. (2002). *The Map: A Beginner's Guide to Doing Research in Translation Studies*. Manchester: St. Jerome.
Zanettin, F. (2013). Corpus methods for descriptive translation studies. *Procedia – Social and Behavioural Sciences* 95, 20–32.
Zethsen, K. K. and Askehave, I. (2006). Medical communication: Professional–lay. In Brown, K. (ed.), *Encyclopedia of Language and Linguistics*, 2nd ed., Vol. 7. Amsterdam: Elsevier, 644–649.
Zethsen, K. K. and Montalt, V. (2022). Translating medical texts. In Malmkjær (ed.), 363–378.
Zielinska-Elliott, A. and Kaminka, I. (2017). Online multilingual collaboration: Haruki Murakami's European translations. In Cordingly, A. and Frigau Manning, C. (eds.), *Collaborative Translation: From the Renaissance to the Digital Age*. London: Bloomsbury, 167–191.
Zwischenberger, C. 2022. Online collaborative translation: Its ethical, social, and conceptual conditions and consequences. *Perspectives* 30(1), 1–18.

Organizations and Online Resources

American Bible Society. www .americanbible.org/ (accessed 5 June 2024).
American Society for Testing and Materials (ASTM) International. www.astm.org (accessed 26 January 2024).

American Translators Association. www.atanet.org/ (accessed 24 January 2024).

British Medical Journal. www.bmj.com (accessed 24 January 2024).

British National Corpus (BNC). www.english-corpora.org/bnc/ (accessed 30 January 2024).

Canadian Hansard. www.ourcommons.ca (accessed 22 November 2024).

Chartered Institute of Linguists (CIOL). www.ciol.org.uk (accessed 22 November 2024).

Chartered Institute of Linguists (CIOL). *Professional Code of Conduct.* www.ciol.org.uk/code (accessed 20 November 2024).

Code of Good Subtitling Practice. /www.esist.org/wp-content/uploads/2016/06/Code-of-Good-Subtitling-Practice.PDF.pdf (accessed 24 November 2024).

Court of Justice of the European Union. https://curia.europa.eu/jcms/jcms/Jo2_10740/en/) (accessed 28 February 2023).

CRITT Translation Process Research Database (TPR-DB). https://sites.google.com/site/centretranslationinnovation/tpr-db (accessed 22 November 2024).

Ethnologue: Languages of the World. www.ethnologue.com (accessed 11 July 2022).

EUR-lex. https://eur-lex.europa.eu/homepage.html (accessed 24 January 2024).

European Commission. Checklist for Outgoing Translations. https://commission.europa.eu/system/files/2016-11/translation_checklist_en.pdf (accessed 22 November 2024).

European Higher Education Area (EHEA). Diploma supplement form. http://ehea.info/Upload/document/ministerial_declarations/EHEAParis2018_Communique_AppendixIV_952782.pdf (accessed 24 January 2024).

European Union Careers. Applications Tests. https://eu-careers.europa.eu/en/selection-procedure/epso-tests (accessed 18 November 2024).

Globalization and Localization Association. www.gala-global.org/ (accessed 24 January 2024).

Institute of Translation and Interpreting (ITI). www.iti.org.uk (accessed 7 June 2024).

Institute of Translation and Interpreting (ITI). How to become a translator. www.iti.org.uk/starting-out/how-to-become-a-translator.html (accessed 24 January 2024).

Microsoft Bing Translator. www.bing.com/translator (accessed 22 November 2024).

ProZ.com. www.proz.com/ (accessed 26 January 2024).

Sandberg Translation Partners Ltd. https://stptrans.com/nordic-translation-specialists/ (accessed 10 January 2024).

SIL International. www.sil.org/tags/summer-institute-linguistics (accessed 5 June 2024).

Sketch Engine. https://sketchengine.eu (accessed 5 June 2024).

Smartcat. Translation jobs: Top 15 websites for freelance work 2024. www.smartcat.com/blog/top-15-websites-to-get-freelance-translation-jobs/ (accessed 22 November 2024).

Society of Authors. Guidance on relay translation. www2.societyofauthors.org/wp-content/uploads/2020/05/Guidance-on-Relay-Translations.pdf (accessed 20 November 2024).

TOBII eye-tracker. www.tobii.com (accessed 5 June 2024).

Tomedes Translator's Blog. What has the United Nations done for the translation industry? www.tomedes.com/translator-hub/what-united-nations-translation-industry (accessed 22 November 2024).

United Nations Careers. https://careers.un.org/home?language=en (accessed 24 January 2024).

United Nations Department for General Assembly and Conference Management (DGACM). Translation. www.un.org/dgacm/en/content/translation (accessed 7 June 2024).

United Nations General Assembly (1948). Universal Declaration of Human Rights. www.un.org/en/about-us/universal-declaration-of-human-rights (accessed 22 November 2024).

Verband deutschsprachiger Übersetzer/innen literarischer und wissenschaftlicher Werke (VdÜ) (Association of German-Speaking Translators of Literary and Scientific Works). https://literaturuebersetzer.de/ (accessed 25 January 2024).

Worldometer. www.worldometers.info (accessed 22 November 2024).

Index